WITHDRAWN

The Art Song

The Art Song

JAMES HUSST HALL

UNIVERSITY OF OKLAHOMA PRESS
NORMAN

Certain of the musical examples in this volume have been reproduced by permission of the publishers and copyright owners, as follows: By permission of Rouart, Lerolle et Cie.: Henri Duparc, *Phidylé* (copyright 1911 by Rouart, Lerolle et Cie.), p. 164; Francis Poulenc, *Les Ponts de Cé* (copyright 1944 by Rouart, Lerolle et Cie.), p. 186. By permission of G. Schirmer, Inc.: Ottorino Respighi, *Nebbie* (copyright 1939 by G. Schirmer, Inc.), p. 20; Hugo Wolf, *Gesang Weyla's* (copyright 1904 by G. Schirmer, Inc.), p. 119; Richard Strauss, *Morgen* (copyright 1904 by G. Schirmer, Inc.), p. 127; Henri Duparc, *L'Invitation* (copyright 1912 by G. Schirmer, Inc.), p. 163; Achille Claude Debussy, *Mandoline* (copyright 1912 by G. Schirmer, Inc.), p. 174; Debussy, *C'est l'extase langoureuse* (copyright 1939 by G. Schirmer, Inc.), p. 177; Peter Tchaikovsky, *Pilgrim's Song* (copyright 1899 by Willcocks & Co., Ltd.), p. 193; Rimski-Korsakov, *Eastern Romance* (copyright 1917 by G. Schirmer, Inc.), p. 195; Rimski-Korsakov, *In Silent Woods* (copyright 1917 by G. Schirmer, Inc.), p. 196; Modest Moussorgsky, *Little Star* (copyright 1917 by G. Schirmer, Inc.), p. 202; Moussorgsky, *Hopak* (copyright 1910 by G. Schirmer, Inc.), p. 204; Sergei Rachmaninoff, *The Isle* (copyright 1917 by G. Schirmer, Inc.), p. 209; Alexandre T. Gretchaninoff, *Over the Steppe* (copyright 1917 by G. Schirmer, Inc.), p. 211; Vaughan Williams, *Silent Noon* (copyright 1939 by G. Schirmer, Inc.), p. 249; Charles T. Griffes, *By a Lonely Forest Pathway* (copyright renewed, assigned 1937 to G. Schirmer, Inc.), p. 274; Griffes, *Lament of Ian* (copyright 1918 by G. Schirmer, Inc.), p. 276; Wintter Watts, *Wings of Night* (copyright 1921 by G. Schirmer, Inc.), p. 279; John Alden Carpenter, *The Sleep that flits on Baby's Eyes* (copyright renewal assigned 1942 to G. Schirmer, Inc.), p. 283; Samuel Barber, *The Daisies* (copyright 1942 by G. Schirmer, Inc.), p. 288. By permission of Carl Fischer, Inc.: Bainbridge Crist, *Into a Ship Dreaming* (copyright MCMXVIII by Carl Fischer, Inc., New York. Copyright renewed), p. 278. The example from Charles E. Ives' setting of *The Children's Hour*, p. 286, is used by permission of the composer.

TO
My Singing Lady
F J H

Foreword

IN THE BROADEST INTERPRETATION of the term, Art Song might include such varied forms and methods of joining words and music as a Greek *skolion,* a troubadour's *cansó,* a *chanson* by Dufay, any of Schütz's *Symphoniae Sacrae* for solo voice with *continuo* and instruments, a *Lied* by Schubert, and a *mélodie* by Poulenc. Such inclusiveness reminds one of Friedrich Niecks' ample definition of program music as encompassing not only all illustrative instrumental compositions but all vocal music. In that which follows we shall be content with the conventional meaning of the term Art Song, limiting our discussion essentially to self-contained secular compositions scored by individual composers for solo voice with lute, harpsichord, or pianoforte accompaniment. Even within such limited boundaries the wealth of material is overwhelming. The choice of each composer and each song included has been made as objectively as possible, the author not being concerned here with forwarding the claims of what he may personally regard as unjustly neglected composers and songs.

The author is deeply indebted to Dr. W. H. Taeusch, dean of the College of Wooster, and Dr. Daniel A. Harris, associate professor of singing at Oberlin College, for their painstaking examination of the manuscript and their many helpful suggestions.

JAMES HUSST HALL

Oberlin, Ohio
February 15, 1953

Contents

The Art Song

CHAPTER I

Problems of the Art Song

W<small>HO</small> has not been gladdened by a child singing at his play? His melody of the moment, so slight in range and span, he hums over and over again. Without form and without meaning the song has bubbled forth unconsciously. In the childhood of the race, under much less advantageous conditions, song must have sprung up in such a simple and spontaneous fashion. It seems reasonable to suppose that as soon as man became differentiated from beast, song came into being as a means of emotional expression, for song is not only the birthright of man, but it is an immediate and satisfying method of expression and intensification of feeling. This native response to emotion has remained through the ages one of the most distinguishing features of songs that endure. The very simplicity and directness which are at the base of song have tended to restrain its makers from the intricacies, involvements, and abstractions that have frequently marked the courses of other media and forms. The naturalness of vocal expression and the inevitability of the joining of words and music is illustrated in the history of music in that long stretch from the beginning through the Renaissance, when man was almost entirely concerned with vocal music. The same impulse that results in the art song had already found expression in folk song, liturgical chant, madrigal, motet, and those larger hybrid forms of oratorio and opera.

The basic aim of song is not mere formal beauty, but rather characteristic beauty. Song is a dual art and at its best there is a fusion of text and tone. Melody and the span of its phrases, harmony and the color of its chords, form and the shape of its being

—all result from the text, which, prior to song, stood alone, but now in song finds a fuller meaning. The great Elizabethan William Byrd has phrased this idea beautifully in the title of his last set of madrigals published in 1611: *Psalmes, Songs, and Sonnets: some solemne, others joyful, framed to the life of the Words.* Pause on that word "life" and stress it afresh, for not every poem or every setting attains that which is the goal of song. Not separate factors, words and music, but rather the union of the two, an act of creation, a miracle such as Browning described when "out of three sounds he brought forth not a fourth sound but a star."

Composer and interpreter alike approach the song through the poem. They study its structure, the movement of the verse, the organization of its lines, rhyme, and stanzas. These are important, for the poem gives form to the music. However, the duality of song, text and tone, poses severe problems in the creation of a design that satisfies the requirements of both poetic and musical forms. Despite the factors that they have in common, both existing in sound and in time, we can push too far the parallels between their rhythms and designs, for the form of music is one and that of poetry another. The adjusting of the one to the other, the eternal compromise that must occur whenever two arts are joined, demands a sensitiveness to balance so that the sanctity of neither music nor poetic form is violated, nor the identity of either submerged.[1] The music must not only give wings to the words of the poem but must have a certain life of its own. It must be understood in terms of music, free, spontaneous, intelligible per se. No amount of brooding over a poem with keen calculations as to its setting can alone create a song. There may be many solutions, but behind each that brings satisfaction, there is the unerring instinct of a sensitive soul.

By convention and with justice one speaks of instrumental

---

[1] For a stinging presentation of the view that any musical setting of poetry injures the tempo and meter of the verse and at the same time constricts the music, see R. H. Schauffler, *Florestan, the Life and Works of Robert Schumann*, 384–88.

design, such as the sonata and rondo, in terms of a preconceived plan. There is a certain universal need of unity, variety, and coherence that results again and again in a design which, despite its thousands of variations, is still recognized as basically "sonata." One might contend that this could hold in the world of instrumental music where ideas are perfectly free to command the form that they will. If such highly individual and opposed ideas and moods as those found in the first movement of Mozart's *C Major Symphony* and in the *D Minor Symphony* by Beethoven are classed as sonata, why should we wonder that a similarity of musical design is discovered in the settings of poems as opposite in idea and mood as Shakespeare's *Who is Sylvia?* and Goethe's *Heidenröslein?* It is true that the form of the ideal song is dictated by the poem and that each song creates its own design. Although countless variations are possible, the basic form of an Art Song falls in one of three classifications: strophic, *durchkomponiert*, ~~and~~ and a composite or modified strophic.

The strophic follows the common pattern of folk song, in which the same music is repeated for succeeding stanzas. Such a form is most frequently summoned by a lyric poem in which essentially a single mood or emotion is maintained. The crystallization of this mood in music must be broad and general, conceived in terms of the whole. "Love's longing" may be the underlying sentiment, but the poet will reveal this in various lights and shadows. His stanzas will not be monotonous repetitions. The lines and accents will be varied, the word of greatest meaning not always falling in the same position within either the line or the stanza. The musician, however, must deny himself any detailed illustration of the poet's subtleties. The composer must seize upon the dominant sentiment and be content with a musical complement which is not too sharply focused. The strophic form is highly satisfactory purely from the standpoint of music; indeed, its most customary structure of AABA is often employed in instrumental music, where it is called "song form." Its very completeness often blinds the composer and audience alike to its limitations in the fusing of text and tone. In most cases the poem is emotionally warmed by the strophic form, but the fusion demands a whiter heat than is possible in exact repetition of pattern. That the form appears as valid as frequently it does, is due largely to the interpreter whose sensitive skill colors and tempers the melodic phrase in varying fashion, according to the meaning of the text. One might paraphrase Lowell and say that "the song without the singer is bare."

At the opposite pole from the strophic type stands the through-composed form. Indelibly associated with German song, the German term *durchkomponiert* is commonly used. The reader may have been confused by the different ways in which he has found this word spelled in English texts. The variety is due to the word which follows or is understood; for example, the German word *Lied* ("song") is neuter and therefore the modifying adjective agreeing in declension ends in *es*. The German word for form (*Form*) is feminine and in use with this term we find *durchkomponierte*. Used independently, the form of the past perfect participle, *komponiert,* is often employed. It is this last which we shall use hereafter to designate music which does not repeat, the musical phrase reflecting as closely as possible the phrases of the poet.

There has been a marked tendency in the later development of the form for the composer to be so intent not only on capturing the meaning of each phrase, but on the illumining of each word, that his subtle, detailed translation has often lacked a unifying continuity. At its worst, phrases tend toward angularity and distortion; and the niggling niceties of melodic inflections and constantly shifting meaningful harmonies prevent us from "seeing the woods because of the trees." At its best, the music matches the poetry; they are true colleagues, each contributing in equal proportion or like degree, *pari passu*. For the strophic song we noted that the composer must be content "with a musical complement which is not too sharply focused." Adjusting this figure to the *durchkomponiert* form, one might refer to it as a panoramic song. The camera, instead of trying to capture the whole scene in a thousandth part of a second, is so placed that it brings a small part of the scene into a sharp, clear image and slowly turns to record in faithful detail every other part of the scene. The problem of the *durchkomponiert* song is more than the invention of separate phrases that are faithful to the changing sentiments of the text. The musical form cannot be sacrificed to the poem. It is difficult to make the sum of the details of illustration equal the emotionally and structurally unified "whole" of the song. Such a form, at least in theory, is the ideal.

Between the poles of the strophic and the *durchkomponiert* lies a large area which shifts in its allegiance, attracted now to one and again to the other. The form that results is a composite, or as it is frequently described, "modified strophic." The unifying factor of repetition is employed, but at some moment in the course of the song, usually at the emotional climax, the composer is compelled to break the pattern. He introduces new music that more closely and fully reflects the sentiment of the poet's particular lines.

In addition to these generalizations regarding the aims of song and the forms that result, we must consider briefly the voice part and its support. One of the chief distinctions between folk and Art Song is that instrumental accompaniment as well as vocal melody is essential to the latter. Naturally, in the early cultivation of the Art Song, interest was almost entirely concentrated on the voice part. Melody had been growing on the broad base of the rhythm and inflection of the spoken word. Yet the authority of Greek philosophers, Christian churchmen, and Florentine scholars could not curb the flight of song. Melody not only deepened the channels of speech, but overflowed its banks into a world of its own. The love of the sheer beauty of the voice itself resulted in a virtuosity illustrated two thousand years before Vittoria Archilei ornamented the monodies of Caccini, and this despite Caccini's and Bardi's caution to "have

7

care not to maim the words."[2] When the Art Song came into being, there was already waiting a sensitive and cultivated medium for its vocal expression. The mission of the song, however, is not the exploitation of the virtuoso, and the melodic line of the early Art Song may appear poverty-stricken in comparison to its use in other media. Basically, the melody pattern of song springs from the text. The length and width of phrase, its diatonic, chromatic, or intervallic emphasis, the pace and the duration of its separate members, the dynamics—all are the result of the dictation and suggestion of the words. Ernest Newman in his *Study of Wagner* holds that the function of "vocal music is broadly speaking in the end to present the verbal sense in another and more intensified form; its function is to replace speech utterance in music."[3]

The natural result of this transfer is a declamatory type, the short detached phrases of recitative. But song is much more than this, and the emotion that wells up from the heart touched by the poet's lines is seldom content for long with the broken phrases of recitative. Contrast is afforded by the smooth, long-breathed *cantabile* phrase. There had been considerable expression in such sweeping lines in the florid liturgical chant, where the voice frequently expanded a single vowel into an embroidered melisma. Any factor of the art when employed in free, expressive composition rarely remains true to a single type for long; and melody in the Art Song moves freely from the declamatory to the *cantabile,* often merging the principles of both in a single "phrase." A good melodic line is an emotional necessity of the Art Song and no amount of explanation of subtle intellectual matching of melody and words can ever make the ear and heart forgive a melodic line that is barren and unintelligible musically.

[2] D. Ferguson, *A History of Musical Thought* (2nd ed., New York, 1948), 243: "For as much as the mind is superior to the body, so far superior are the words to counterpoint; as the soul must guide the body, so counterpoint must take its rules and laws from the words."

[3] E. N. Newman, *Study of Wagner* (New York, 1899).

8

Although the accompaniment is an integral part of the Art Song, the interest in the voice part was so great that its accompaniment was for long little more than a prop or a duplication of the voice in harmonic terms. Gradually it emerged from its subservient position and, from a balance between vocal and instrumental parts occasionally illustrated in the late eighteenth century, the dynamic assertiveness of the newly welcomed pianoforte brought new importance to the accompaniment. Composers found the piano a flexible medium that could intensify the melody; and to the meaning of the text the new instrument could contribute much through its own world of harmony, modulation, and rhythmic figuration. Preludes, interludes, and epilogues came to offer their instrumental comments. Melody and accompaniment became closely interwoven. The old status of master and slave no longer held. Frequently the tables were turned. In the late nineteenth century came the climax in the development of the Art Song conceived largely from the instrumental angle, with the voice considered as but one of the lines of the texture. It may well be that today, in a period of choral renaissance, the independence and excessive importance attached to the instrumental part may yield to a more just and wholesome and balanced relation between voice and accompaniment. Many evidences of this are present in contemporary song.

No matter by what method one breaks down an experience in the world of art, he realizes again and again that the mystery of its beauty has somehow slipped from his analysis. The divine mystery may be experienced but only partially revealed. In the world of the Art Song one may study the component parts; he may examine the structure, relate text to melody, analyze the harmonies and modulations, phrase and parse every item that forms it; and yet he must discover that strangely enough the whole is greater than the sum of its parts.

CHAPTER II

Italian Song

THE creation of a vital art form is never the matter of a moment. It never springs into being in full maturity like Athena from the head of Zeus. Yet many writers, excited by the great gifts of Schubert, have extravagantly proclaimed him the inventor of the Art Song. Both his sympathy for and his emphasis of the Art Song were new, but it would be as rank an injustice to call him the "Father of the Art Song" as to accept for the literal truth the poetic compliment often paid to "Papa" Haydn as the "Father of the Symphony." The roots of the Art Song are spread deep and wide; they intertwine with the folk song, *rondeaux* of troubadours, arias, cantatas, and a hundred other sources from which nourishment was drawn. It is always historically interesting to trace the beginnings of a form—to "discover" in the Noh plays of ancient China a systematic use of leitmotif, or to find in the classic Greek dramas of Aeschylus the forerunners of Peri's *Dafne.* Although historically exciting and of great value, the aesthetic results of the search for prototypes are frequently dulling. Let me assure the reader that we are not here interested in a review of "The Art Song before the Art Song." With but a bow to a pioneer and an allusion to a few productive forces that gave identity to the form, we will cut through the entangling beginnings and proceed directly to Italian song of the seventeenth and eighteenth centuries.

Just as the actions of men are probably never due to a single motive, so an art form is never the result of a single need. In search of adventure and in response to emotional needs not satisfied by existing forms, man explored ways that led toward the Art Song. The songs of the trouvères, the rising of the cantus to the topmost singing voice, the ayre which, though "apt for voices or viols,"[1] soon tended to invite a solo voice accompanied by instruments—these are some of the paths that point the way. It was John Dowland, "that nightingale of that tight singing isle," who liberated the ayre. The fact that he, as well as Luis Milan, was a virtuoso lutenist is significant, for this instrument which in medieval use had played a single-line melodic role, accustomed to being assigned a contrapuntal part in an ensemble, had in the sixteenth century become harmonic-minded. Chords could be easily sounded by the player who often was also the singer. It was an intimate instrument and, since it was easily carried about, was equally at home in the great hall or out-of-doors. Considerable freedom and independence are found in the lute accompaniments of songs of the great Spaniard Luis Milan, appearing in print in Italy as early as 1535.

In a period filled with change we find a strange crossing of paths and purposes. The single chordal-minded instrument takes the place of an ensemble, and at the same time the solo singer is substituted for the chorus. Richly woven polyphony yields to an apparent single strand of harmony. This emphasis of the individual is one of the richest fruits of the Renaissance. The serious artist no longer needed to hide his identity within an organization; he could cultivate his own style and proudly sign his own works. Aristocrat and artist alike, restrained for centuries by the strong hand of the church, had won new freedoms, political, religious, and intellectual. The range of subjects which now could be treated was vastly extended. The painter worked with equal zeal to represent Venus or the Virgin; the musician found like pleasure in setting either the secular verse of a madrigal in the vernacular, or the Latin prose of a motet. The spirit of the times called for the Art Song, which could at once satisfy the

[1] E. H. Fellowes, *William Byrd* (Oxford, 1932, 87, "Psalmes, Songs, and Sonnets; some solemne, others joyfull, framed to the life of the words: Fit for voyces or Viols." (London, 1611).

demand for expression of the secular world of the individual by the individual, and could offer a natural medium for the combination of voice and instrument in the new harmonic texture.

As the accompanying instrument, the lute gradually retired into the background and the harpsichord rapidly came to the fore. Improvements of the keyed instruments led to the pianoforte, whose dynamic flexibility and rich tonal resources continually strengthened its position as the normal accompanying medium of the Art Song. The new harmonic texture, for which these instruments were so apt, had been developing from the period of the *Ars nova*. There is justice, however, in calling the sudden and dramatic cultivation of this style at the end of the sixteenth century the "Monodic Revolution." Urged forward by the desire to discover music fit for drama, Galilei, Peri, and others wrote actual vocal solos accompanied by simple harmonies. The scholarly ideals of these innovators, who agreed with Plato that music should be "first of all language and rhythm, and secondly tone,"[2] were soon forgotten by their followers; but the form and texture, which they sponsored, developed and dominated Italian music for more than a century.

The theater ruled the world of music, even the church being tainted by it. As the composer cultivates the broad, sweeping strokes needed for the opera, he appears to stifle the fineness and intimacy necessary for the Art Song. The record stands that not one of the great song writers has been a successful opera composer. Yet in the first full tide of Italian opera there is little of high tragedy and tumult, and actually the distinctions between the various forms for solo voice, within and without opera, are slight.[3] In an age of experimentation, titles must not be taken too seriously; aria, arietta, canzona, canzonetta, madrigal, and cantata have many points in common both in form and in style.

In the first text of illustrations of the new monodic style, *Nuove musiche,* 1602, Caccini entitles as a madrigal his charm-

[2] W. J. Henderson, *Early History of Singing,* 98.
[3] A. H. Wodehouse, "Song," in *Grove's Dictionary* (3rd ed.), V, 21.

ing apostrophe to the loved one, *Amarilli*. The sustained melodic line is supported by a *basso continuo,* the Italian term for the thorough-bass, with figures indicating the harmonies which formed the core of the improvised accompaniment. The delicate yearning beauty of the ideas, the clear cut design of ABCBC codetta, the distribution of keys with the relief of the dominant center for the B, and the refrain, so sensitively vocal, with the gleam of the major that comes as a shaft of sunlight, and so intensely emotional as it steadily ascends to the climax—all make this one of the greatest of early art songs. There is no faltering in design, no stumbling in tonal sense, and its emotional meaning and pure beauty need no translation for modern ears. In Caccini's day it was the custom for singers to add their own improvised ornamentation (*gorgia*). The top line of the example, drawn from Schering's *Geschichte der Musik in Beispielen,* No. 173, represents a Baroque interpretation of the melody (middle score) of *Amarilli.*

A _ _ _ _ma _ _ril_li   mia bel _ _ _ _ _ la, Non cre-

The Roman Carissimi did much to systematize the new monodic materials. Great advances were made in unifying the more extended aria-like melodic portions and the loosely speech-rhythmed recitative divisions of the cantata. Carissimi's instinct for clear tonal, melodic, and structural patterns, that helped him "to build better than he knew," is illustrated in *Vittoria mio core.* Entitled a cantata, this work is less elaborate and extended in its alternations of divisions than many examples of the form, and in truth illustrates one facet of the development of the Art Song. With joyous abandon Carissimi has echoed the poet's verse that tells of the victory and freedom the heart feels when at last able to ignore, even to scorn, the wiles and smiles of the false lady. Following an old rondo form, the virile refrain idea is contrasted by the repetition of the same couplet resulting in an ABABA form. Note the symmetry of the phrases and the clear-cut blocks of keys. The refrain idea, strangely enough when one thinks of the energy and sentiment of the text, moves first to the darker side of the key, to the sub-dominant, the second phrase modulating to the dominant. The succeeding phrase repeats the beginning for unity's sake, but its cadence expands into a roulade, the florid sweep of the voice that the Italians loved and cultivated so much. In the contrasting idea, note the balance of the strong chordal melody and its diatonic cadence, which carries it into the dominant, from which the energetic principal theme springs back again into the tonic.

Preceding examples have been titled madrigal and cantata. Our next illustration, Caldara's *Come raggio di sol,* is an aria. We must recall that the age of high differentiation and formalization had set in, but that the barriers between forms were not insurmountable. Our choice of examples has been dictated by the spirit of the music, seconded by its availability in print and on records. One is reminded of the old troubadour's complaint about the churchmen who "followed the mode and spoilt the tune." Excuse us then if we have not chosen a *canzona,* for many a *canzona* so titled is less truly an Art Song than Caldara's most famous aria. As expressive and sustained as is the melody, the true distinction of *Come raggio di sol* lies in the depth and directness of its harmonic meaning, realized over the insistent throb of its repeated bass. Chords are rich and filled with tension; yet, as they create the atmosphere for the song, they never become mawkishly sentimental, but sustain a dignified, even noble pathos. Despite the variety of daring harmonies the tonal plan is closely ordered and the first half of the song closes in the domi-

nant. The last part does not retread the path of the first, although
it is unified by rhythmic figure and repetition of the broad ending cadence, now in the home key. Everything contributes to
its rich expressiveness, yet noteworthy are the phrase *mentre del
mare* (m. 13–15)[4] and the Neapolitan-sixth, eleven measures
from the ending. As the sun's golden rays rest on an ocean
whose calm surface does not reveal the wild tempests waking
beneath, so laughter and apparent contentment may hide a heart
borne down by grief.

Such depth of feeling is rare indeed among a people who at
that time were quite content with an abstract beauty that moved
between a rather mechanical bustle and brilliance and an exquisite becalming grace and tenderness. Alessandro Scarlatti is
the great codifier of all the principles established by his predecessors. Yet he is more than this, for he frequently rises above his
damning facility. Marks of both his complacency and his daring
are found in the arietta, *Se Florindo è fidele*. Clearly Scarlatti is
more interested in the patterning of his ideas than in faithfully
matching the poet's lines, for the declamation is far from fault-
less. Most intriguing is the rhythmic pattern, with the pair of
phrases of three bars separated by a single measure that anticipates the repetition. The cadence extends the phrase to seven
measures, which are echoed. The simple sunny harmonic course

---

[4] The abbreviation *m.* will be used for measure, *m.* 1 referring to the first complete measure or bar of the song.

of tonic-dominant is clouded as the B idea enters with a wavering single line in the accompaniment answered, *imitando,* by the voice alone. The interlude that follows starts with the initial off-step syncopated phrase as if this were to repeat the section. Instead, the rapid modulation to the dominant introduces a new longer-phrased idea, broken by a dropping fifth mirroring the word *preghi.* A sequence makes a gesture towards the home key, when an unexpected turn reintroduces the fluttering and clouded figure of B, before at the parallel minor, now at the level of the relative minor of the dominant. The first section is repeated, followed by the *imitando* B in the parallel minor. Most frequently there was a lift of the third in the realization of the last chord, a *tierce de Picardie,* which brought a gleam of light to the ending.

Giordani's arietta, *Caro mio ben,* has become a symbol of the *bel canto* style. This loose term literally means "beautiful singing" and refers to a style of singing which emphasizes a broad, flowing, and flexible legato line. The term is frequently used today to mean the type of music which demands the above style of singing—a slow, sustained, broadly flowing, essentially diatonic lyric melody supported by simple chords. It was not always thus, for the term earlier included the florid style with brilliant *fioriture.* The great popularity of *Caro mio ben* is certainly not due to the verse which assures the loved one that absence makes the heart grow fonder—and sadder. Nor can its favor be due to the matching of these lines by the composer. Rather it is the slight varying of beautifully molded symmetrical phrases, rich and smoothly rounded, that creates a feeling of well-being and satisfaction in simple, dignified lyric beauty. Of the subtleties, note how in responding phrase the accompaniment begins, the voice's entry being delayed a measure. The extension of the first full cadence in the voice is a unifying factor, repeated at dominant level in the B section. The mood is so sustained that one scarcely realizes the varied design of A A′ B C A′ C′. The last cadence is delightful in its restraint.

Of value may be a summing up of characteristics of Italian Art Song of the seventeenth and eighteenth centuries. The dominating factor is the love of the voice as an instrument, rather than as a medium of speech. This physical delight in the sensuous sound of the voice is often the beginning and end of the composer and his audience, and such an attitude rarely results in a close and subtle interpenetration of text and music. Fortunately the poems are usually simple in mood and the beauty of a general intensification gives much satisfaction. Melodies are conceived in terms of the voice. A graceful sustained line, with phrases that cohere and seem to be not only logical but inevitable, usually rides on the crest of the simply felt harmonic support. Factors in this grace are the closely bound diatonic movement, and that when skips occur they seldom strain beyond the nearest chord member. The range in lyric song is slight as contrasted with the opera, where feats of virtuosity frequently demand control of the stratospheric regions. The support of the voice for the most part is rather perfunctory and seldom rises to an equal place with the melody. In the echoes or *imitandos,* the accompanist is warned *colla voce* or *col canto.* There are difficulties in judging the accompaniments as most of them are realized from the figured bass. Too frequently in modern editions the realization is a "concert transcription," whose lush romantic harmonies are often beyond the boundaries of the simple grace and expressiveness of the period.

Later Italian Song

ACCOMPANIED MONODY, which had been the basis for the early Italian baroque opera as well as song, was destined for luxuriant cultivation in the former medium and dwindling interest in the latter. The glamour of the theater and of drama with music, which quickly yielded to the taste for display and feats of virtuosity, attracted the best efforts of composers. Music for church and chamber played secondary roles. The simple lyricism of accompanied song could not compete with the showy theatrical-ism of opera. In such a period the cultivation of the Art Song in Italy was stimulated neither by audience nor by other rewards. Thus the Art Song passed through a long barren period, with only an occasional blossom, from about 1725 (the time of the death of A. Scarlatti) to 1850.

The rise of nationalism, as one facet of romanticism in the nineteenth century, had a different meaning for Italy than, for example, Russia. Musically Italy had been independent for centuries, but politically she was a pawn, groping for national unity. One reflection of this nationalistic tendency was the spirited development of folklike song, which captured too often only the outward shell of the real folk song. At their best, as in *Marie! Marie!* and *O sole mio* by Eduardo di Capua (d. 1917) or the ever popular *Funiculì, Funiculà!* by Luigi Denza (1846–1922), one finds that the people's songs ring true and Italy has almost accepted them as folk songs. At another level is Giovanni Sgambati's *Separazione* ("Parting"), an old Italian folk song transcribed from the collection of the Neapolitan Guillaume Cottrau (1797–1847).

Highly characteristic of the lyric genius of the South are many of the songs of Francesco Paolo Tosti (1847–1916). Despite Tosti's residence in England and his receipt of a knighthood, his settings of English texts, such as *Good-bye,* are as Neapolitan as his *Mattinata.*

Serious delving into native forgotten masterpieces was another expression of the growing nationalism. Francesco Malipiero (1882-) described himself as a lover of his art "seeking to defend the music of the past out of sheer love for it."[5] His scholarly editions of Monteverdi and other early masters stimulated interest in other composers than the current favorites of the opera world, and Malipiero's compositions, though colored by his studies, are no mere echoes of the past.

Perhaps that charge could best be leveled at Stefano Donaudy

[5] G. F. Malipiero, "Mephisto," *Musical America,* August, 1951.

(1879–1925), whose ingratiating melodies are so much like the *canzoni* of the eighteenth century that had he chosen he might have fooled his public as Kreisler did for many years with his "transcriptions." Donaudy, however, entitled his collection *XXXVI Arie di stile antico.* Characteristic of the animated songs is the *canzona, Spirate pur, spirate,* and of the sustained cantabile arias, *O del mio amato ben.*

Ottorino Respighi

IN A MANIFESTO of December, 1932,[6] Respighi (1879–1936), Pizzetti, Zandonai, and others expressed their opposition to all modern art devoid of human content but rich in cerebral puzzles. Respighi's music is generally warm and rich in sentiment, and, although there are noisy and rhapsodic pages, there is an overall feeling of serenity in his work. His belief that "the romanticism of yesterday will again be the romanticism of tomorrow"[7] was strengthened by studies abroad, under Rimski-Korsakov in St. Petersburg and Max Bruch in Berlin. Inspiration came also from French impressionists. The various factors of Respighi's style were fused and became his very own; they rested upon a solid classical feeling for structure learned from his Italian masters, Martucci and Torchi.

In Respighi's varied contributions, song holds an important place, more than half a hundred songs appearing between 1906 and 1933. Among the first issued is the most frequently programmed, *Nebbie* ("Mists"). The poet Ada Negri summons both the mood and the picture to which Respighi was responsive. Mists rise over the moorlands. Ravens float by on black wings. Naked branches raise themselves in prayer. In anguish a forsaken soul wanders.

The slowly rising scale growing in intensity is the natural response to the rising mists. Having reached its height, the de-

[6] *The New York Times,* January 7, 1933, p. 11, col. 4.
[7] *Ibid.*

Le neb.bie son.nolen.te Sal.go.no dal ta.cen.te Pia.no

scending pattern symbolizes the gliding ravens. A modified repetition follows (m.11–14), omitting the hesitant beginning of the first stanza; the voice continues (m.15–16) where the piano had commented before. New material, freely centered about the octave cadence of m.5, is here heightened with vivid harmonic and dynamic contrasts (m.18–19). The voice murmurs the close of this division and in m.23 resumes the latter half of the strophic pattern with final measures repeating a ghostly *"Vieni!"*

Contrast is offered in the rich chords of the accompaniment, the opening section above center in pitch, which later is deep and dark. The firmness of structure is strengthened by a hidden tonic pedal present in all but eight chords, and the moment of strongest rhythmic tautness is based on octave swings of this same tonic (m.13).

The poet of *Nebbie* pictures in *Nevicata* ("Snowfall") the fluttering and dancing snowflakes, which silently fall on fields and streets, on rooftops and gardens. Yet, surrounded by such peace, the heart is stirred by memories of a love long forgotten.

The ceaseless sixteenth-note motion, with a generous use of an *ostinato* pattern doubled at the octave, *ppp,* supports an undulating voice line, which takes seven, nine, then only five measures for the same unusual verse pattern, whose fourth line is one two-syllable word.

Pioggia (1909) with its pattering and nimble figures suggestive of its title, *Rain,* makes the third of Respighi's most popular nature songs.

One finds in Respighi delightful variety. He can be gay with the suggestive swing of *Invito alla danza* or somber as in *Ballata,* Boccaccio's improvisation over the grave of the beloved. Respighi can be "experimental" as in *Mattinata* with its double bell-like *ostinati* or as in the three *Vocalises* of 1933. Refuting all clichés of recitative is a setting of a bit of poetry by Aganoor Pompili in the style of Maeterlinck, *E se un giorno tornasse.* Unbarred, free in melodic line, apparently undisciplined harmonically with minor triads on all but the fourth of a chromatic scale (and only three of these triads appearing more than once), rising and falling parallel higher-seventh chords with two augmented triads along the way—all contribute to a successful experiment.

Ildebrando Pizzetti

PIZZETTI (1880–) succeeded Respighi as teacher of advanced composition at the St. Cecilia Conservatory, Rome. In his turn, Pizzetti has become the "Dean" of Italian composers. His influence has been extremely healthful, for he has never been a faddist and has ever been alert to the voice from within. The worship of beauty alone has never satisfied Pizzetti, who has penetrated beneath the lines of the texts he has chosen.

"Melody," he stated, "is emotion translated into musical sounds."[8] The melody may be drawn with a few straight lines or luscious curves, whatever is appropriate to the mood which may be prolonged beyond the duration of the word itself. Sound in structure, skilled in drawing a flowing line, and sensitive to harmonic color, Pizzetti has found song an attractive and intimate medium.

His most illustrious pupil, Mario Castelnuovo-Tedesco, believes Pizzetti's lyrical *I pastori* (1908) to be "the most beautiful

8 "Music and Drama," *Musical Quarterly,* Vol. XVII (October, 1931), 426.

concert song of the last fifty years, and the most perfect musical expression of D'Annunzio's poetry."[9] D'Annunzio in *Dreams of Distant Lands* recalls how in September the shepherds of the Abruzzi leave the hills to follow the ancient paths to the wild Adriatic. The sun makes the wool as blond as the sand. The poet imagines the tramping of the flocks and the sweet sounds. "Ah! why am I not with my shepherds!"

In the broad swing of the 6/8 meter, a shepherd's pipe motive leisurely curls and repeats at a lower level. Most of that

which happens in the 109 measures of this spacious song is derived from this motive, which appears at different pitches, in different voices, and in different lengths (as the augmentation at m.19–26). Much is made of the interval of the major second (m.65) drawn from the basic motive. There are suggestions of a primitive pentatonic and other modal tunings. Metric freedom is reminiscent of improvisation, the pulse in the 2/4=6/8 of the voice not always coinciding with that of the 3/4=9/8 of the accompaniment. The piano score in more than half of the song is spread upon three staves, in part to accommodate the tremulous center and the sustained pedals. There are subtle repetitions; the section at m.52 begins like that at m.19 but soon finds new paths. Little ornamental additions as in m.36 and in the cadence of the voice at m.54 bring delight. "Sweet sounds" tinkle like little bells (m.93–98) with a high B-flat, tonally lonesome.

[9] M. Castelnuovo-Tedesco, "Pizzetti," *Book of Modern Composers* (ed. by D. Ewen, New York, 1942), 203.

Pietro Cimara

Cimara (1887–), active in Italian opera productions, has composed many songs of melodic charm and transparent design. In the popular *Fiocca la neve* ("Snow is falling"), the poet Giovanni Pascoli brings us a scene of snowflakes softly falling. Within, a cradle is gently swinging while an old woman sings to a weeping child: "Around your little bed are lilies and roses like a beautiful garden." The child falls asleep. Slowly the snowflakes are falling, slowly, slowly.

Cimara's use of the figure of a falling second in every measure except in those of the final cadence seems a bit excessive, despite the obvious programmatic purpose. Some variety in treatment is offered in the swinging interplay of hands in the accompaniment of the middle section (m.23–32), the lullaby. This is in the parallel major, hinted at in the raised third of m.9. A suspensive feeling is projected in the last vocal phrase which ends on the fifth. The mood is reinforced by the accompaniment's final cadence in which the raised note is not the third, but the tonic, a plagal cadence with lowered third of the subdominant moving to the tonic minor triad.

Mario Castelnuovo-Tedesco

A stream of songs has issued from the Florentine Castelnuovo-Tedesco (1895–), and a long stay in the United States has not dammed the source. Gifted with an astonishing facility and a deeper understanding and wider compass of poetry than many of his countrymen have evidenced, Castelnuovo-Tedesco is a central figure in modern Italian song. He hesitates not at all at a sonnet from Dante, Shakespeare, or Milton. Any verse, from Petrarch to Guiterman, is grist for his mill. Like most facile writers, Castelnuovo-Tedesco has undoubtedly written too much, and like many facile moderns his scores are occasionally involved.

His sensitiveness to the accent and color of words is copiously illustrated in his cycle of *Shakespeare Songs*. The appeal of Shakespeare is universal, and a modern musical setting of his lines should not be condemned because it does not sound Elizabethan. *Springtime* (1921) is none other than *It was a Lover and his Lass*[10] from *As you like it,* Act V, scene 3. The composer's one suggestion of early color is in the first vocal phrase where there is a modal tinge. There is an ecstatic spring to the refrain, "In Springtime," when the accompaniment swirls up to repeat the vocal line; a "bird" trills in the tenor and the stanza is capped with festive cadence, echoed and closing suspensively for entry of the succeeding strophe.

In Sonnet LXI, *Benedetto sia 'l giorno,* Petrarch having received from Laura some favor—a glance or greeting—gives expression of his devotion. Blest be the day, the month, the year, the moment, the place when two lovely eyes held me fast. Blest be the coming of love, even her wounds and despair; and blest be my thoughts which are so much of her that naught else exists.

This setting (1933) with its joyful, fervent rolled chords in the first division suggests a lute. A contrasting section (m.18–28) anticipates "blest be the sighs and tears" with a tenor line (in the piano), whose motives are frequently symbols of sighing

ch'io chia_man_do il no_me di mia don_na ho spar_te

(m.18) and grief (m.23). With m.28 there is a free return of

[10] To compare Castelnuovo-Tedesco's setting of *It was a Lover and his Lass* with that of Morley, see Chap. XX, 227 below.

the opening. The piano, marked *quasi scampanio,* brings a growing excitement in the ringing bells, which at last rise through two octaves in a chain of sixths and thirds, the tenor meanwhile slowly descending, while the voice doubles its motion as it drops down the scale. The little epilogue brings back the rolled chords of the opening, but adds a sixth to the final tonic chord.

Casella, long a leader of the Italian school, now appears more cosmopolitan than the younger generation and, indeed, than many of his contemporaries. Considering the trials that Italy has passed through since World War I and the attendant political, economic, and social changes, it is surprising that a more revolutionary kind of music has not captured the scene. Undoubtedly there is much experimentation going on, but few examples of radical technique in song have made themselves known. Although freed from melodrama's strangle hold which long delayed the advances of the Art Song, the Italian through temperament and tradition is still susceptible to the lyricism of *bel canto* and the sweep of a hearty tune.

CHAPTER III

Early German Song

THE German term for song, *Lied,* was applied as early as the thirteenth century to a form of three divisions. The first two the Minnesingers called *Stollen* (props) and these made the *Aufgesang* (fore-song); the third section, which was usually contrasted in meter and melody, was termed the *Abgesang* (concluding song). This bar-form, in the analysis of Alfred Lorenz,[1] m m n, and the recapitulation bar-form in which a part of the *Aufgesang* recurs as an ending, greatly influenced the structure of later music.

Song, however, was not the privilege or property of the nobles and the courts; it was the heritage of the people. To the *Volkslied* (folk song), in diatonic simplicity and symmetry of phrase and in the naturalness of strophic form, had been confided the joys and sorrows of the people. The individual composer, especially as the folk effort of expression declined in the seventeenth century, frequently accepted the *Volkslied* as the foundation for his individual music-making. The technical characteristics of the resulting *Volkstümliches Lied,* an Art Song in the folk style, are those of the *Volkslied* raised to a higher power. The accompaniment, which, though frequently used in the folk song, had been improvised, was here set down in simple harmonies, chords whose top line was not a mere duplication of the voice part. Heinrich Albert (1604–51) has often been called the "Father of the *Volkstümliches Lied.*" His followers were legion;

---

[1] A. Lorenz, *Das Geheimniss der Form bei Richard Wagner* (4 vols., Berlin, 1924–33). For a concise statement of the core of the theory see "Syllabus for Music, 101, 2, 3" (3rd ed., Chicago, 1939), 47–48.

however, many find the flowering of this school in J. A. Hiller (1728–1804) and J. F. Reichardt (1752–1814). In its simplicity and inevitability this short Art Song found a warm response from the people. There lingered, however, in the "higher" circles a suspicion concerning the serious artistic worth of such a slight and obvious thing. Despite a certain national prejudice in favor of the native folk song style, the aria and ode were considered the more worthy of serious attention and these commanded the interest of the most gifted composers.

This snobbery in part explains the relative indifference of the eighteenth-century German composers to the Art Song. It is always interesting, even though largely useless, to surmise what would have happened had Bach's genius been focused even for the shortest period on the Art Song. Suppose his second wife, the highly musical and gifted soprano, Anna Magdalena, had been more enthusiastic about the two little lieder which she copied in her notebook than about the arias which preceded them. And well she might have been when one notes the haunting beauty of the cadences and the deeply personal sentiment of the text of *Bist du bei mir* ("Wert thou with me"). One can dismiss as a trifling though moralizing bit of humor the first *lied* in her notebook, *Erbauliche Gedanken eines Tabachrauchers* ("Edifying reflections of a pipe-smoker"), which likens the clouds of smoke that roll quickly away to the brevity of life itself.

One can not lightly pass by the second song, *Bist du bei mir,*[2] which has a dignity and spaciousness quite beyond its short span. Its forty-five measures seem few indeed, scored in single lines on the two staves: the top for the voice in the soprano clef, signature three flats, and the lower in the F clef, the harmonies so obvious that no figures were added to the bass. The design is closely knit. The first section is four measures plus five, the beauty of the cadence extended and closing in the dominant, with the return to the tonic in the replying section. With the

[2] Bach *Gesellschaft,* XXXIX, 309.

third line of the poem, *"Ach, wie vergnügt,"* enters a contrasting idea and key, the relative minor. The compelling logic of Bach penetrates his smallest works and one notes that the last phrase of the middle section is none other than the haunting cadence of the initial section. The return of A is subtly contrived in exactness except for the opening phrase, which stems both in text and melody from the preceding section. Despite the composer's instrumental conception of tone, the singer is grateful for this independent lied. Although not unique, it stands almost alone in the work of this master and his illustrious contemporary, Handel. Their interest in cantatas, masses, operas, and the like called forth hundreds of solos for all voices, but these were not art songs. Bach's son, Karl Philipp Emanuel, considered the song more seriously than had his father, and his settings of some of Gellert's *Geistliche Oden und Lieder,* as well as his theorizing in the preface to the collection printed in 1758, led Bitter to call him the "founder and creator of the German lied,"[3] while Reissman holds him the "father of the *durchkomponiertes Lied."*[4] Although both claims appear extravagant, the latter half of the century brought a growing interest in the song.

The classic masters Haydn and Mozart each wrote about forty songs, although one must admit these hold a most unimportant position in their total contribution. In the story of the Art Song, however, their lieder are significant.

Haydn

ALTHOUGH Haydn's conception of tone was essentially instrumental, he was far from unaware of the beauties of the voice. One recalls his early years in Vienna as an accompanist to the great singing teacher Porpora; at Esterhaz, the young deputy Haydn was contemptuously referred to by the old intendant

[3] *Oxford History of Music* (Oxford, 1904), V, 328.
[4] *Ibid.*

Werner as a mere "scribbler of songs."[5] Evidently Haydn did not possess the proverbial "composer's voice," for he sang his own songs more than once at royal parties in London. And it was while there in 1794–95 that he composed two sets of six *Canzonettas,* several of which have ever since given delight. The original English texts, written and adapted by Mrs. John Hunter, were soon translated into German, and the songs appeared in the Viennese collection of Haydn's German lieder. The text, whether in English or in German, was not of too great moment to the composer. One could scarcely expect the peasant Haydn to be a connoisseur of poetry, and, excepting an adaptation from Shakespeare, he was never spurred to composition by the verse of a great poet. Yet, despite his choice of poems and his decidedly instrumental conception of tone, Haydn's genius was so all-embracing that his songs not only gave impetus to a form sadly in arrears, but occasionally anticipated the inspired methods of a Schubert or a Loewe.

We are so accustomed to *Gott erhalte Franz den Kaiser* in adaptations as a church or national hymn that it is difficult for us to realize that it was written as a solo song. Haydn had admired the English use of *God Save the King,* and at his suggestion the poet Haschka wrote the verse for which Haydn composed music that expressed his simple, full reverence for his emperor and his land. In 1797 on the Emperor's birthday, February 12, the air was sung not only for His Royal Highness at the *Burgtheater* in Vienna, but in many other assemblies. It was instantly accepted by the people, and has remained one of the world's best-known melodies. Its natural, inevitable melodic line has led Tappert and others to point out similarities to Croatian and other folk melodies.[6] Nothing, however, has robbed it of its deep fervor and noble simplicity.

Undoubtedly the most frequently sung of Haydn's songs is the canzonetta, *My Mother bids me bind my hair.* The verse by

[5] K. Geiringer, *Haydn, A Creative Life in Music,* 57.
[6] Wodehouse, "Song," *Grove's Dictionary,* V. 70.

Mrs. John Hunter was originally titled *Pastorale,* and it is occasionally called *Shepherd's Song.* Mrs. Hunter had first set this verse to an *Andante* from a sonata by Pleyel, a not infrequent practice, a number of Haydn's instrumental melodies having had verse adapted to them. One of the chief reasons for this song's deserved popularity, beyond the lilting freshness of its melody, is an equality between the voice part and the accompaniment seldom attained in this period. The accompaniment in Haydn almost always doubles the voice, either absolutely or in a slightly figured fashion.

The accompaniment here duplicates the voice more than one suspects, for Haydn has ingeniously woven his lively rhythmic patterns about the voice line. The chief charm of this accompaniment lies in the little interludes and cadences. Here scales sweep up or down, in thirds, octaves, or tenths; the little "kick" of the cadence at the end of the introduction is enjoyed twice as the dominant is reaffirmed in m.26. Highly artistic are those measures in which a simple arpeggiated accompaniment supports the broken line of the voice, as at the end of the stanzas. The voice announces a gay, lilting phrase moving to the dominant by its eighth measure. In the next four measures the voice drops through an octave, with repetition of a four-note pattern at its original level and then extended in cadence in the lower half of the scale. There follows a halting and broken pattern with the two-note descending figure, long associated with Bach and the

Ach, a _ ber ach   das Her _ ze mein seufst: weh!

Mannheim school as a "sigh." But note the replying phrase, "While others dance and play," which calls forth an ascending legato in the voice and exciting movement in the accompaniment. The difficulties that frequently arise with translation of the text are illustrated in the German, where the syllables of nouns, verbs, and adverbs are broken by rests. One recalls the Italian phrase, *Traduttore traditore* ("Translators are traitors"). There is no great depth in this song and the compassion of neither singer nor audience is roused for the maiden. In fact all are glad that Lubin went away, for the song is a joy to sing and play.

Of deeper hue is *The Spirit's Song,* in which the Spirit counsels the lamenting loved one to grieve not, for the lover's "Spirit wanders free and waits till thine shall come." This text spoke to Haydn, who romantically painted his tonal canvas in dark, lugubrious shades dramatically broken by shafts of light. In solemn tread the opening unison phrase rises, each time to rest on a sustained chord. At the repetition of the first phrase the voice belatedly joins with its warning "Hark." The short interlude (m.24) and transition (m. 34) are such as one frequently finds in his quartets and symphonies. With the words, "All pensive and alone," (the B idea), a complacent phrase in the relative major is challenged by the text and the voice responds in more angular phrase, even skipping an octave. Following transition, the quiet B idea now appears in the sub-dominant ("I watch thy speaking hands"), but drives toward the home key where the very first phrase of the song reappears, intensified in its repetition. The voice in its second "Hark" moves into new worlds, supported by new harmonies; its range is extended as the voice sweeps downward an octave and a fourth. Its last phrases are broken, as if the pathos were almost too much to bear. This song remains great to the end, where a unifying factor is observed in the epilogue, for the tonic pedal embellished with a turn is drawn from the interlude just preceding B, in which the same note and turn appeared *above* shifting harmonies.

Mozart

IT CANNOT be claimed that Mozart gave more attention to the Art Song than Haydn. One would suspect that the Italian aria so marvelously developed by the younger master, both within and without his operas, would militate against any just solution of the problems of song; nevertheless, Mozart's conception of tone as vocal and his God-given sensitiveness to any problem he touched bring the song nearer to the joining of truth and beauty. His thirty-four songs, of which only seven were printed during his life, were composed from 1768 to 1791. In choice of texts he was a bit more fortunate than Haydn, although it still seems astounding that Mozart selected but one poem from Goethe, while Haydn ignored entirely that poet's great storehouse of lyrics yearning for music.

Das Veilchen is not one of Goethe's great poems, but it inspired Mozart to attune his music to the changing sentiments of the verse. The composer read a dramatic tragedy into this Anacreontic love poem, wherein the sweet and lovely violet's dreams of being plucked and honored by the fair shepherdess are shattered, for in passing the shepherdess presses beneath her feet the unnoticed violet that in dying thus finds joy. The song begins with no great distinction, the accompaniment announcing a tune-like melody which is immediately repeated by the voice. Here, however, the older style is denied and the tune no longer commands and continues its merry way. Now in the dominant, the shepherdess enters, and an independent, bounding staccato figure in the accompaniment pictures her tripping grace. A bright interlude reaffirms sentiment and key. As the violet ponders its heart's desires, the key and mode are momentarily clouded. Then the brightness of the major returns with an active Alberti bass and a right hand that follows the voice and adds to its rapture "flowery" turns. It is here that the quiet lyricism is transformed into a dramatic scene.

Mozart, a man of the theater—this song was written on June

8, 1785, just before *Le Nozze di Figaro*—interprets the situation
with recitative, the tension heightened by the changing harmonic and rhythmic patterns of the accompaniment. The cadential phrases beginning with *"und sterb ich denn"* re-establish
the tonic that has been absent since the first division of the song.
So closely ordered and unforced have been the key changes, we
have been aware only of the natural movement of the song. In
these final measures the song resumes a lyric joy. Note the widening sweep of the voice as it mounts in the climax to the tonic, the
emphasis on the word *"sie."* Note also the way that this is
matched by the increased activity of the accompaniment. It was
with *"zu ihren Füssen doch"* that Goethe closed the poem.
Unsatisfied with this rather bald narrative ending, Mozart repeats two phrases of the poem describing the violet; the first,
"das arme Veilchen," is sung *a piacere* over an arpeggioed dominant seventh; there is a hold, over the quarter rest, and then *a
tempo* appears the first repetition within the song, the three
closing measures of the opening strain. Despite this slight reminiscence, the song is *durchkomponiert,* the freedom with which
the composer matched the poet making it one of the early masterpieces of song.

One may admire greatly *Das Veilchen*, yet love more the
simpler but thoroughly characteristic *An Chloe*, or *Die Ver-
schweigung*. These two songs were jotted down in 1787 when
Mozart's mind was so filled with ideas that it is not surprising

to meet phrases here and there that we have met in works of his more frequently heard. *An Chloe* is introduced by six measures, in two-part writing save for the final stamp of the cadence. The principal idea is charmingly poised on the dominant, swinging thence to tonic with echoing replies as the cadence gently falls. In repetition Mozart chromatically varies the melody. The second idea enters in the dominant, its most engaging feature being the extended cadence. After a return of the first section, new material, C, in a broken rhythmic pattern, *"den berauschten Blick,"* enters in the sub-dominant. Much of the closing section is freely based on A. A little operatic and not entirely expected is the flourish of four measures during the last repetitions of *"aber selig neben dir."* The accompaniment then repeats the introduction, its first two measures stated twice, the second time an octave higher; in both, the voice adds a counter-melody to the cadence. The whole joyous song is like a composite of Mozart love ariettas.

The lyric that tells of the love of the reticent Damon for Chloe closes each stanza with the sage observation that "he is so young, and she is so fair, no more need be said." This little song of nineteen measures is without repetition of pattern, except at the close of the first and the last of the three divisions, when the accompaniment repeats the two-measure cadence with that little touch of variety that marks the artist. Although the voice is doubled almost constantly in this strophic song, generally the accompaniment in Mozart attains a fuller independence than heretofore.

Beethoven

THE FREQUENT criticism of Beethoven as an awkward writer for voice stems largely from a few passages in his bigger works where voices vie with instruments. The composer, intent on what he wanted to express, momentarily confused his media and impatiently commanded them to do the "impossible." In his mind's ear he had heard, and thus he was impatient with complaints of singers or players, as may be illustrated by his rebuke to Schuppanzigh, the eminent leader of the group that introduced many of Beethoven's string quartets: "Does he imagine that I think of his wretched fiddle when the spirit is upon me?"[7] In composing a song, Beethoven steeped himself in the poem, caught its meaning as a whole, and seriously set out to translate it into tonal language. Among his seventy-nine lieder there are some trifling songs, but by the high ethical seriousness of the texts, by their musical worth, and even by their number, about double that of Haydn or Mozart, one recognizes that with Beethoven the Art Song is no longer a mere diversion, an idler in the salon. This changing attitude toward the song is most important, for until the feeling prevailed that the artistic worth of a work was not to be measured by its length or the number of participants, the song could not emerge as a medium and form of the first rank.

This does not mean that either Beethoven or his public valued his songs as highly as his symphonies. Nor has the judgment of that day changed, for, except in rare cases, composer and public to this day have felt the song overshadowed by larger instrumental works. It is difficult for many to realize that a sketch in red chalk by Michelangelo is worth a great deal more than a Canaletto scene of Venice, large enough to cover the wall of a banquet room. However, it would be a madman who would claim that the sketch of Michelangelo was equal to his wonders on the ceiling of the Sistine Chapel. Michelangelo's sketches, Beethoven's songs, are but sparks from the anvils of Titans. Both were at their best when faced with the difficulties of shaping those gigantic fantasies that had troubled their profound, creative spirits; both worked best when not cramped by small spaces. It may well have been an artistic "claustrophobia" that led Beethoven once to admit to Rochlitz that he did not like to write songs.

[7] R. H. Schauffler, *Beethoven, the Man who Freed Music* (New York, 1933), 180.

35

However, in *Adelaide,* the most important of his early songs, composed 1795–96, Beethoven did not allow his fancy to be confined within the usual short space of a song. One must recall that the distinctions between vocal forms were not yet clear. Mere length never becomes the standard by which the classification is fixed, no more so than that the range of a voice determines its classification as tenor or baritone. By their quality or timbre ye shall know them. *Adelaide* has the length (ten pages, or both sides of a twelve-inch record), the freedom (parallels no song form), and the paragraph structure (six large divisions) of a solo cantata or aria. With Krehbiel, I like best the term which the author Matthisson used in a note to his poem in the 1825 edition of his works. There he characterized *Adelaide* as a "lyrical fantasia."[8] He added that of the various musical settings "not one of them put the text so deeply in the shadow" as Beethoven's, which is a high left-handed compliment from a poet. The melody of the song is amiable; the pulsing triplet figure of support is at times meditative and lulling; again, it rises in ecstasy in the apostrophes to the loved one, and still again attains solo position in suggestive program music reflecting waves, breezes, and nightingales. The recurrence of the name of the loved one is treated with magical variety. The *allegro molto* division resembles one of those many-paragraphed codas of the master's sonatas. The brusque change of meter, the answerings of voice and piano, the relentless drive towards climax, and the whispered cadence—all were prompted by the lyric and dramatic suggestions of the text which Beethoven so spaciously interpreted.

Not only to Matthisson's poem *Adelaide* did Beethoven bring its finest setting, but in his Opus 48 are found the definitive settings of six of the poems from Gellert's *Geistliche Oden und Lieder.* These poems appealed to Beethoven's deeply religious character. The most widely known of all his songs is *Die Ehre Gottes aus Natur.* Some of the joy and refreshment, the con-

[8] Ludwig van Beethoven, *Six Songs* (New York, 1902). With critical notes on the songs by H. E. Krehbiel. Schirmer's Library of Musical Classics, Vol. 618.

solation and inspiration which Beethoven sought again and again in nature, he found expressed in these lines and the music which they called forth is of a heroic grandeur and elemental simplicity. The melody is of severe strength in its chordal and diatonic line, and so sustained that it could best be satisfied by the tireless majestic tone of an organ diapason. The accompaniment of huge chordal blocks marches along four-square. It is small wonder that it is heard most often in choral setting, for few are the soloists who can measure up to Beethoven's demands.

In marked contrast is Beethoven's treatment of Carpani's text, *In questa tomba oscura,* which appeared as the sixty-third and last in a volume of settings of the same text by different composers. Among others commissioned by a Viennese patroness to make their contribution to this strange volume were Cherubini, Salieri, and Zingarelli. *In questa tomba oscura* is the embittered cry of a spirit who seeks the peace of death and commands her who was faithless during his life to disturb not his ashes with her poisoned tears. The solemn tread of the first division recurs, but with a repeated *in questa* at the beginning and with coda of a two-fold *ingrata.* After the repressed grimness of the opening, the middle section rises naturally to dramatic fervor, the rich dissonant chords of the accompaniment *tremolando* adding to the intensity of the emotion. The march of the bass starting in m.7 on the tonic (original key A-flat), reaching the dominant below two measures later, offers a bit of scoring that must have been due to the limited range of the piano of that day. Although the six octave piano (C_1–c'''') had appeared, more common were the five and one-half octave instruments with F_1 the lowest note. Since, at the time, Beethoven could not in the original key go lower than the bottom F in the beginning of m.8, he perforce breaks the tread of the bass octaves and has to be content with the single upper F-flat. It seems legitimate here for accompanists to continue the octaves to the dominant.

The Opus 83, composed around 1810, contains three songs, the poems by Goethe. Nineteen—almost a quarter of Beethoven's songs—have texts by Goethe. Not only was the musician drawn towards the poet (Rolland has a whole book regarding their "relations"),[9] but Beethoven was the first musician to sense deeply the worth of these poems. The romantic stress of the highly personal finds illustration in a poem, *Wonne der Wehmuth*, born out of the sorrow of separation from Lilli. Goethe has expressed in these few lines what Beethoven had often experienced, tears of unhappy love. After exaltation, the sting of bitterness and yet the pleasure of remembrance is so great that the cry is for the tears to remain. Beethoven's great loneliness and his search for the "immortal beloved" well up through these lines in music that is filled with poignant beauty. The repeated phrase, *"trocknet nicht,"* takes but half a measure, the accompaniment continuing with a solo line of descending scale. In this song, so short of length, so great in value, the accompaniment in thirteen of the twenty-three measures rises to solo position. The voice and piano are true complements, in an interplay

suggestive of Schumann. Yet within its short space we are led back to the first phrase in the home key (m.16); so rich, however, is the inspiration that only one measure is an exact repetition. There is a quiet tenderness in the few measures of the coda; in its final measure, the descending scale motive of m.1 sinks resignedly through to the tonic.

9 R. Rolland, *Goethe and Beethoven*.

An die ferne Geliebte

THE CONSTRUCTIVE genius of Beethoven, which shaped anew every instrumental form, found intriguing problems in the world of song. His musical impulse, stirred by the needs of the text, caused him to either accept or adapt and individualize all the designs at hand except the ballad, which rather strangely remained foreign to his nature. What is more natural than that he, who found the song a rather small and fragile domain, for he loved most the breadth and sweep of the symphony with a whole series of movements for orchestra, should bind together a half-dozen of these little songs and thus create for the first time a song-cycle.

The one example of such a procedure, *An die ferne Geliebte,* is Beethoven's most original contribution to the Art Song.[10] Just below the title in the first edition is printed *"Ein Liederkreis von Al. Jeitteles."* A garland or circle of songs! Then follows the name of the poet Jeitteles, a young Viennese medical student. The prominence thus given the poet is almost as new as the organization of the six settings into an unbroken musical cycle, which is truthfully characterized on that same title sheet as being *"Für Gesang und Piano-Forte."* The piano is seldom content to remain a mere prop for the voice, and the new emphasis on the instrument must have made this cycle appear to some like a group of piano pieces with a voice obbligato. These mood pieces are so intimate in style that Friedländer likens them to the old Italian house cantata,[11] and Krehbiel is reminded of Goudimel's harmonizations of the old Psalm tunes written "for the enjoyment of God at home."[12] They are extremely personal in intensifying the moods of the lover thinking on his distant beloved. In the third piece the lover sings to the clouds and brook and birds;

[10] A. W. Thayer, *Life of Ludwig van Beethoven* (ed. by H. E. Krehbiel, New York, 1921), II, 343.

[11] M. Friedländer, *An die ferne Geliebte,* 53.

[12] See the historical and critical notes by H. E. Krehbiel, Schirmer's Library of Musical Classics, Vol. 617, iv.

in the fourth, he laments that in May when the birds are nesting and all lovers are delighting in the spring of the year, he still must be lonely; and in the sixth, he hopes that the yearning of his songs will waken a response as his loved one sings them at twilight. Each song has its own function, and the study of keys, speeds, meters, and dynamic levels in the cycle is valuable. A word only regarding the terminal movements which are distinguished by problems of design.

The very first phrase cost Beethoven considerable concern, for it is found in many versions in his sketch books, the interval of the drop on *spähend* tried at the third, fifth, and sixth, but most frequently at the seventh. The eight-measure melody of

longing is followed by a two-measure lilting refrain, closing suspensively and followed immediately by the voice's eight-measure melody. The accompaniment, however, is changed, and we recognize what is rare in song form, a theme with variations. Beethoven had tried this freely in the earlier *Busslied* of the Gellert *Spiritual Songs*. Here, however, he holds the voice to the repetition of the theme five times, a slight but most poetic modification made in the fourth stanza where, on the word lieder, the voice arches over a third in an expressive triplet. The importance of the last song does not lie in the squarish first division or in the rather instrumental and formal development of the coda, but rather in the poetic and physical binding together of the whole cycle by the natural return of the first theme. Of the host of cycles that follow in Beethoven's train, none has greater unity in structural design.

Moser, in *Das deutsche Lied*, has taken the directions which Beethoven placed at the beginning of the song, *In Resignation*, as the key to the interpretation of all of this master's lieder: *"Mit Empfindung, jedoch entschlossen, wohlakzentuiert und sprechend vorzutragen"* ("To be sung with feeling, yet resolutely; well accented and enunciated").[13]

[13] H. J. Moser, *Das deutsche Lied seit Mozart*, I, 101.

CHAPTER IV

Schubert

B Y universal consent Schubert is the symbol of the Art Song. His forerunners had regarded it as unimportant, but none of his successors could think of song as a trivial medium. Yet none of these later master composers made contributions to song of as much importance as Schubert's gifts even to chamber music or to the symphony. Nor was Schubert of second rank in these fields. The world's acceptance of him as the symbol of song is due not entirely to the abundance and perfection of his songs, but in part to the fact that they are the beginnings of a new order. The song was not new, but Schubert's attitude toward it was. Irresistibly drawn to the song, he showered upon it his greatest gifts. With earnestness he attacked each problem afresh, for his very lack of academic training freed him from traditional solutions. Certainly, he tried on the mantle of Zumsteeg[1] in a few childish exercises, but he soon cast it off and remained throughout the rest of his short career peculiarly himself.

The intensity with which Schubert applied himself and the reckless extravagance with which he spent his ideas were directed by a sensitive poetic spirit. With all these powers he wrought the miracle of raising a relatively obscure art form from infancy to high maturity within a few years. There seems to be no parallel for this in the other arts even though one recalls the rapid flowering of Greek art and the wonders of Italian painting revealed by Giotto. The progress of operatic and instrumental forms from 1600 to 1825 is relatively clear and gradual,

[1] D. F. Tovey, "Schubert," *Heritage of Music* (ed. by H. J. Foss, London, 1927), I, 89.

but the history of song is filled with great voids, with scattered and tentative essays, and then, in Schubert, a sudden blinding efflorescence. How appropriate is Seraphicus, Schubert's Christian name usually omitted in the shorter form of Franz Peter. In truth he was one of the celestial beings gifted with love and light and ardor.

How unprepared his generation was for this new art is evidenced by the fact that it was not until 1819 that a Schubert song, *Schäfers Klagelied,* was publicly sung in Vienna. Yet Schubert had already poured forth the large majority of his more than six hundred lieder; in the year 1815–16 alone he had composed about two hundred of them. The public's taste had to be cultivated, and the greatest agent in advancing Schubert's cause was the baritone Johann Michael Vogl. An admired operatic singer, it seems almost paradoxical that Vogl should have been drawn to the simple and unaffected beauties of these songs, so fresh and free from catering to mere vocal effects. Vogl was drawn not only to the songs but to the composer. One may describe their holidays of 1819 and 1825 as the first concert tours of a lieder singer and accompanist. From Salzburg, Schubert noted that "the way in which Vogl sings and I accompany, so that for the moment we seem to be one, is something quite new and unexpected to these good people."[2] Although Schubert was commenting upon the performance, his words suggest cardinal factors in the making of the songs. All parts contributed to an indivisible whole. What Vogl sang was a new poetry. What Schubert played was a new instrument.

The year of Schubert's birth (1798) saw the formal inauguration of the new German romantic movement with the first issue of the *Athenaeum,* in which the brothers Schlegel stated the principles of romanticism. This was in part a protest against the neo-classicism championed by Goethe, following his Italian journey. The earlier work of this greatest of German masters belongs to the period of *Sturm und Drang,* which in its fresh ex-

[2] O. E. Deutsch, *The Schubert Reader* (tr. by E. Blom), 458.

43

uberance and meaningful personal sentiment is at one with romanticism. The great rushing movement towards freedom—political, social, and artistic—found in poetry one of its greatest outlets. After a long and sterile period, Germany was filled with poetry, and it was Schubert's fortune to be born at such a time. He was not too particular in his choice of poems; he accepted largely what came to hand, Schumann commenting that "he would have gradually set the whole of German literature to music; he was the man for Telemann, who claimed that 'a good composer should be able to set wall-advertisements to music.'"[3] What fortune then that he happened on many of the lyrics of Goethe in the first tumult of his genius. In all Schubert set seventy-three poems of this master, whose genius is summed up by John George Robertson: "No other German poet has succeeded in attuning feeling, sentiment and thought so perfectly to the music of words as he; none has expressed so fully that subtle spirituality in which the great strength of German lyrism lies."[4] But change "poet" to "musician" and substitute "poem" for "music of words" and the tribute is fit for Schubert.

We have a clue to the way in which Schubert accompanied Vogl, for he once complained of the "accursed thumping which even eminent players adopt, but which delights neither my ears nor my judgment," and he wrote that "the keys under my hands sang like voices."[5] The new world which had been opened by the piano was gradually being explored. Beethoven had revealed new glories—but "there is one glory of the sun and another glory of the moon."[6] Schubert reveled in this instrument's capacity for sustaining tone so that it "sang like voices." Such a simple, even bare, support as that of *Heidenröslein* sings and gives ample, sustained support. Another stock pattern, illustrated in *Who is Sylvia?* appears very tame in the almost ceaseless repetition of the chords in eighth-note motion; yet to this

[3] R. Schumann, *Music and Musicians* (tr. by P. Rosenfeld) (New York, 1946), 114.
[4] Encyclopaedia Britannica (11th ed.), XII, 187a.
[5] Deutsch, *The Schubert Reader*, 436.
[6] First Corinthians, xv, 4.

the new instrument gave dynamic surge. Color, a wide and immediately responsive range of volume, a smooth *cantabile* or a "curt and crepitant" *staccato*—all that is commonplace for us was a rich, new, expanding experience for Schubert and his world. The song could never have developed as it did without this new instrument.

Schubert's comment on his accompanying of Vogl, "for the moment we are as one," is suggestive of the way this master fused all the elements of the song into an indivisible whole. Poem, voice, instrument, melody, harmony, rhythm, design— they became one. There was no unjust emphasis on any one thing. In their union is the strength of Schubert. The poem is no mere peg on which to hang a piece of music, nor is the music so subservient to text that its own musical life and meaning must be sacrificed. One of Grillparzer's sketches for an epitaph for Schubert strikes the root of this: "He bade poetry sound and music speak. Not as mistress and maid, but as sisters the two embraced above Schubert's head."[7] The purpose behind this equal collaboration is the creation of a mood, the generative source of poem and music alike. The older German term of *Stimmungslied,* a song intended to produce a certain state of mind in the hearer, might justly be used for all of Schubert's lieder.

What went on within Schubert when he was in the act of fusing poetry and music, we can never know. His disturbing answer to one who asked him how he composed was simply that as soon as he finished one work he began another. Of the externals, we have evidence that relates the process to one of clairvoyance. No testimony is more revealing than that of Spaun, who in his *Memoirs* recounts how he and Mayrhofer one afternoon in 1815 went to see Schubert and found him "all aglow reading the *Erlkönig* aloud from a book. He walked up and down the room several times, book in hand, then suddenly sat down, and, as fast as his pen could travel, put the splendid ballad

---

[7] E. Istel, "Schubert's Lyric Style," *Musical Quarterly,* Vol. XIV (1928), 575.

on paper. As he had no piano we hurried over to the Convict School, and there the *Erlkönig* was sung the same evening and received with enthusiasm."[8]

The setting of the ballad is so vivid that part of Schubert's method of interpretation appears clear even in an objective analysis. His music for this interpolated song in Goethe's *Singspiel, Die Fischerin* (1782) has been subjected to repeated analyses and comparisons to Loewe and others. How niggling it seems amidst all its truth and characteristic beauty to focus the light on the false accentuation of the third line of the third stanza, *"Manch' bunte Blumen sind* an *dem Strand,"* in the Erlkönig's first enticement of the child. If one scans this and the very first line of the narrator, *"Wer reitet so spät,"* he discovers that even in a declamatory song the composer, having launched upon a vital musical illustration of mood, cannot always rein in his idea to match exactly the meter of the verse. Schubert may be said to stand more than halfway between the eighteenth-century musician who often rode roughshod over the verse and the composer of the latter part of the nineteenth century who was ever painfully exact in declamation.

Goethe's ballad, except in the first and last stanzas which give the setting and the dread ending, reveals the characters through conversation. These rapid phrases of dialogue, demanding a through-composed setting, tend to break down the line and unity of the composition as a whole. Schubert seized upon the ride and the storm to give not only a realistic background but also to bind the dialogue and narration together. Upon this background he drew the principal characters with such vividness that we are torn by the terror of the child, moved to compassion for the father and to hatred for the Erlking. The background figure of an octave, repeated in triplet motion for the galloping horse, is reinforced by an upward swirl followed by downward shuddering thumps, the symbols of the storm. These figures drive forward relentlessly, except when the voice of the

[8] H. T. Finck, *Songs and Song Writers*, 72–73.

Erlking wheedles the boy. Then, in a suave, sustained melody in the major mode, accompanied first by a dance figure and in his second entry by flowing arpeggios, the phantom masks himself. When, however, he reveals himself for what he is and would snatch the child, the tragedy is intensified by the continuation of the ride motive and its dynamic increase from a *pp* to a *fff* within a seven-bar phrase. The only other moment where the ride motive does not bring its unifying motion and color is during the final three measures. The upward march of the bass has led to the strangely distant chord of A-flat (original key, g), its very obscurity heightened by a distinct break in style, for here the score is marked *recit.* The piano sustains the distant chord and then is silent as the voice in simple cadence moves to the tonic; the instrument replies with a quiet, but tension-filled, diminished seventh which still seems far from home. Following a pause the voice closes on the dominant with the dread words, *"war todt,"* and the piano gives the fierce stamp of finality with a detached cadence, V7–I, marked *andante.* These last measures contain the only modifications of measure and tempo, and amidst the exciting depiction there is a surprising balance.

The narration at the beginning is approximately equaled by that of the ending, and their total measures are about the same as those of the phantom, or the introduction and interludes. The father's assurances are much shorter and their irregular phrase lengths are indicative of Schubert's intent to depict the text rather than fill the customary number of measures. Perhaps the most obvious means of characterization is that of pitch, the *tessitura* of the father, low, and that of the boy, high; the unearthly Erlking exceeds both in range and abandon. The methods by which the tension is increased are most direct. The distress of the child's cry to his father is sharpened by biting dissonance (m.42), and his increasing fear is marked by the rise in pitch, each appeal a tone higher (m.73, 98, 124). The Erlking is compliant and his levels also ascend (m.58, B-flat; m.86, C; m.117, E-flat). The uncanny power of Schubert in striking directly to the heart of the character is illustrated in the Erlking, whose first song is filled with calm assurance; in the nervous flow of this tragedy, its fifteen measures seem very spacious. When next he promises dancing and singing and laughter, even with the repeated and intensified refrain of the last line of the stanza, in his eagerness for his prey his song is compressed to ten measures; his last threatening promise takes but seven.

This great masterpiece waited six years for public performance. Since Viennese publishers would not accept it because there was no market for an involved song with a difficult accompaniment, Spaun sent it on to Breitkopf und Härtel at Leipzig. They found it so unlike the style of the violinist Franz Schubert they knew that they returned the music to him. He not only disowned but characterized the song as "claptrap."[9] *Erlkönig* was published by subscription in 1821 as Opus 1.

Gretchen am Spinnrade

A WHOLE YEAR before *Erlkönig,* Schubert's sympathy for Gretchen had been roused as he read Goethe's *Faust.* There in her garden muses Gretchen as she spins. Her peace is gone; yet she dreams of her lover, his noble form, his radiant smile, his commanding eye, his hands, his kiss. The spinning wheel begins its circling motion, and over its monotonous hum the voice

sings a sad sweet refrain. These are the two constants: this nine-bar refrain beginning each of the three sections of the song, and its first half recurring as an echo in the coda. The pattern of introduction-refrain-interlude-stanza is used three times, but

[9] Tovey, "Schubert," *Heritage of Music,* I, 83.

Schubert intensifies the scene by increasing, (first), the length (23, 39, 44), (secondly), the distance of the modulation (mediant, flatted fifth, flatted second), and, (thirdly,) the tension of both harmony and melody. The second stanza is a free variation of the first, but the third is essentially entirely new. Its gradual rise in repetition of pattern leads to a thrice-repeated phrase before it leaps a fifth to the climax; the last two phrases reinforce the climax by repetition. As superb as is the climax, even greater insight is revealed in the emotional height of the song at the ending of the second section, and in the drop back to the gray level of a half-recalled refrain in the coda. In the former, as Gretchen has pictured in her mind's eye the beauty of Faust, her heart quickens; and as she recalls his kiss, she is lost in remembered rapture. The whir of the wheel is stopped, the undulation

of the melody arrested, and on a sharp dissonance all is suspended. Deep in the bass at the lowest level of the song, the dominant pedal sounds and Gretchen is pictured as returning haltingly to her work.

How a lad of seventeen could sense the subtler meanings of this scene and then divine music that would sustain and deepen its whole emotional world can never be explained. That miracle, with many more that match it, is Schubert!

49

Heidenröslein

As ONE LOOKS upon the facsimile of Schubert's score of this lyric,[10] he wonders how so slight a thing could mean so much. Schubert scored but sixteen measures, placed a repeat mark, and then wrote underneath to the left the text of the second stanza and to the right the third. It appears so bare; there is no introduction, only the simplest sort of accompaniment alternating a single note in the bass with a two- or three-note chord in the right hand. Its melody lies within an octave and its rhythmic pattern is crystal clear. Goethe's seven-line stanza is matched by Schubert with a fourteen-bar melody, spatially and tonally balanced by four-bars tonic, six-bars dominant, four-bars "refrain" tonic. To this is added a gaily tripping two-bar instrumental reply, which serves as interlude between the stanzas. Goethe's lyric tells how the rose in her beauty attracted the boy, who heeded not the rose's warning that her thorns would prick him. Vainly she opposed him. They both suffered. Schubert caught at the surface beauty and outward music of the poet's lines, which he translated into a sparkling melody as inevitable as a folk tune. In pure strophic form, the music must serve for the first stanza epitomized in the word *Freuden* (joys) (m. 10), as well as for the final stanza, where the burden of the song is *leiden* (suffer).

Du bist die Ruh'

As so OFTEN in reading a poem which he was about to set, Schubert here chose a phrase which for him was the essence of the poet's song. Thus he could ignore the byways where the poet's fancy led and concentrate on the dominating mood. Schubert interprets Rückert's apostrophe to love as the giver of peace, and the music is colored entirely by this feeling. In utter simplicity, a gentle rocking of sixteenth notes begins, and if one were not searching for the secrets of Schubert, the introduction's

[10] E. Bücken, *Die Musik der 19 Jahrhunderts* (Potsdam, 1928), 47.

lulling effect would conceal its seven-measure phrase. With the entry of the voice, a four-bar phrase is repeated, answered by a more dissonant four-measure pattern, whose complement modestly starts the same; on the word *mein* (m.22), however, its line dips a half-step below the parallel point, on the word *voll* (m.18), and leads back to home key, with two bars added for cadence. An interlude of five bars over a tonic pedal closes with its last measure of sixteenth-note motion in the bass, offering one of those slight but sensitive Schubertian contrasts in keyboard color and spacing. Then follows an exact repetition of the voice part and an interlude for the second stanza. The third stanza begins as before, but its second measure introduces a new melodic line which steadily rises; it is supported by new harmonic color and the first notation by Schubert for dynamic change (m.57) from its highly restrained *pp*. A measure of rest follows this bold phrase, whose poetic figure of "light" must have led Schubert to this modified strophic or composite form. Further, the poet's third stanza, containing but three lines, differs from the others. The song is resumed with the simple quiet cadence of the other stanzas. A new interlude of two measures leads to repetition of this short third stanza. As the voice sings its last phrase, the piano breaks into an imitation of its melody, its last echo closing directly in simplest cadence.

It would seem indefensible to ignore the song cycles of Schubert as here we must do. If one were to consider them, it would have to be as complete cycles. There are no great new problems solved within them and there is a significant amount of second-rate Schubert among the forty-four songs. In the problem of organization it is true that the unconscious creative artist often "builds better than he knew." The analysis of Thomas Archer,[11] following in the footsteps of the Lorenz method, however, seems more fanciful than the composer. Archer discovers in *Die schöne Müllerin* a free rondo with prelude, and in *Win-*

---

[11] "The Formal Construction of *Die Schöne Müllerin*," *Musical Quarterly*, Vol. XX (1934), 401–407.

terreise an exposition (Nos. 1–8), development (Nos. 9–20), but no reprise—since the madness of the hero precludes a logical goal (Nos. 21–24). There is a pleasant tenderness in the story of the miller's apprentice following the babbling brook, which is vividly contrasted to the stark hopelessness of the dejected lover midst the winter's frost and snow. Either cycle roused Schubert to a few master songs, but he was always more uneven in a cycle of movements than many other master musicians. Indeed, if one takes any successive dozen songs, not to mention twenty or twenty-four as in these cycles, he will discover that Schubert strikes all around the clock. He could not always strike twelve.

Der Doppelgänger

WE CHOOSE for final consideration one of the six Heine lieder. The choice is difficult, for this new poetry which Schubert found in the "Home-Coming" sequence in the *Buch der Lieder,* published in 1827, stirred him to a new kind of music. Six months after the composer's death, Haslinger published the Heine songs, together with six settings from Rellstab and one from Seidl in a volume he titled *Schwanengesang.* Schubert explored many new paths in his last year. His settings of Rellstab's *Ständchen* and *Aufenthalt* represent the poles of an earlier discovered world; his music for Heine's *Am Meer* and *Der Doppelgänger* take us to a new continent. Bie holds the latter to be the charter of modern song.[12]

Schubert never did hew closer to the line than in *Der Doppelgänger.* There is a stark intensity in the repetition of the ominous chords of the four-bar motive that serves not only as introduction but as an *ostinato,* which supports in its stubborn, deep, gruff color the free declamation of the troubled voice above. Note the spacing of this motive with its melody tripled, the inner parts insisting on a dominant pedal. Six times it is repeated thus. The voice is well rooted in this dominant, too, and as it

[12] O. Bie, *Das Deutsche Lied,* 64.

moves forth again and again, only to return, it reminds one of the reciting tone of a chant. Although within a strictly metrical frame, the voice seems to declaim freely the poet's lines. Unadorned, the turn of m.21 is an intensification; the voice is servant alone of the sorrow and terror that grips the lover returned to where his love had dwelt. Lost in his grief, he is startled by the presence of another beside him. In terror he recognizes the figure is his phantom double. Why does it return to mock him? The voice has risen in fear as it recognizes the phantom (m.41), and the accompaniment has suddenly turned in a new variant of its basic four-measure pattern to a tense, thick harmony untouched before and made more impressive by a command for *fff*. Immediately, it sinks back to home key and a quiet *piano*. But the burning distress of the question of the lover to his ghost twists the harmony and melody, and the world seems less ordered than before as in the epilogue the returning four-measure leitmotif leads not to a hollow V^6_4 without third, but veers to a full chord on the flatted second (Neapolitan color). There is little light in the raised third of the final chord. This is a new

music. It is a strange union of a rigid pattern like that of a passacaglia and the freest kind of declamation that hovers between recitative and *arioso*—a strange union of pure mood and dramatic situation, a *Dramatic Lyric* in much the same way that the term was applied by Browning.

CHAPTER V

Loewe

THE only portion of the seventeen-volume *Gesellschaft* edition of the works of Johann Karl Gottfried Loewe (1796–1869) that remains green is the collection of ballads. It is not unusual for a man to be remembered for a single novel or statue, although it is seldom that such a work causes his name to be coupled with that of Dickens or Michelangelo. Loewe's name, however, is not only frequently paired with that of Schubert, but the gifted and industrious *Kapellmeister* of Stettin is often awarded the palm in ballad-making. In truth, it is Schubert who is essentially known for but one ballad, although he wrote several in his early years, the only period in which he was attracted toward this form. Every year the performances of his setting of Goethe's *Erlkönig* not only far exceed the total of performances of all the ballads of Loewe, but it is musically, psychologically, and emotionally beyond the more calculating northerner. But one swallow does not make a summer, and we go to a dozen or more ballads among the five hundred lieder of Loewe for the orthodox principles of the art ballad.

This term, or that of "modern ballad," is used to distinguish the consciously conceived poetry and music of the nineteenth century which stemmed directly from the earlier ballads. The earliest narrative songs are lost in a distant past. They were shaped and varied by succeeding generations of the folk; minstrels recited and sang the verse which may often have been fashioned to fit an existing dance tune. Hence, one explanation of the word "ballad" as derived from *ballare* (dance).

The musical characteristics of the early ballad are essentially those of the folk song; their melodies are unvaried in strophic repetition, the symmetrical phrases shaping a short, simple, and often tonal–rather than modal–structure. The direct forerunners of Loewe, such as Zumsteeg, Reichardt, and Zelter, were usually content to maintain the older forms. The title of *Romance* frequently appears upon ballads of the last half of the eighteenth century, although the romance, which lies halfway between lied and ballad, emphasizes the lyrical mood, the narrative of the dramatic event being incidental to it. The true fundamental of the ballad is the story of a struggle between conflicting forces. The fact that the poet is only the narrator restrains him from emphasis of the subjective and reflective. He strikes directly into the story, which is allowed to unfold simply and directly; all its action which may suggest a tabloid music-drama, all its overtones of sentiment which belong to the lyric—these must be transformed into narrative. In its impersonal presentation, epic, dramatic, and lyric elements may be joined, but the epic must predominate. It was not only in the recognition of this as of prime importance, but in the discovery of a convincing musical translation for it that the genius of Loewe was revealed.

Loewe uses the strophic form as a basis, but he moves freely within and without it, permitting the narrative to mold the design. Each of the opposing characters or forces has its own musical symbol, a sort of leitmotif, generally first stated in the voice, but freely changed and developed rhythmically, harmonically, and melodically both in the voice and accompaniment. Loewe's melody often settles down into a rather complacent *volkstümliches* pattern. At its best it is supple and suggestive, and most rarely brilliant or florid. His accompaniments are frequently content to support the voice, the topmost line of the rather full chords duplicating the melody. But it is not for this that we remember him. One notes with delight the ballads in which the accompaniment plays a major role, independently expanding the motives and sketching in pictorial backgrounds. In addition, and less objective, is the intensification of mood, the importance of which is noted by Goethe who wrote: "The ballad requires a mystical touch, by which the mind of the reader is brought into the frame of undefined sympathy and awe which men unavoidably feel when face to face with the miraculous or with the mighty forces of nature."[1] Loewe often succeeded in creating this mood of the legendary and its world, peopled with knights or spirits, good and evil.

Many feel that his first flight was his highest, for his Opus 1, composed in 1818 and published in 1824, contains *Edward, Die Wirtin Töchterlein* and *Erlkönig*. Schubert's setting of this last was published in 1821, but it was composed in 1815. In addition to coincidence of opus number, the choice of key is the same, G minor, and there are broad similarities in the use of the major mode for the King, low *tessitura* for the father, high for the child, and recitative for the ending. One might expect greater truth of declamation in the studious Loewe than in the impetuous Schubert, but we discover that in the King's first appeal to the child, Loewe, like Schubert, stresses *an*. One notes the change of meter in this division, and when the measure returns to 9/8 and is continued for the King's second entry, the repetition of the same melody in new measure brings many false accents. In the first phrase alone *"Willst"* has too little stress, and *"seiner"* and *"mit"* as well as the length of *"Knabe"* are unduly emphasized.

The magic spell of the Erlking over the shuddering child is woven of a simple arpeggio, the symbol of the natural world itself. Loewe marks that it should be "stealthily whispered and alluring." Its support is a pedal in bass and alto, a *tremolando* above of fifth and third in sixteenth notes, while the tenor doubles the voice. Many have pointed to the arpeggio as the fitting depiction of the ghostly Erlking, as the voice of the wind, as a magic spell. Its plain pattern serves for all the entries of the specter. This is a rationalistic interpretation as understood by

[1] A. B. Bach, *The Art Ballad*, 32.

56

Komm, lie_bes Kind, komm, geh' mit mir

the narrator or the father who could not perceive this misty shape. To the boy, however, as to Goethe and to Schubert, the King was all too real.

As Sir Donald Francis Tovey wrote, "Schubert uses melodies as pretty as the Erlking's promises."[2] The first two measures of Loewe's accompaniment set up a tremulous stir, and then the bass rises through two octaves in a loping figure of the ride. A more agitated figure of a ride motive appears just before the second entry of the King and returns for the final stanza of narrative. Except for the father's last "assurance" to his poor child, the tonal plan has been tightly knit about home key. Now, however, as if in reckless desperation, in five measures four keys are touched, each a major third lower; the last brings the octave full cycle but now in major mode. The succeeding two measures heighten the tension as the bass expands its leap to an augmented sixth, which leads to a I_4^6, supporting free recitative of the voice. Note its broken line, each word separate; note, too, the care in scoring as the word *"Kind"* passes and a strangely suspensive dominant is left sounding alone in the tenor. In place of the sharp finality of Schubert's ending with its direct cadence, the four measures of Loewe's descending line sound like an eloquent threnody.

It may appear to some that Loewe has been exalted and then directly debased in the comparisons to Schubert. Critics still de-

[2] Tovey, "Schubert," *Heritage of Music*, I, 90.

bate the virtues of each as illustrated in this superb ballad and most would agree that it is Loewe who, in his "objective firmness," has not forced the boundaries of the ballad style.

Much greater is Loewe's setting of *Edward*. Schubert's strophic setting of this ballad is far from his best, and certainly Loewe's Op. 1, No. 1, has no rival. Sprung from Scottish soil, so rich in ballads, this story of mother and son was discovered by Herder in Percy's *Reliques;* translated lovingly by one who treasured these folk legends, the tragedy lost nothing of its sweeping intensity. The questions of the mother and the answers of the son mark natural divisions in the form. Yet this very alternation makes unified continuity difficult, and nowhere is Loewe more convincing in his genius of fusing word and tone into an organic whole. The choice of separate themes for mother and son is natural, and their difference is sharpened in the first divisions by change of meter, a 6/8 for the mother, a 2/4 for the son; the themes are varied in repetition. Most interesting is the introduction of the son in bare, clumsy harmony, the voice doubled by the bass; for his second reply the voice now moves in thirds with the bass. The transition to a new meter, C, which from its introduction through to the ending is common to both personages, is made by the son beginning his third answer in the 6/8 measure of the mother. Gone is his sullenness, and in a sudden wild directness the murder is confessed. Key, meter, melody, accompaniment—all are new and form a vivid climax, which in an eight-measure codetta sinks into deep gloom.

The second large division of the ballad opens with the mother's fourth question, a sharp rhythmic figure whipping forward the accompaniment, first above for the mother, and then in the bass for a different theme of the son. The fifth pair of questions and answers somewhat parallels the second in being a variation of themes directly preceding. In the fifth answer, the intensifying and heightening force of the motive is lost and the voice joins the bass in a falling scale, its last half dropping eerily in whole steps, in free sequence repeated, but only after a twice-stifled and tormented groan of "mother." With new rhythmic variations and modulation to home key, the sixth division leads to the coda. Here the mother's theme varies but slightly the broken phrases of the third question; but now it is harmonically inflected to the second key. A dramatic pause follows, and immediately in the first key and with some likeness to his confession, the son shouts his curse; the vocal line is sustained while through five successive measures the accompaniment pelts the arpeggiated tonic chord in sixteenths; thence, it moves outward to a rolled diminished seventh with an immense hollow between right and left hands. In terrible wrath and anguish, and with magnificent directness, the voice brokenly drops from tonic to dominant, *"ihr riethet's mir!,"* and again the interpreter is challenged by the interjection, "O," which he must color differently each time.

With a nod toward the old Mastersingers' lied, one may analyze this ballad as consisting of two bars and coda, each bar comprised of two *Stollen* and *Abgesang,* each of these in turn corresponding to a question and answer of the verse.

Question and Answer:	1	2	3	4	5	6	7
Ideas:	A B	A'B'	C D	E F	E G	E H	C'J
Measure:	9		37	69	94		127

Edward is grim and dour, a masterpiece in mood and structure that moves irresistibly to its terrible climax. It is one of the finest flowers of the northern ballads, by a master who once proudly wrote from Vienna, where he had sung this very work, "Herr von Vesque, proposing my health, called me the North German Schubert."[3]

3 Bach, *The Art Ballad,* 84.

CHAPTER VI

Schumann

S CHUMANN's approach to music is strikingly different from that of his forerunners, who were destined for music from infancy. Long delayed in practicing the piano, Schumann's ingenious device for hurrying nature generated new obstacles that turned him toward a composer's career. To this he brought a deeply imaginative nature that had drunk deep of romantic poetry and novels. He could see eye to eye with their makers; their world was his world, which Schumann proposed to translate into tone. Naturally his first choice of a medium was that which he knew best, the piano. For it he created a distinctly new idiom which so completely satisfied his musical yearnings that he did not score for any other medium from his Opus 1 (1829) through Opus 23 (1839).

Then he saw a new heaven; he had seen visions before as he had been stirred by Jean Paul and enraptured by Johann Sebastian. But this new vision was Clara! His marriage to Clara Wieck, so long opposed by her father, was in legal process of being sanctioned; and after many years of both eager and anxious waiting they were wedded on September 12, 1840. As the year opened, piano pieces which he had offered to his Clara no longer seemed sufficient. What was inevitable was that he should burst into song. The sentiments of his own love he found only partially expressed in the poems of his romantic contemporaries. He would not only give voice to their words, but he would support and enhance them with music for a piano, whose magic he had been discovering in the past ten years. In a letter of February 19, 1840, he said: "I am now writing nothing but songs, great and small." He expressed his delight in this as compared to instrumental composition and realized what men ever since have found to be true, as he noted, "I have brought forth quite new things in this line."

Wherein the newness? Like the true romanticist Schumann claims a place all his own. No one more truly drank from his own cup. There is little that is worn or trite in the 138 lieder of 1840. From the choice of the poem to the instrumental epilogue, one discovers highly individual touches. Schumann once wrote of a new kind of music which Chopin had voiced in his *Préludes*: "In every piece we find, in his own refined hand, written in pearls, 'This is by Frédéric Chopin'; we recognize him even in his pauses and by his impetuous respiration."[1] And, as surely, we recognize Schumann in even his shortest songs.

The central clue to Schumann's style is the combining of all parts into a whole. Any one factor may be observed apart and found to be in its own terms imperfect or incomplete. The most obvious illustration of this is in Schumann's concept of the song not as for voice with accompaniment, but as for voice *and* accompaniment. Both are imagined at the same moment. Their values are at least equal and often Schumann illustrates the ever growing tendency since Schubert to make the accompaniment emotionally more important than the voice. The term accompaniment, meaning a subsidiary part, is highly inappropriate for most of Schumann. His pianoforte almost invariably assumes a major role. No longer does the piano merely support and form background and occasionally say a line of its own; now there is dialogue, and the voice and pianoforte intertwine; again, to the piano is assigned a whole soliloquy or a penetrating remark on the poet's real meaning, only half-revealed through his words in the singing voice. Introductions, interludes, and epilogues were never so important. Quite unlike any previous treatment accorded the epilogue is that given by Schumann. His use of the coda of the song is somewhat like that which

[1] G. C. A. Johnson, *A Handbook to Chopin's Works* (London, n.d.), 171.

Beethoven realized in the coda of the sonata. Their spheres and intentions are quite dissimilar, but both masters extended the coda's boundaries from a mere clinching of the argument by a firm cadence to the introduction of new and important ideas. In Schumann's lieder, whether the ending repeats or comments upon a principal motive or whether the close seems a natural but new extension and flowering of the poet's lines, the epilogue is felt as far more than a satisfying musical coda. Here is a poetic rounding-out of thought and mood. The singer must recognize it as such, for otherwise he will chafe at the new importance of the pianoforte and its last phrases. Indeed there are few of Schumann's songs which focus the final attention of the public on the singer. Many of the songs are like the short pianoforte sketches in that they are so delicate and intimate that they generally ignore the public, and the interpreter is left communing with himself.

The student of these songs will find many illustrations of rich harmonies, now bold, now veiled. He will discover most subtle and ingenious introductions of foreign or dissonant tones; syncopations and anticipations have much more importance than heretofore. There are few realistic or external program figures; even in the songs of nature it is the mood behind the scene which Schumann tries to capture. The texture varies from a loose filigree to compressed polyphonic development. His sensitiveness to poetry often leads to freedom in design, with few examples of pure strophic. Yet in the shortest and freest sketches there is evidence of a love of unity and symmetry, most frequently secured by motival repetitions, rhythmic, melodic, and/or harmonic. There were many in the eighteen forties who agreed with Robert Franz, no mean master of the song himself, that Schumann's lieder were "piano pieces with superadded vocal part."[2]

It was not of such songs as *Der Ring, An den Sonnenschein,* or *Frühlingsnacht* that Franz wrote. Schumann can write

[2] Finck, *Songs and Song Writers,* 125.

rounded phrases for the voice and whether the line be diatonic or skipping, sustained or madly running, the melody feels vocal and holds the center of the stage. But there are songs of Schumann in which the voice has little sweep, and even a short phrase may find its completion in the piano; or a slightly longer phrase may be symmetrically answered by the instrument. The short phrase, interrupted or not, tends to be repeated at different levels. There are poems which are matched with folk-like melodies; others tend toward free recitative. Most unusual is that of *Ich hab' im Traum geweinet,* in which the voice is unaccompanied during half of the song.

One is inclined to belittle the voice because of the new importance given to the piano, especially its interludes and epilogues. In a volume of fifty-five of Schumann's most frequently sung lieder,[3] there are but two in which the measures of piano "solo" approximate those for voice. Strangely enough, in both, *Nun hast du mir den ersten Schmerz gethan,* Op. 42, No. 8, and *Hör' ich das Liedchen klingen,* Op. 48, No. 10, the measures are almost equally divided between voice and piano; but the first is not a fair example, in that it is the ending of the cycle *Frauenliebe und Leben,* in which the epilogue is not for a song, but for a cycle. By repeating the music of the first of the eight songs, Schumann suggests the widow in her grief turning back through the years to picture her hero as when first his image filled her dreams.

Thoroughly characteristic of Schumann is the grouping of songs in a cycle. Earlier he had gathered together short pianoforte pieces and had loosely bound them under a poetic title. With similar freedom he made a circle of songs (*Liederkreis*) from the poems of a single poet, as in Op. 24 and Op. 48 (Heine); Op. 35 (Kerner); Op. 37 (Rückert); and, Op. 39 (Eichendorff). A certain unity results, but in none does the series of songs form one piece of music. In his second cycle of twenty-six songs, seven poets are represented. The title is a delightful fancy—*Die*

3 Schirmer's Library of Musical Classics, Vol. 120.

Myrthen ("Myrtle Leaves"). Instead of our traditional orange blossoms, the German bride wears a wreath of the myrtle's shining evergreen leaves and sweet-scented white flowers, once held sacred to Venus. The cycle was for his Clara, to his beloved bride.

Widmung

FOUR OF Schumann's finest songs are in *Myrthen,* and we shall stop a moment with each. The first of the set is one of his most joyous love songs, *Widmung* ("Dedication"), the poem by Rückert. The first division is all fire and intensity and glows with its apostrophe to the loved one. The prelude is only a measure, just enough to set a jubilant figure swinging; then eagerly the voice enters with a firm melody, in which the accompaniment cannot resist joining, while still maintaining its swinging figure. The second division has the quality of a trio, and although of the same tempo, the longer note-values of the melody, supported by the chordal accompaniment pulsing in triplets,

Du   bist die Ruh,'   du   bist   der Frie_den,

give one the impression of great breadth and depth. The enharmonic change to the major third below the first division of the song is restful to the ear. The first phrase of this trio, *"Du bist die Ruh',"* reminds us that this poet used the same words for the beginning of a love poem which called from Schubert one of his finest lyrics. The transition anticipates the return, as over a dominant pedal the accompaniment sets swinging again its original figure. The return is shortened by two measures, and the cadence, placed a third lower, does not have the lift of the exposition. This gives to the last phrase greater assuredness and dignity; the accompaniment drops its eighth-note figure and reaffirms the voice except in the last, where the latter's jump of a sixth is thrilling. The epilogue in its repeated cadence continues but softens the mood.

Der Nussbaum

THE COUPLETS of Mosen's poem tell of a maiden who is lulled to slumber by the rustling leaves of the nut tree that whisper a bridegroom will come next year. The song grows out of the first two measures which reappear exactly as a *ritornello* eight times and in modified form several more times. Its sixteenth-note arpeggio motion is a poetic, but not realistic, suggestion of the breeze which stirs the leaves. The melody of the pianoforte is answered by the voice, the accompaniment continuing in lacy broken chords. The second vocal phrase moves to the dominant, but in a measure leads back to the mesmeric *ritornello*. The fourth couplet, *"Sie flüstern von einem Mägdlein,"* is new, and although the following couplet appears as a return, its close is new and extended; this leads to a coda whose ten measures quietly rise and fall over a tonic pedal. The dreamy sentiment of the song is a miracle of monotony.

Die Lotosblume

SCHUMANN's first songs, the Op. 24 *Liederkreis,* were settings of poems by Heine. In them the composer failed to scale the heights he reached, with apparently effortless ease, only a few months later in music for verses of the same poet. The Op. 25, No. 7, *Die Lotosblume,* is the joining of Heine and Schumann summoning what Shelley once described as

Some world far from ours,
Where music and moonlight and feeling
Are one.[4]

In fancy Heine sees the moon's light, which wakes the lotus flower that blooms and glows and trembles as she joyously reveals herself to her lover, the moon.

The accompaniment begins with a gentle repetition of the tonic chord in six-four position, much loved by Schumann, and the top line of the chords now and again doubles the melody. The voice in a close, diatonic line gradually rises to a climax, followed by a three-fold cadence, the accompaniment echoing the second, and deep below supporting the last. The very first phrase illustrates one of the infrequent lapses of Schumann in declamation, as he breaks the verb in two, separating *"ängstigt"* from its reflexive *"sich"* by a half-measure of silence and bringing undue emphasis on the latter. Schumann was fond of interrupted melodic phrases, and most frequently if the pause was of an appreciable duration, the piano part sustained the interest by continuing or answering the voice or by introducing a new element. The last is found here, with a bit of melody rising in the bass; its value is greater than would appear, for this is an accompaniment which, except for the final cadence, is concerned only with a rich harmonic support. The best illustration of Schumann's broken melodic line is in *Allnächtlich im Traume,* where there are eight phrases in the eleven-measure stanza, with the second offering false declamation similar to that in *Die Lotosblume.*

Du bist wie eine Blume

THE MOST FREQUENTLY set of Heine's poems is this exquisite lyric from the *Buch der Lieder,* and the most frequently sung of the

---

[4] "To Jane: The keen stars were twinkling" (stanza four). Indeed Shelley's lines are equally true of the magic that Schumann and Eichendorff produce in *Mondnacht,* Op. 39, No. 5.

settings is Schumann's. Small wonder, for its twenty measures create a flawless gem. Above an almost constant sixteenth-note pulsing chordal accompaniment, the voice matches four lines with four phrases, balanced, yet with a persistent continuing line which leads to the dominant. The rising duo in bass and alto at this point guides the course back to home key, and the voice repeats the melody of the first half of the opening stanza. The accompaniment which began with its three-note chords of the right hand, sustained by a deliberate bass pitched about and below center, now rises the octave, the left hand joining in the active pattern. Now the essence of Schumann's lyricism is perceivable as the last two phrases call forth a new music. Note the interweaving of pattern between voice and piano, and that it is to the latter that the climax is given. In the melodic fall from this the voice joins; then follows an epilogue rich in softly dissonant colors, the topmost melodic line reluctantly coming to rest.

Die beiden Grenadiere

ALTHOUGH HE IS essentially a lyric composer, in the catalogue of Schumann's works it is surprising to find how frequently he banded together in threes, ballads and romances. Schumann was not a man bound to hard and fast distinctions, and with romantic fervor he permitted the poem to lead him to its goal, which only then became his. If *Die Löwenbraut* is closest to the ballad traditions of Loewe, *Die beiden Grenadiere* is a much more natural fruit of Schumann's tree. Heine's ballad tells of two soldiers of the *Grande Armée* who, freed from a Russian prison camp, were returning to France. En route they heard of the Battle of Waterloo with the defeat of their army and the capture of Napoleon. In his sorrow one grenadier thinks on death as his wounds burn. The other soldier's thoughts turn to his wife and child who would perish without him. The first veteran scorns such sentiment for family when his Emperor is captive. But death is near, and he asks his companion to see that he is buried in France with the Cross of Honor, gun, and sword. Then, as a sentinel, he will await the return of his Emperor and rise from the grave ready to defend him. The effect of Schumann's setting is that of music which is constantly shaping itself to fit the dramatic narrative, that is, as *durchkomponiert* dramatic ballad. In truth the strong and martial theme, A, used to introduce the characters, and its musical complement, B, m.10–19, with accompaniment in grave-appearing half-notes, return, and with slight variation seem meant exactly for the conversation of the soldiers. Note the variation of the accompaniment as A enters the third time, *"Was schert mich Weib,"* the growing intensity is marshaled by increasing speed, the new triplet figuration in the accompaniment of B, and finally by volume. Repeated four times and serving as transition is the two-measure phrase, m.53–54, with its syncopated accompaniment of but a measure's length, the bass of the second an octave higher.

Then as a symbol of French patriotism, Schumann has the grenadier swear his loyalty to the tune of *La Marseillaise,* the accompaniment marching along in sturdy column-like chords, and the major mode most brilliant. Twice woven into this is an extension of the sixteenth-note motive of m.2. Probably Schumann had in mind this climax and made his first theme such that the introduction of the national hymn seems musically inevitable. The last six measures offer another illustration of the way in which the musician reads between the lines of the poet. There is nothing in Heine's poem to indicate anything other than a heroic ending, as the soldier visions his Emperor again the victor; and thus it is usually treated by the singer-actor. But the soldier has twice told us that his time is near. He has been buoyed up by his excitement, but his strength is not sufficient. His last phrase Schumann marked not *allargando,* but *ritardando.* This is not a heroic ending of grandeur, but a transition and decline to the slow, sustained, drooping chords of the epilogue, whose last two measures are *adagio.*

Dichterliebe

THE BEAUTIES of the poetry of Heine and the music of Schumann are joined in the sixteen songs of this cycle, although one naturally places the garland as a crowning glory on Schumann's head. Heine was little more interested in the musical translations of his poems by Schumann than Goethe had been in those by Schubert. Even if the advance in the poet's appreciation of the composer was slight, there was a thoroughly new attitude of the musician toward the poet. Franz Liszt writes of Schumann as a dweller in the worlds of both music and letters; heretofore music and letters had been separated as by a wall, and any contact had been after the fashion of Pyramus and Thisbe.[5] Heine's lyrics were just such as Schumann would have written had he been able to compose in verse as he did in tone. Thus he was drawn to a new poetry whose span was often very short, whose subjects were intensely personal, filled with sentiment, now exquisitely veiled and delicate, again aflame with the cynic's sneer. It was not merely the "text, but the context" which Schumann subtly divined. He seemed to be the poet's "double," following him in his most extravagant fancies and often extending his meanings, intensifying his moods.

One section of the *Buch der Lieder* is the *Lyrical Intermezzo* in which the poet confesses he has poured his anguish and revealed his heart. There is no plot, no action; the poems flow from a heart which only occasionally sings of a love without sorrow; there is a haunting refrain of the faithlessness of the loved one. Remembered joys turn into bitter wounds that rankle. Choosing the first four of these poems in sequence and then skipping among the remaining seventy-one for twelve more, Schumann personalizes them by inventing the "poet" and entitling his selection *The Poet's Love*. He thought of these songs as being sung in sequence, and the passage from one to the next,

[5] F. Liszt, *Gesammelte Schriften* (Leipzig, 1882), IV, 115. An English translation of a part of this is in *Musical Quarterly*, Vol. XI (1925), 615.

although direct and without transition, may be romantically exciting but never tonally startling.

The suspensive cadence at the end of the first song, *Im wunderschönen Monat Mai,* has often been chosen as an example of Schumann's freedom and responsiveness to text. Certainly the words are neither abrupt nor inconclusive; but the motive, which is but half completed in the piano and finds its true goal in the voice, may represent the poet's meditation on that happy May day, when he pledged his love. What was more natural to Schumann than to repeat the questioning motive of the introduction in the final measures, and let the cadence fall where it might. This was a cycle, and the second song flows without a ripple from this cadence; but Schumann does not continue in this vein, and the only other venture in uniting the separate songs is at the close of the cycle, where the epilogue of No. 12 is repeated and expanded. The reason for the choice of this particular epilogue is not as apparent as was the repetition of the first song in *Frauenliebe und Leben,* previously commented upon. There is a mock-heroic air in the last of the songs, *Die alten bösen Lieder,* where the "poet" sings that a coffin large enough to hold his bitter songs and sad dreams must be bigger than the great Heidelberg cask (49,000 gallons) and longer than the bridge at Mainz. But in the last stanza recurs the burden of the cycle—love and pain—and as the *adagio* changes to *andante espressivo* and to major mode, its key is a half-step higher than in its original statement and a fifth higher than that of the opening of the cycle. But its mood is in the "right" key and it is the perfect poetic completion of a superb cycle. Numbers 1, 13, 14, and 16 have already been noted, and from the others we choose No. 7 as illustrating a facet of Schumann upon which we have not touched.

Ich grolle nicht

HEINE WAS NOT content with this single outburst of bitterness, as he repeatedly and vehemently swears that he would not complain though his heart should break, for he saw through all her outward richness a heart filled with wretched night. The following poem in the *Lyrical Intermezzo* repeats the phrase, *"Ich grolle nicht,"* and pictures further the loved one in her angry pride, but admits that his misery is like unto hers.[6] Heine's imagination had not needed the spur of reality. However, from "great grief he fashioned this song"; he had loved his cousin Amalie, but she had married for money rather than love.

It is not strange to find this intense despair in Heine, but it is astonishing to find Schumann able to match it. His music is painfully sharp, a passionate and tragic outburst. Only in the last five measures does the bass give up its stern march in half-notes, and terrifically relentless is the downward diatonic scale through an octave and a sixth (m.22–28). Only in the last meas-

ure does the relentless drive of repeated chords in eighth-note motion find completion in a gruff cadence, where each chord is cut sharp and clear and separated by an equal block of silence. By the strong accents on the first of each series of four chords and by the emotional tension one feels in the biting dissonances, the song is ever pushed forward. The vocal phrases are short, stifling in their contempt. Schumann once wrote to Clara: "By

6 L. Untermeyer, *Heinrich Heine, Paradox and Poet*, 77. ("Yes, you are wretched, and I do not mourn.")

melody I mean something different from Italian airs which always seem to me like the song of birds—pretty to listen to but without any depth or meaning." The melody of this song is neither *cantabile* nor *recitativo,* but its dramatic declamation has elements of both and certainly has depth and meaning. Its design is like that of *Du bist wie eine Blume,* the second stanza (m.19) repeating the first nine measures and then moving to a new ending, followed by codetta and epilogue (m.30–36). The two songs represent opposite poles of Schumann's genius; the warm and tender, even hesitant lyricism of *Du bist wie eine Blume* finding expression much more frequently than the direct and passionate tragedy of *Ich grolle nicht.*

CHAPTER VII

Franz

THERE was a day when Franz was always placed beside Schubert, Schumann, and Brahms. After disasters overtook Franz and helplessness forced him to resign from various posts at Halle, widespread benefit concerts that yielded some $25,000 relieved him of financial worries. Such interest and sympathy was aroused not by the sad fate of a faithful functionary of Halle, but rather by the composer of little songs which had sung their way into the hearts of his generation. Rivals for the people's affection, Abt and Jensen, have since faded almost beyond hearing, and even the star of Franz no longer appears to be of first magnitude. The same qualities of truth and beauty which Franz's contemporaries discovered in his songs are found in them by this generation; but the truth, though as honest and sincere, and the beauty, though as pure and undefiled, do not disturb us so deeply.

I suspect that many have been unconsciously influenced in their judgment of Franz by the tiny range of his art. The same charge of minuteness used to be leveled against Chopin,[1] and the two artists have many other points in common. As early as 1855 Liszt, in a discerning essay on Franz, drew many interesting parallels between these artists. Since then the one has waxed and the other has waned. This change has not been due to the occasional use of the larger forms by Chopin. A receptacle for salt by Cellini may well be worth a couple of bad cathedrals; a twenty-measure prelude by Chopin or lied by Franz is more to be prized than many a symphony. As perfect as are these songs

[1] Liszt, *Gesammelte Schriften*, IV, 223–25.

of Franz, they issued from a nature that confined itself to a world of narrow boundaries, a nature that could not effuse or soar for more than a moment at a time. If one, like him, will not rebel at these limitations, then there may be discerned the reasons why a select few still place Franz with, and not below, Schubert, Schumann, and Brahms.

Franz reminds us of the ancient Roman god Janus, who is represented as facing both forward and backward at the same time. Franz was a romanticist, and it was the warmth and freshness that Schumann found in the bundle of twelve lieder sent him by the hesitant composer that led Schumann, without Franz's "knowledge or desire," to send the songs to a publisher. Upon their publication in 1843, Schumann, in his *Neue Zeitschrift für Musik,* reviewed the Opus 1 as not an isolated product but bearing "an inward relationship to the whole development of our art during the last ten years."[2] Franz is hailed as the profound interpreter of the new poetry in a "noble and new style," for the performance of which one needs "a poet as well as a singer."

Franz was a part of the new romantic movement, but his nature was such that he never permitted himself to be carried into the middle of its turbulent stream. He was ever stopping to test his own music and trying it over to see "if it be in tune" with the fundamentals he had learned from Bach and Handel. Equally sensitive was he to the old chorales and folk songs. His attitude toward the art takes us back to the Minnesingers; he once wrote that his songs "must not excite, they must bring peace and atonement."[3] Frequently years passed while he was shaping and reshaping a little song; and since his fastidious taste could not abide a smudged copy he kept rescoring the song to have a clean sheet.[4] The opus numbers from the first (1843) to the last, Opus 52 (1884), bear little relation to the actual period

2 Schumann, *Music and Musicians,* 241–42.

3 Like this is the composer's statement that "the ethical side in my songs is the chief thing," "Franz," *Grove's Dictionary,* V, 309.

4 Facsimile of *"Auf dem Meer," Songs of Robert Franz* (Boston, n.d.), xviii.

of composition. Franz said that he had never had "enough vanity to add the date and year" to his songs.[5] One can understand why such a modest soul was vexed by the preposterous charge that he made up his name by joining the first names of Schumann and Schubert. Actually his family name was Knauth, but his father, in order to distinguish that branch, had accepted the name Franz. At the time of the composer's marriage in 1848 royal permission was granted to retain the name.

Franz was a sweetly stubborn man who, once having set his course, doggedly held to it. Much as he admired Schubert, he felt that the Viennese master's strongly dramatized scene and exuberant rush of melody often exceeded the boundaries of song. Some of Schumann was either too violent, too bitter, or too humorous for Franz's taste. A common meeting ground was a reflective dreamy mood, tinged with melancholy. Franz was always searching for poems, which, as he expressed it, made "music grow out of the text." He never set a ballad, and his avoidance of this, as well as his predilection for the highly personal, contemplative lyric, led Ambros to characterize him as a *Stimmungslyriker,* one concerned with moods, not situations.[6] In a letter to Liszt dated September 29, 1855, Franz freely acknowledges the part that the new poetry played in his music-making, writing: "The poet furnishes the key to the appreciation of my works; my music is unintelligible without a close appreciation of the sister art; it merely illustrates the moods, does not pretend to be much by itself . . . The word is steeped in the tone, or forms, as it were, the skeleton which the sound clothes as its flesh. Therefore, it is easy to sing my songs if the vocalist saturates himself with the poem and thus endeavors to reproduce the musical content."[7]

Franz's illustration of the text was not detailed. He let the crosscurrents of the poetry play upon him until they had re-

[5] H. Kleeman, "Robert Franz," *Musical Quarterly,* Vol. I (1915), 497.
[6] *Ibid.,* 499.
[7] Finck, *Songs and Song Writers,* 138. See Liszt, *Gesammelte Schriften,* IV, 221, for extension of this.

solved themselves into a central mood, and this was what streamed forth into music. He never enforced his interpretation upon the poetry, but rather tried to get behind it and reduce its essence to a musical motive.

The song grows from this germ. It expands and flowers rapidly under the lyric concentration and honest craftsmanship of a devotee of Bach. Occasionally there is a counter or answering theme, and these phrases move between the voice and accompaniment; generally there is a heightening process with frequent use of sequential repetition. At the top, the line curves back, and, though never with violence, the final cadence comes to rest via unexpected harmonic paths. The design that such methods bring is almost invariably a strophic form. Occasionally the last stanza calls forth some change, perhaps a new counterpoint in the accompaniment. Schumann had called upon Franz to build "more stately mansions,"[8] but Franz remained content with short, strophic songs. But, like the miniaturist, he reveled in the challenge to fine and exquisite workmanship. If Franz could never write large, he could write exceedingly fine.

The almost invariable use of strophic form may well have been due in part to Franz's deep love of the old German folk songs and chorales. Not only did their structure become second nature to him, but one discovers melodic, rhythmic, and harmonic turns that could not have been used so naturally except by one whose musical speech had been permeated by the idiom of the church and folk. Sometimes the sources of these turns are physically apparent; again one may feel only the spirit or idealization of the original. Franz once wrote that Handel had been his model, but of the *bel canto* of the Italians, which he admired in this master, we find little. Essentially, Franz's melody is simple, diatonic, and moderate in range. His songs were conceived for mezzo-soprano, and since the range was never excessive, Franz felt that any transposition was unpardonable; for him, the color and meaning of the song were changed by a shift

[8] O. W. Holmes, "The Chambered Nautilus" (stanza five).

of key. This is but another evidence of the purist, for whom the dotting of the i's and the crossing of the t's in his own works were sacrosanct.

Philipp Spitta and many later musicologists were certain that Franz, with the best of intentions, was too free in his realizations of Bach's scores, and had mistakenly crossed the i's and dotted the t's. If then the original key of the song meant so much to the composer, we may be certain that any modulations within its measures were not haphazard, but planned with great regard to both word and tone. The composer held that modulation was more effective than melody in emotional development. Since the designs are short, excursions to other keys must be few and not too distant. Much admired was a modulation up or down a small or large third. Sometimes the tonality wavers; and frequently joined with either the major or minor mode are phrases in the old ecclesiastic modes.

A sensitive shifting within these three regions is found in *Die Lotosblume,* Op. 1, No. 3, with a touch of the Dorian in the haunting, upward-inflected phrase (m.5–6) and dropping chain of sixth-chords leading to a major mode, a large third below the opening. Moving in and about the Phrygian mode, *Es klingt in der Luft,* Op. 13, No. 2, was marked by the composer *"Im alten Tone."* There has been considerable emphasis on the modal and contrapuntal qualities in Franz. Both are present, but not in the degree one would expect from the criticisms. The great majority of the lieder are thoroughly harmonic, though far from "hurdy-gurdy, sing-song writing." All the most usual supporting patterns are found, but Franz treats each type with remarkable variety and ingenuity. The old *volkstümliches* straight chord support, in which the top line doubles the melody of the voice (*Widmung,* Op. 14, No. 1), has variants in which the melody is in the alto (*Aus meinen grossen Schmerzen,* Op. 5, No. 1) and the accompanying chord off-beat; and the voice may be doubled in both tenor and soprano (*Meerfahrt,* Op. 18, No. 4). When the melody is duplicated in the bass, the chords of the right hand most frequently are syncopated, or extended in broken triplets as in *Ja, du bist elend,* Op. 7, No. 6, whose dramatic interpretation by Wagner was disliked by Franz.

Auf dem Meer, Op. 6, No. 1, illustrates the non-doubling bass on the beat, with syncopated chords in the right hand. Different patterns of broken chords are occasionally employed (*Die Lotosblume,* Op. 1, No. 3; *Nachtlied,* Op. 28, No. 3). An independent melody is carried on by the accompaniment of *Am leuchtenden Sommermorgen,* Op. 11, No. 2, and this also illustrates the unusual hollow spacing between the right and left hands often found in Franz. Unique in design, range, accompaniment, and melody is *Der Fichtenbaum,* Op. 16, No. 3, the contrast of the dream of the palm tree bringing a glittering accompaniment, and the flatted sixth an exotic color. Even in the simplest accompaniment (*Bitte,* Op. 9, No. 3), Franz is free to vary his pattern, and it is the melodic flow of a cadence or the actual countering of a melody that brings a feeling of polyphony. There are bits of canonical imitation, seldom more extended than in *Kommt feins Liebchen heut'?,* Op. 25. No. 4. His harmony is leavened with polyphony and tinged with modality.

Louis Ehlert has a famous paragraph in *Aus der Tonwelt* in which he is perplexed concerning the place of Brahms in the world of song. How would the newcomer compare to the great three, Schubert, Schumann, and *Franz,* each of whom created a distinct style as easy to distinguish as a poem of Schiller's from one by Heine or Uhland. "A Brahms lied is not always conceived for the voice with piano accompaniment: often in place of the latter could be substituted an orchestra or quartet, and the voice might be replaced by a cello or oboe. This likewise is often true of Schumann, seldom of Schubert, never of Franz."[9] Thus Ehlert held Franz to be the greatest of all, not in the power of invention, but in the disposition or planning of his song. Franz ever remains true to his medium; his are songs for voice and

[9] L. Ehlert, *Aus der Tonwelt* (N.p., 1880), 242 ff., cited in part in Finck, *Songs and Song Writers,* 141.

piano, the two so bound together that they fuse into one. Schumann sensed the need of "a poet as well as a singer," and for gaining the most of a song's delicate, intimate beauty he added, "they will please best sung when alone and at evening."[10]

Für Musik (Op. 10, No. 1)

IN MOOD AND hour of day this poem of Geibel would have pleased Schumann as it did Franz. As the shadows darken and the stars appear, the night trembles with a spirit of longing. Through a sea of dreams the soul seeks peace and offers its whole devotion. To music? No. Rather, to the loved one, the title suggesting only that these are lines "for music." The pattern is built on the opening two-measure phrase which reappears twice within the eight-measure stanza, each time the sequence at a higher pitch. In each of the phrases the melody has fallen from the half-note crest of its tiny wave, sustained by a cadence from six-four to root position, but always strangely suspensive in feeling.

The fourth and last phrase begins on the same point as had the third, but instead of falling, leaps a fourth to the tonic; yet a flatted seventh at the beginning of the measure and a I_4^6 on the second beat, where the voice stops, maintain a feeling of suspense. The color of the accompaniment has added to this, having begun with a I^6 and closed with a I_4^6; poised above the center of the keyboard (original key, G-flat), the melody doubles in the alto and echoes in off-beat chords in the upper part of the right hand. The return of the pattern for the second stanza is simply prepared by a V^7 on the third quarter of m.8 and by a melodic anticipation of the tonic on which the voice and the thumb of the right hand begin their duo, *unisono*. The third stanza offers variations which one comes to expect in Franz; the accompaniment is much fuller, the melody doubled in octaves; harmonies of the odd-numbered measures are altered, and a new countertheme woven in the tenor. The line of the voice is

[10] Schumann, *Music and Muscians*, 242.

79

Die sich dir er - - - ge - - - - ben

changed and marches straight up to its half-note. The greatest change of all is the extension of the final cadence, as the voice arches to unusual heights for Franz and comes to rest in a fully rounded, conclusive cadence.

Es hat die Rose sich beklagt (Op. 42, No. 5)

THE SIX-LINE STANZA from the Persian of Mirza-Schaffy, translated into German by von Bodenstedt, is divided by Franz, and his setting of the first three lines is repeated strophic fashion. One might expect irregularities of phrase lengths and patterns in a composer's translation of a three-line stanza into music; with this particular poet one might anticipate suggestions of Eastern color. With Franz, however, the extraneous is stripped away and he strikes deep to the heart of the subject which is revealed in simple beauty. His strophe is the usual eight-measure length, the most normal expectation for a quatrain, but certainly not for a tercet. The "fourth" phrase is most naturally assigned to the piano which introduces a questioning, wistful two-measure subject in the minor; the voice then joins and the second phrase leads to the tonic major. But Franz has avoided a square-cut cadence by introducing the seventh in the chord, which refuses to change though offered a second chance. The third phrase follows the preceding pattern, beginning ana-

crustically and closing on a seventh chord. Climax is reached
with the final phrase when the voice swings upward through an
octave and gently comes to rest. In mounting to the climax, note
the melodic lines which clash on the word *"ihr,"* e-flat, f, g-flat
(original key, D-flat), sounding all at once; the cadence which
follows is romantically rich in the tenor line, a sixth below the
chief melody, which is sounding in three voices. A four-meas-

den ihr der Lenz ge-ge-ben ha-be

ure epilogue is made of the piano's opening phrase followed by
a modification of the voice's first phrase, ending wistfully with
the third of the tonic chord at the top. Thus Franz expresses the
complaint of the rose that all too soon her perfume fades; but
the poet soothingly assures her that through his songs her sweetness will find life eternal. Yet the epilogue tends to make us
think about the passing of beauty rather than its permanence.

Half a dozen of the most frequently sung lieder of Franz
merit analysis. Though each has its own beauty, one finds similarities to the two examples just reviewed. Thoroughly characteristic is *Aus meinen grossen Schmerzen,* Op. 5, No. 1, in its
gentle fervor, its general pattern of short phrases with the last
cadence extended, its modification of strict strophic form with
the first half closing in the dominant and the last part of the
final stanza a new and rich diatonic melody with the cadence
in the tonic, and the short epilogue's reaffirmation with the basic

phrase. The accompaniment is one of Franz's favored patterns, the right thumb generally shadowing the voice, and after-beat chords with generous thirds and sixths gently rocking the song forward.

Widmung, Op. 14, No. 1, and *Bitte,* Op. 9, No. 3, are characteristic of another facet of Franz. The simple, rather full chords support a melody which needs but one chromatic, and that one to enter momentarily its most closely related key. Liszt wrote: "Since this composer loses himself so far in the conception of the sentiment that it often becomes a religious act, the result is that many of the songs bear the type of sacred music." The difficulties of choosing in this garden of lieder remind us of what many have observed: the general level of excellence in the some 275 songs is very high. The range of subjects and moods chosen is rather narrow. Yet Franz was not without dramatic feeling. The Eichendorff *Romanze, Und wo noch kein Wand'rer 'gangen,* Op. 35, No. 4, is *durchkomponiert,* programmatic, and includes *tremolando,* three different tempo designations, and even an *allegro vivace.* Ambros characterized it as an "entire romantic opera *in nuce* [in a nut shell]." The song at which Wagner marveled, *Ja, du bist elend,* has been mentioned. More gloomy, less vigorous, is the most frequently sung of Franz's dramatic lieder, *Im Herbst.*

Im Herbst (Op. 17, No. 6)

THE POET Müller's thoughts were here quite unlike those of Keats who sang of autumn as "A season of mists and mellow fruitfulness," when all fruit is filled with "ripeness to the core."

> *Hedge crickets sing; and now with treble soft*
> *The red-breast whistles from the garden croft;*
> *And gathering swallows twitter in the skies.*[11]

Müller was more attuned to Byron who wrote,

[11] J. Keats, "To Autumn" (stanza one).

FRANZ

My days are in the yellow leaf;
The flowers and fruits of love are gone,
The worm, the canker, and the grief
Are mine alone![12]

Müller dreads the season of autumn, for it is filled with memories of when the world was blooming and sweet, when "once twain we did roam. . . . But now I walk alone! My love is false! Oh, would that I were dead!" For Franz this is a large "time-canvas," to use a term of Walford Davies.[13] Its forty-four measures, however, break up into 14+14+16; the second is an exact repetition of the first, the third beginning as before leads to a bold, broad, stinging climax. Franz began the song with a grim unison march up the minor scale to the fifth, where it is broadened in time and harmony for the ascent to the tonic. The second phrase is an intensified repetition, and the descending pattern of the third phrase is made even darker by the doubling of the voice dropped to the tenor. The increasing intensity of the succeeding phrase is aided by the clear, syncopated accompaniment, freed from reinforcement of the vocal line.

The ending of the poet's stanza, *"O Weh!"* ("O Woe! Alas!"), is no mere rhetorical flourish for Franz. He paints it in purples and blacks, the two-note phrase wailing, and underlined by sombre, strange-colored chords that give a feeling of heaviness as they tardily move first in one hand and then the other. This phrase is like an interpolation, a dramatic "aside," and Franz completes the stanza's course by a sweeping cadential phrase, repeating the words of the last line. The final stanza, having begun as the first, is broadened to a *più lento,* and, as the lover recalls that once the world was so sweet, the cadence streams into the tonic major, the only bright color in the song. The second phrase is varied and echoed in the accompaniment. Then after a half measure's silence follows *largo,* the biggest (eight tones) and most sonorous (*ff*) chord in all Franz. Even more

12 Lord G. G. Byron, "On my thirty-sixth year" (stanza two).
13 W. Davies, *The Pursuit of Music,* 68.

83

extravagant, but quite justified and meaningful, is the contrast between the climax and the final phrase. The voice has mounted to A-flat, supported by a Neapolitan 6/4, *ff*; then, an octave and a sixth below, *p*, the voice resumes its journey in weariness and dejection. The fall of the drama is swift, only two measures in length and a minor third in range.

CHAPTER VIII

Liszt and Mendelssohn

Liszt and Mendelssohn—names that gradually became symbols of innovation and tradition, musicians who were equally and extravagantly idolized by their vast public! Their contribution to the world of song, rich and varied as it is, changed the course of song little; their belief in song and championship of it, however, accelerated greatly the public's interest in, and sympathy for, this art form. Mendelssohn, Sir George Grove held, introduced the German *Lied* to England; his songs and duets were home and concert favorites everywhere. Long before Liszt had composed songs, he had made familiar some of the lieder of Beethoven and Franz through his own poetic transcriptions,[1] which he frequently included in his own pianoforte recitals. From Schubert alone he reset fifty-seven songs. One of his most effective transcriptions is of Mendelssohn's *Auf Flügeln des Gesanges*. The singer of "mere" songs was making headway and the path was wider and less thorny, because Mendelssohn and Liszt went that way.

Liszt

Liszt was in a very real sense of the phrase a man of the world. Though Hungarian by birth, he was at home in every capital of Europe. Indeed, it became easy for him to "speak" in "inter-

[1] What more natural then than to find Liszt later occasionally issuing simultaneously a song and his transcription of it for pianoforte. Some, like the *Liebesträume*, are rarely heard as songs. The No. 3, *the Liebestraum*, is a setting of Freiligrath's *O lieb so lang du lieben kennst*. More familiar in pianoforte transcription too are the *Tre Sonetti di Petrarca*.

national clichés." He wrote songs in several languages, but German predominates. In this he is a symbol of a host of foreigners who were naturally attracted to the German *Lied*. Among them were Russians, Scandinavians, and, even Americans—for some excellent early songs of both Edward MacDowell and Charles Griffes were settings of German poems.

It would be profitable to compare Liszt's settings of Goethe's *Mignon's Lied: Kennst du das Land* with Beethoven's settings, or match Liszt's tonal-translation of Heine's *Du bist wie eine Blume* with that of Schumann. We would discover that the Abbé does not fare badly. When one compares his setting of Goethe's *Wanderer's Nachtlied: Über allen Gipfeln ist Ruh'* with Schubert's fourteen measures of spacious peace and perfection, one observes how the course of song had tended away from the fresh wonder and musical spontaneity of "childhood," to the more troubled literary consciousness of a later age. Indeed, this increased care in reflecting not only the general mood but the inner meaning of individual words, with a "keener psychological use of harmony and counterpoint, constitutes the fundamental difference between modern art song and lieder."[2] Bainbridge Crist, in *The Art of Setting Words to Music,* maintains the two can never be the same. His illustrations of the modern Art Song, however, begin with Debussy. Alfred Einstein maintains that Liszt "discarded the compact lied form in favor of the rhapsodic though still, as a rule, not formless presentation, thereby originating the modern song."[3] It is to a great extent, however, a question of degree.

Returning to Goethe's *Wanderer's Nachtlied,* one finds that in this instance Schubert was more general and Liszt more particular in setting words. In two of Liszt's most admired songs there is little detailed word setting. *Es muss ein wunderbares sein,* the poem by Redwitz, is simple and sincere, as general and

[2] B. Crist, *The Art of Setting Words to Music* (New York, 1944), 5.
[3] A. Einstein, *A Short History of Music* (2nd ed., New York, 1938).

as German as a lied should be in Crist's distinction. Liszt's setting of Victor Hugo's *O quand je dors* has the general elegance and charm of a French romance. More characteristic is the setting of Lenau's *Die drei Zigeuner,* which introduces a strain of a Hungarian czardas. The form is fluid as the symphonic poem which Liszt established, and each of the three gypsies commands a section, tonally responsive to the scene. It is the violinist whose agile brown fingers summon a czardas; the smoke that curls from the pipe of the second and meditative gypsy is mirrored in the accompanying figure; the last is sleeping, but for him, as for the others, there is his own refrain of a gypsy dance. As Liszt gathers Lenau's lesson—that when life is most troubled one may recall how the carefree gypsies thought not of the morrow but fiddled and smoked and slept away the day—the composer has offered an optional close fourteen measures before the end. This is even harder to explain since the poet's lines would not then be concluded.

Liszt however felt that the public would prefer the earlier close to the more extended and dreamy coda. The virtuoso Liszt's concern for the public accounts for some strange artistic slips in a composer who generally treated his poet or subject rather scrupulously. One is reminded how Franz, in a letter of October, 1873, expressed joy that Hueffer had linked his name with that of Liszt, with whom, despite the differences of method, he felt a closer affinity than with Schubert or Schumann. Franz agreed that Liszt and he were "first of all poets, and only secondarily musicians," and wrote that only on this basis "further organic progress of song seems possible."[4] Here again Liszt offers difficulties of classification, for he belongs as much to the painters as to the poets. It was his strong intuitive musicianship that often saved him from the worst pitfalls set by pictorial and literary will-o'-the-wisps.

[4] A. Aldrich, "Robert Franz on Schubert and Others," *Musical Quarterly,* Vol. XIV (1928), 410.

Die Lorelei

THE LEGEND of the betrayed maiden who threw herself into the Rhine and became a siren, luring many a boatman to his destruction, is the foundation of various art works. Heine's poetic version of this tale has called forth some twenty-five songs, the one by Friedrich Silcher having the status of a true folk song loved far beyond the banks of the Rhine. Its tune is so good that one is scarcely aware of the awkward emphases of text; and like a folk song each of the six stanzas is set to the same lilting music. Liszt felt the drama and saw the pictures of the legend and these he set forth vividly.

It was in the summer of 1841 in the idyllic island retreat of Nonnenwerth in the Rhine, just a few miles north of Remagen, the famous bridge-crossing of World War II, that Liszt meditated on Heine's poem. Heine creates an atmosphere for the legend by personalizing the despair of one who is gripped by this ancient story. This opening stanza Liszt translates into a tense (diminished sevenths), orchestrally minded (as celli with off-beat chords of accompanying strings), eight-measure piano introduction. The first two lines of the poem are set in a free recitative, whose last two phrases repeat the mood-bearing word, *"traurig,"* in more sustained melody. With the *allegretto,* only fifteen measures from the beginning, Liszt employs a third metric signature. Here is introduced a new motive, B, of two eighths (completing the first stanza); there follow eight bars of sinuous transition leading to a 9/8 and the parallel major in m.31. This flowing figure is the Rhine motive, C, which by m.50 has responded to the last rays of the sun which light the mountain's summit (modulation to V^b). *Una corda,* ppp, the bass supports, with chords repeated in triplets, a sweet *cantilena* first announced in the pianoforte (m.50).

Note the slight but effective changes of this melody when the voice replies. As the golden comb glitters, a modulation begins, the key a minor third higher taken in m.61, the voice curl-

Die Luft ist kühl   und   es   dun _ kelt

ing about the tonic in a suave "double turn," illustrating *"Sie kämmt ihr goldnes Haar* [she combs her golden hair]." The accompaniment as well as vocal line becomes more involved, driving toward a change in key, meter, and tempo in m.73. Two measures later the *agitato* B motive (first appearance in m.15) returns, intensified by a triplet repetition of a single note in the alto, its pitch rising as the voice tells of the sailor, who is so entranced by the vision and the singing of the Lorelei enthroned above (note the literal height of m.83–84), that he sees not the reefs. Busy *tremolandi* and deep chromatic swirls (m.85) push toward the dread climax as the angry waters swallow both boat and boatman. To come away from this high tension and drop quickly back to the pensive atmosphere of the beginning is difficult. But it is thus that Heine's last two lines command: "And this with her singing the Lorelei has done." Four measures of a rising arpeggio, followed by a long silence, have cleared the storm; the voice returns with the same recitative as in m.9. The B motive, having already served for the tumultuous climax, is now barely sounded, C entering in m.107 and in the relative major. The whole division appears as a recapitulation, but the Rhine section is a little long for the repetitions of Heine's last two lines. Liszt extended them, however, but permitted an optional cut of ten measures starting in m.110! The coda (m.124–31) reinforces the sweetness of the Lorelei's song by romantic harmonies, and, as the voice slowly drifts upward to the tonic, the accompaniment reaches in the last measure the tonic chord which is slowly arpeggiated.

Mendelssohn

MENDELSSOHN SCARCELY ever touched bold heights or soul-stirring depths in his music. Critics have tried to account for this by relating the untroubled course of his life. Born in and sustained by riches, never suffering from lack of ideas or the technique with which to express them, an enthusiastic audience always awaiting each new work—what is more natural than that the artistic output should be genial and elegant. If it be so, however, let us recognize that it was not merely a reflection of an unruffled life, but rather a creative imagination that preferred to move in such pleasant worlds. All of his music is in the temperate zone, but there are fewer interruptions of its tranquillity among the songs than in any of the other media.

There are seventy-nine lieder in Mendelssohn's catalogue, but five of the early songs were by his sister Fanny. The opus numbers spread all along the years. Surprising is the recurrence of bundles of six, seven sets of lieder so appearing; and in sixes are the eight books of the *Songs Without Words,* the organ sonatas, and several issues of part songs. He must have felt this to be his lucky number, or perhaps it is just another evidence of his orderliness. These songs are marked by grace and charm. For present tastes they are too obvious, the composer having been content with the surface of the poems. The melody has a pure beauty of its own, and one must grant to Mendelssohn a keen sensitiveness to what is vocally natural. The voice part almost invariably dominates the scene, the accompaniment lacking distinction in its support. It seems strange that this great admirer and revealer of Bach should have practically closed his songs to the life and vitality that some counterpoint would have brought. His harmonies are simple, their consonance little-disturbed by any strong or sustained dissonance. Strophic form prevails, its course marked by harmonic logic, its seams observed from afar. Mendelssohn is guilty of no sins of taste or workmanship in his songs; they are a sort of distinguished but harmless variety of *Kapellmeister* music.

Auf Flügeln des Gesanges

THIS IS THE only Mendelssohn song frequently sung, and it is even more frequently played. Written at Düsseldorf in 1834 while Mendelssohn was municipal head of the music, it was dedicated to Fräulein Cécile Jeanrenaud who was soon to become his wife. The poem is from the richest single treasury of lyrical poetry of that generation—Heine's *Lyrical Intermezzo*. This, the No. 8, is Heine in one of his most innocent moods. In imagination he bears his loved one on wings of song to a haven on the distant Ganges. There they will be bowered in flowers, with roses and violets, and the lotus gleaming in the moonlight. Ah! would they were there resting under the palms, in love and quiet, dreaming a peaceful dream. In only four measures is there any cessation of the accompaniment's ascending arpeggio pattern in sixteenths, starting anew every half-measure of the 6/8 *andante tranquillo*. It suggests the lapping motion of a barcarolle, and its even pace is never once modified in the composer's markings.

Floating on the crest of the arpeggio waves, and most rarely dipping under their surface, is a gracious and limpid melody, perfectly natural and devoid of artifice. Let us note but two unusual features. There is a marked prominence of the third of the key, more than a quarter of the melody centering on it. More surprising is the appearance of the tonic only twice in the melody, at the end of the first (and second) stanza and in the next to the last cadence of the final section. Even though no *rallentandi* are marked, Mendelssohn has brought the effect of them by scoring longer note values in the melody, as in closing cadences of both sections (m.19–20, 33–36) and in the beautifully suspensive coda (m.38–42), slowly dropping to the mediant. The division of the five-stanza poem into 2+2+1, the music for the first pair of stanzas being exactly repeated, demands a modification of the pattern or the introduction of new material for the fifth stanza. The ease with which Mendelssohn has incorporated both elements, the old and the new, is suggestive of his role in history. The first phrase of four measures is melodically the same as that of stanza one, though the accompaniment is slightly changed; the second phrase opens with the figure of m.14, but this is repeated a step lower, the last eleven measures being new.

Cornelius and Jensen

THERE IS SOME logic in concluding this chapter with a few paragraphs regarding Cornelius and Jensen. Both were attracted to the new dramatic music of Liszt and Wagner. Cornelius, very intimate with both Liszt and Wagner, despite his gentle and rather feminine nature was strong enough never to lose his artistic independence. In a letter to Hestermann, December 25, 1849, he writes: "I do not dig in other people's fields, or adorn myself with others' feathers."[5] The poems of most of his lieder are his own; in him are joined the poet and musician.

The song cycle, Opus 3, *Trauer und Trost* ("Grief and Consolation"), so called from the titles of the first and last (sixth) songs, is a setting of his own verse. The second and third songs, though unrelated in text, dramatically reveal the keen, penetrating, psychological powers of tonal illustration. In *Ein Ton* ("The Monotone") the voice actually intones the verse at the same pitch throughout. It is the wondrous tone which the bereaved one imagines to be the breath which escaped from trembling lips. "Is it the melancholy sound of the bells which followed thy spirit's flight? This tone rings so full and clear as though it enclosed your soul, as though you lovingly bent down and sang

[5] E. N. Newman, *More Studies of Famous Operas* (New York, 1943), 44.

my pain to sleep." Cornelius's interpretation of this is no tour de force. The voice does not overdramatize the sentiment, but simply and unfalteringly declaims the text as if lost in meditation on these wonders. The piano seems little constrained by the fixed tone, about which it weaves in an almost constant eighth-note motion a rich and warm comment; its epilogue leads naturally to the magic tone which it sounds alone, lets fade, and then tenderly repeats.

In the succeeding song of the cycle the process is reversed, the piano maintaining the tonic through all but the last phrase. The voice sings its melody in such independence that only three times does it touch the tonic, so constantly sounding in the accompaniment. The recurring tonic must be the symbol of the door to the dream world which the poet pleads may open, that there in its mystic grove he may hear the sweet words and taste happiness again.

The best loved of the Cornelius songs are the *Weihnachts-lieder*. These gentle and intimate mood-pictures seem ever fresh and pure, some of the loveliest bits of sentiment that adorn the season of Christ's birth. Again the poems are the composer's own, and each of the six songs of this Opus 8, composed in 1856, has its own charm. Technically the most intriguing is *Drei Könige* ("Three Kings have journeyed from the Eastern land"), in which the brightly shining, guiding star suggested to Cornelius, who was seldom drawn to the old music as he was to the poetry of olden times, the old German Christmas chorale, *Wie schön leuchtet uns der Morgenstern*. The piano sounds the chorale, only slightly modified as at m.19–23, where the hauntingly beautiful and irregular pattern of the chorale, with its repeated "Jesu," is twice poetically extended a measure, as if there were a hold at the end of each "Jesu." From the beginning the voice blossoms forth in a perfectly free countermelody.

No less ingenious but to me more winsome are the last two songs. Number 5 contrasts the free melodic recitative with a flowing refrain. The last of the cycle, like its companions, brings no feeling of a prosaic metric pattern, although the designs in-the-large throughout are quite regular. As the voice sustains the last note of the second phrase, the piano sets rocking a gentle refrain, which brings in each later appearance some key and melodic change.

The *première* of Cornelius's opera, *Barbier von Bagdad,* under Liszt's direction at Weimar on December 15, 1858, was the focal point of a mounting opposition to the director who, following the demonstration, resigned his post. He recommended and the duke accepted as his successor Eduard Lassen (1830–1904). Like Liszt, he was a foreigner to the scene, but his artistic career was spent in the German orbit, far from his native Copenhagen. Many of his songs are graceful, warm, and filled with sentiment, qualities which are found in most of the lyricists of that day. Of greatest distinction among them and to be listed beside Franz and Cornelius is Adolf Jensen (1837–79). His first song, Op. 1, No. 1, *Lehn' deine Wang' an meine Wang'* ("O lay thy cheek against my own"), the No. 6 of Heine's *Lyrical Intermezzo,* has maintained its hold. It can easily be cheapened and made into a gushing sentimental song; in a performance fair to the composer the melody is warm and natural, the harmonies richly romantic, the form crystal clear. Certainly the mood of Heine's intimate and love-filled verse has not been overreached in this setting. Vying in popularity with it is Op. 24, No. 4, *Murmelndes Lüftchen* ("Murmuring Zephyrs"), a cradle song from the *Spanish Song Book* by E. Geibel and Paul Heyse. Tender, fresh, filled with a light fancy, the voice sings a graceful melody, its first division doubled by the pianoforte an octave below, while above, the right hand weaves its arpeggio arabesques "with gentle motion and as delicately as possible," as the composer asks.

CHAPTER IX

Brahms

THE fame of Brahms has never been greater than it is today. While he was living, men debated his right to a place among the master composers, and occasionally a dissenting voice is heard now. In the last chapter we noted the problem which Ehlert faced as he evaluated Brahms to determine whether or not he deserved a position beside the established triumvirate of Schubert, Schumann, and Franz. The "big noise" of the period, though, was Wagner; ears accustomed to his luxurious fullness found Brahms' music thin. Many were so blinded by the light that streamed from Wagner that they thought Brahms lived in a land of perpetual shadow. Typical of much criticism of the time is the space given by L. C. Elson, writing in 1888 a *History of German Song*. To Brahms he granted a single paragraph, while Wagner received two chapters.

I presume that Brahms' position would be little changed had he never written a single song for voice and piano, for his orchestral and chamber works would assure him a high place. Yet—and in this he joins hands with Bach whom he loved and from whom he learned so much—had Brahms never written anything for instruments, he would still be counted among the masters because of the wealth and beauty of his vocal works. He found abundant opportunity for practical experience with voices; he directed choruses both of women and of men, for whom he wrote considerable music. Nor was he unacquainted with the solo voice, for he appeared frequently through the years as accompanist for Julius Stockhausen and Frau Amalie Joachim, two of the finest lieder singers of the nineteenth century. Brahms knew intimately the melodic lines of Bach and Handel, of Schubert and Schumann. If then he molded the warm, supple, living medium of the voice into new patterns, it was not that he was ignorant of the accustomed ways, but rather that he divined new ones.

Brahms was relatively indifferent to the titles of his works, and his 194 compositions for one voice, with piano accompaniment, were issued as *Gesänge, Lieder, Romanzen,* and *Gedichte.* Included in this number is the Op. 84, captioned *Romances and Songs,* for one or two voices, with pianoforte accompaniment, but always heard as solo songs; excluded is Op. 91, *Two Vocal Pieces,* for voice, with pianoforte and viola accompaniment. Among the thirty-one opus numbers, he used a mixed title seven times, five of these for *"Lieder und Gesänge,"* between which there appears no difference whatsoever. The term *Gesänge* is found on the first three issues of six songs each and intermittently through Op. 72. Brahms finally settled upon the term *Lieder,* and only this term is used for the last collections, from Op. 85 to Op. 121, titled *Vier ernste Gesänge.* The song never lost its attraction for him; while still in his teens he wrote the first set, Op. 3, (1851), and the last music which he sent his publishers was Op. 121, dated May, 1896. (The eleven *Chorale Vorspiele* composed in the same May and June appeared posthumously.)

There is no such profuseness as one finds in Schubert's outpouring of 137 songs in 1815 or Schumann's 138 lieder in 1840. In Brahms' flood year of 1868 only twenty-five songs were issued. Since the creative artist often does his best work when the stimulus is the imagination, not reality, we can understand bachelor Brahms' attraction to and success with love poems. Yet Brahms was not without the friendship of women. Most ideal was his admiration for Clara, the widow of Robert Schumann, who had brought Brahms to the notice of the world. Most stimulating, in her penetrating criticisms of his manuscripts, was Elisabeth von Herzogenburg. But most exciting emotionally were Agathe von Siebold, whose voice Joachim likened to the tone of an Amati violin, and, later, Hermine Spies, a pupil of Stockhausen. Moser centers in them two periods of bloom in the making of songs: 1858–68, Agathe; 1882–92, Hermine. Some of the songs were composed with a particular voice in mind, most notably the *Vier ernste Gesänge* for Stockhausen. A few of the collections are specified for low or high voice, but here again, as in the choice of titles or the substitution of his favored string—the viola—for his favored brass—the horn— (Op. 40), Brahms was not exacting. As a result of his association with Stockhausen, Frau Joachim, and Hermine Spies, as well as his preference for the darker tonal colors and keys, we find more frequent scoring for low voice. Brahms did not mind transposition or transcription of his songs. Faced with the great variety of arrangements of his *Wiegenlied,* he jokingly inquired if it might not be advisable to have one in minor on hand in case the child fell ill. What he could not abide was a performance carelessly dishonest to either the score or, particularly, to the mood and meaning behind the notes.

That same sincerity and earnestness lay behind the choice of the poems which he set. Brahms was little influenced in the selection of a poem by the name of the author. Some have wondered how such a student and thinker could have been attracted to some of the verses he set, and, in turn, why he did not more frequently pick the great poems of the great poets. In general, he held that the more perfect the poem the less chance there was for music to enhance it. Of the seven poems from Goethe and the five from Heine, only one, Heine's *Der Tod, das ist die kühle Nacht,* called forth the great Brahms, and that perhaps was due as much to the subject as to the poetry. Brahms never considered the poem as something apart, but always as a stimulus of musical images, that once roused were put through the refiner's fire. The best account we have of the process is given by Sir George Henschel in his *Musings and Memories of a Musician.*[1]

[1] Published by Macmillan & Co. (London, 1918), 87.

The young singer Henschel had appeared with Brahms in a number of festivals, and once in 1877, as they were traveling from Coblenz to Wiesbaden, Brahms spoke of the problems of the composer. "There is no real creating without hard work. That which you would call invention, that is to say, a thought, an idea, is simply an inspiration from above for which I am not responsible, which is no merit of mine. Yea, it is a present, a gift, which I ought even to despise until I have made it mine own by right of hard work. And there need be no hurry about that either. It is as with the seed corn; it germinates unconsciously and in spite of ourselves. When I, for instance, have found the first phrase of a song, say:

I might shut the book there and then, go for a walk, do some other work, and perhaps not think of it for months. Nothing, however, is lost. If afterwards I approach the subject again, it is sure to have taken shape; I can now begin really to work at it. But there are composers who sit at the piano with a poem before them, putting music to it from A to Z until it is done. They write themselves into a state of enthusiasm which makes them see something finished, something important, in every bar."

In the process of deliberation and reflection some details of the words may have slipped away, but the essential mood was clarified. It was about this that the song crystallized. His was not a methodical A-to-Z or word-to-word setting, not heightened speech, but mood music; music that penetratingly revealed the realm of feeling and fancy whence the words had come. H. C. Colles has pointed out that a song writer is not saved by his good taste in poetry or damned by his bad taste. "It is his taste in music which matters."[2]

One of the strongest factors in the shaping of Brahms' style

[2] H. C. Colles, *Oxford History of Music* (Oxford, 1934), VII, 360.

was the *Volkslied*. He not only played and sang the old German folk songs for his own pleasure, but he took the melodies and with real affection wrote simple, artistic accompaniments, such as are found in the forty-nine *Deutsche Volkslieder,* published in 1894. There are fourteen additional songs set for four voices. Best-known of his work in this field, through the delightful *Sandmännchen,* are the fourteen *Volkskinderlieder* ("The Children's Folk Songs"), 1858, which he wrote for Robert and Clara Schumann's youngsters. Many were the composers before him who had been influenced by the folk song, directly and indirectly, but for none was it more fruitful. In number, Brahms' settings are fewer than Beethoven's "symphonies and accompaniments" for the Irish, Welsh, and Scottish folk songs, published by Thomson of Edinburg. But Beethoven's heart was not in this work. Imagine his being stirred by *Paddy O'Rafferty.*[3] Brahms worked with the music of his fathers; that he considered his settings a labor of patriotic love is evidenced by the fact that they are without opus numbers. There are a few of his art songs which are titled *Volkslied,* as in Op. 14; others clearly show the folk influence, and never does it seem a weak imitation, but rather a natural mode of expression. The folk traits are most obvious in his simplest music, but their natural, simple, robust qualities are present in Brahms' more involved expression. There it is more difficult to grasp. Even the smart music critic, George Bernard Shaw, in his salad days, advanced the untenable thesis that Brahms could sing or think, but not do both at the same time.[4]

The generative force in a Brahms lied is the melody. This is ever of first importance. Whether the melodic line be simple or involved, the form and accompaniment largely hinge on the voice part. Sometimes when Brahms was judging a song, he would cover the top line of the accompaniment with his finger

[3] "Paddy O'Rafferty" is noted in the Beethoven *Gesellschaft* edition as work #224 (without opus numbers): "Twenty Irish Airs."

[4] B. Shaw, *Music in London* (London, 1932), III, 146. "Nature inexorably offers him the alternatives of Music without Mind, or Mind without Music."

and, pointing to the melody and bass, say: "These are what count." He once cautioned Henschel that he "must endeavor to invent simultaneously with the melody a healthy, powerful bass."[5] That Brahms practiced what he preached is illustrated in some of his rough sketches, in which the chief line is the melody, supported here and there by a figured bass. We are familiar with the often illustrated fact that what is strange for one generation may become commonplace for the next. Brahms' melodies, which once were considered strange and unvocal, seem natural enough now, but certainly not commonplace. There is nothing cheap or tawdry about them. They still challenge the skill of the best singers. Brahms is master of the long, sweeping line; he uses all the voice, high and low, and demands a firmly sustained legato in both diatonic and arpeggiate phrases. The former reminds one of the folk song; the latter most frequently skips gracefully within the chord, as at the beginning of the *Sapphische Ode;* or, again, the jumps may be jagged and most angular as in *Der Schmied.* His melodies generally match closely the lengths and accents of the verse, but occasionally the sweep of the melody and its obedience to musical laws carry it beyond the goal of scrupulously just declamation.

Although the melody in the voice dominates the scene, the accompaniment is seldom a neutral background. Indeed, the pianist is inclined to think his part worthy of a central position in the foreground, for Brahms, in treating the instrument in unconventional ways, sets up difficulties with new patterns that seem naturally to merit independent status. One never feels that the accompaniment, however involved the texture, has become a show window for the composer's technical ingenuities. The complexities arise from Brahms' thinking both harmonically and contrapuntally. His harmonies seldom lack originality. They are frequently severe, sometimes noble; they rest upon the solid foundation of a "healthy and powerful bass." Heavy dissonances may appear on the accent, but tensions are seldom

[5] Henschel, *Musings and Memories of a Musician,* 112.

released at once. This gentler dissonance brings a luminous richness to his generally dark, occasionally thick harmonies. Brahms'
harmonies are shot through with melodic interest in the separate
voice parts. The term "healthy," which Brahms noted as an
essential characteristic of a good bass, evidently meant to him
not merely logic in harmonic progressions, but vital melodic
independence. He had a superb polyphonic feeling and the
technique to make it count. Despite the priority of bass and
vocal melody, inner voices are trusted with important things to
say. Nor do these independent strands separate and fall apart.
They all unite to form an organic whole. It is not by chance that
von Bülow's "three B's" has continued to include Brahms. At
one time there were Bruch and Bruckner, whom others had
nominated.

Often sharing with the counterpoint of melodies in the more
detailed accompaniments is a counterpoint of rhythms. Highly
varied are the patterns; Brahms can create a feeling of great
force by vigorous opposition of two rhythms. He loves the vibra-
tion set up by the division of a triple meter into both 3×2 and
$3 + 3$. Again, Brahms may suggest a timelessness through the
failure of a single rhythm to set up its rigid domination or perhaps by a shifting of the metric signature or the stretching out
of a cadence. How effective and lovely these accompaniments
can be, in and of themselves alone, was extravagantly but suggestively put by Schumann, after Brahms had roused him at
Düsseldorf in 1853 by playing some piano pieces and songs,
which resulted in Schumann's prophetic *Neue Bahnen*. Schumann wrote that the songs of this "young eagle" were "songs
whose poetry might be understood even without the words,
though a deep vocal melody flows through them."[6]

A song, to produce such an effect, must have been tightly
organized. There could have been no digressions, nothing extraneous. And not only was it unified in its materials, but also in
its mood. The one should grow out of the other, but not always

[6] Schumann, *Music and Musicians,* 253.

does one find a singleness of purpose as in Brahms. Once more we know the composer's ideas through his counsel to Henschel. On July 12, 1876, Brahms wrote to Henschel, as the latter records in his *Musings and Memories of a Musician*: "Let the song rest, keep going back to it and working at it over and over again, until it is completed as a finished work of art, until there is not a note too much or too little, not a bar you could improve upon. Whether it is beautiful also, is an entirely different matter, but perfect it must be."

With such love for fine craftsmanship, one might expect some cabinet work in dovetailing German words and musical phrases. Of this there is surprisingly little. The sentiment of the words is caught, and the structure that results is built on broad lines. Such a translation of mood into a living organism does not despise the strophic form. Indeed, Brahms glories in it. The form may be varied as in *Vergebliches Ständchen,* where the third of the four stanzas is shifted to the minor. In the three part form, ABA, the re-exposition may be exact (*Ständchen*) or modified (*Wir wandelten*); in either case the introduction of the contrasting idea, B, has seldom been dramatic, and invariably it has led back to the return in a natural and reasonable way. One does not have to study Brahms for a "method in his madness"; his is an Olympian grasp and logic. By nature and training Brahms was "classical." Yet his was a heart "in unison with his time and country," and the play of romantic freedom and waywardness within a firmly controlled design may be found in the short lyric forms as well as in the symphonies.

Liebestreu (Op. 3, No. 1)

BRAHMS WAS apparently indifferent to the effect of his compositions on his public, but his own feeling about this song has been affirmed by Joachim and Schumann. There were earlier songs that had been saved, but Brahms placed at the beginning of his first group of published lieder this setting of Reinick's poem, and

thus "put his best foot forward." Its strength and directness, both
of content and design, the more mature Brahms was seldom able
to match. In this work, a new voice sounded; these were "new
paths." An anxious mother counsels her daughter to cast aside
her love, which brings but grief. The daughter dreamily answers
that her grief will not sink as a stone in the sea, nor will it die as
a flower cut down. After the mother belittles her child's pledge
as mere words, which the wind might bear away, the daughter,
unshaken in her belief, cries that though the winds cleave the
rocks, her vow to her love will forever endure. Each of the three
stanzas is divided between the mother's exhortations and the
daughter's determined replies.

There is little realistic, literal picturing in the music. One
might expect the mother's melody to move in a deeper register
than that of her daughter. Brahms cannot be said to have used
this obvious means of characterization, for although the daughter sings a whole step higher, she also sings a whole step lower
than her mother. A literal declamation of the lines, which are
alternately of four- and three-foot lengths, is denied; the mother's pair of lines, repeated without change, result in a four-
measure phrase; the first and longer line of the girl's reply occupies an orthodox two measures, but the shorter poetic line
brings a longer musical phrase, as Brahms extends the cadence.
In somber key, *molto lento,* the right hand sounds the tonic
chord in $^6_4$ position and, repeating it, sets up a triplet figure that

continues to the end. These chords are the basic harmonic support, and thick (4-part) or thin (2-part), they move up and down and color the song. Only two groups of triplets (joined by Brahms as a sextolet) have set up pulse and mode, when the motive of the song is stated by the bass and, a beat later, answered by the voice. The fundamental unrest and conflict behind the song is summoned by the clash between the triplets and the eighths, and by the dissonant entry of the voice as its F is asserted against the doubled G-flat (original key, E-flat minor) of the accompaniment; the voice's groping upward in eighths coincides with the temporary calm of the quarter note in the bass. Through the mother's couplet, the push and pull of this dissonance and motion continue to the cadence on the dominant in m.5. There the right hand triplet chords move upward, the accompaniment then giving the semblance of a higher *tessitura* for the daughter. The bass now joins the voice, enhancing Brahms' direction of "dreamily."

As the years passed, Brahms left more and more to the singer's judgment, marking scarcely more than a tempo or mood. The early songs, however, were filled with detailed markings, and despite the deletion by Brahms of many of these for a second edition, most editors have retained his earlier aids. Note the degrees in tempo and force by which the song rises to its climax. The second stanza repeats exactly the music of the first, but moves *poco più mosso*. The final stanza is marked still faster, *agitato* and *forte*. The quiet assurance of the girl has suddenly changed to heroic declaration. The strict strophic form, which had been intensified in speed and dynamics, had held its line, but no longer could repetition serve such vehemence. In a new pattern for the final couplet, the voice is more clearly based on the fundamental motive; after such a stretch of lugubrious minor, the vigorous entry of the parallel major is miraculous; the *ostinato* motive of the bass widens to two octaves; the voice mounts to its climax, and in its eagerness the half notes of earlier stanzas have no place; yet this couplet with all its sweep and grandeur is compressed to four measures, ending as never before, on the dominant. The coda which follows tempers the heroic force and impetuous speed of this climax with a continuous ritardando and diminuendo to the very ending. The voice repeats the last four words in a broken line that descends in minor scale from the sixth to the tonic. Three times a sighing two-note phrase is followed by a rest, and, in the third measure from the end, the relentless pattern of the bass is stretched out; and, with its augmentation, the song finally closes, restored in tempo and mode, but spent in its mournful defiance.

Wie bist du meine Königin (Op. 32, No. 9)

THIS is Brahms in a jubilant mood, as he mirrors in his music the warmth and ardor of Daumer's poem, after the Persian of Hafiz. The loved one is a queen, whose smile is as spring, whose magic presence turns the desert into a cool, shadowed retreat. Even death would be joy could the lover but die in her arms. Like a refrain is the ecstatic repetition of *"wonnevoll,"* a word that has challenged all translators, variously approached as "joyfully," "blissfully," "wondrous sweet," "my joy," and "dear delight." The word appears to be too full of meaning, and even Brahms' translation into music differs three out of four times. Each of the four stanzas closes with a twofold cadence of this word, its basic pattern begun by the piano (m.16), the left hand continuing its fundamental role of an upward sweeping arpeggio in sixteenth-note motion, here on a I_4^6. The voice imitates the right hand melody (m.17), while the harmony changes to a seventh chord on the raised fourth, resolving in a conventional, but thoroughly satisfying $I_4^6 V_7 I$. The third stanza finds harmonic and melodic intensifications that lead to a return in m.60. The cadence of the last stanza is begun by the voice (m.75), which now accepts the extension of the second *"wonnevoll"* of stanza three, but adapts it to the original melodic and harmonic pattern.

Brahms' treatment of the varied strophic form is characteristically free and meaningful; in this lied stanzas one and two are identical; when stanza three begins with thoughts of the dead desert, the music shifts to the parallel minor, and the mood is enriched by melodic, enharmonic, and chromatic changes. The opening of the fourth stanza is like the beginning of the poem, but ten measures from the end the melody is altered, colored by the word *"Todesqual"* (death pangs). The measure's rest before the voice's entry with the *"wonnevoll"* is dropped, and the voice assumes the lead in this cadence, which for the first time, as it reaches the goal of the tonic, is not in elision joined by the five-measure introductory phrase. The last three measures bring final assurance with a widening tonic chord. The setting of the first lines undoubtedly brings undue emphasis on *"meine"* and *"Königin"* and too important a break before the phrase is continued. This awkard declamation is not repeated; the ecstatic sweep of the melodic line is apt for the song as a whole, and it is such a gorgeous musical idea that one should not complain.

Wiegenlied (Op. 49, No. 4)

UNDOUBTEDLY THE best known of Brahms' lieder is a simple cradle song which honored a baby born to Arthur and Bertha Faber of Vienna. When Brahms thought of Bertha, he recalled the pleasure she had given him in the summer of 1859 by singing an upper Austrian dance song, which began in the dialect, *"Du moanst wohl, du glabst wohl."* Paying her a most gracious compliment, he used the gently swaying tune of the *Ländler* as background and above it scored a charming, simple melody, as inevitable as a folksong. Originally, there was but one stanza, the poem of great age. Brahms used the text as found in *Des Knabens Wunderhorn.* Brahms was never quite pleased with the phrase *"Im Traum's Paradies,"* but permitted the publishers to issue the song with an added stanza. Every measure of the bass begins with the tonic (original key, E-flat), leisurely leaps upward to fill in the harmony delicately completed by the syncopation—generally in thirds—in the right hand, and then as leisure-ly chooses the right note on the way down to complete the circle. Among these measures of naïve charm, most Brahmsian are m.13 and m.17, where the thirds of the accompaniment move in contrary motion to the voice. The simple lyricism of the *Wiegen-lied's* thirty-six measures (18x2) is as truly Brahms as the 138 measures of *Ruhe Süssliebchen,* No. 9 of the *Magelone* cycle, the subtle and richly varied lullaby which Peter sings to Magelone.

Sapphische Ode (Op. 94, No. 4)

HANS SCHMIDT, who had been a tutor for the Joachims, sent Brahms some of his verses. One of these, which was patterned on the old verse form attributed to the poetess Sappho, caught his fancy. The poetic form consists of three lines like the first:

_ ◡ _ ◡ _ ◡ ◡ _ ◡ _ ◡

Rosen brach ich nachts mir am dunklen Hage,

followed by the last line, an adonic:

_ ◡ ◡ _ ◡

Thau der mich nässte.

Intrigued by these rhythms and touched by the somber, reflec-tive sentiments of the verse, Brahms was inspired to compose a magnificent song. The rhythmic "irregularities" begin with the third phrase, *"Doch verstreuten";* evidently in order not to bring a primary accent on the conjunction *"Doch,"* Brahms delays the entry to the third quarter (m.8) and then alternates measures of 3/2 and 4/2, until with m.13 the interlude restores the duple measure. The melody is a remarkable mixture of disjunct (chordal) and conjunct motion; ten of the twelve notes in the first phrase are members of the tonic chord. Of the two "out-siders," one is the dominant, the other a passing note between tonic and third. In the first stanza, a real tonic pedal sounds in eight of the thirteen measures, and in inner voices the tonic is present in three other measures.

Such statistics for another composer might spell boredom, but above and about such unifying factors Brahms has spread rich variety: the gentle syncopation of the accompaniment changing to quarter notes in the bass, echoed off-beat in the right hand; the darkness of the minor (m.8–9) followed by softly dissonant chords, which in most leisurely fashion round out the cadence. The vocal phrases are long and sustained, the cadence in m.11–13 conceived for an ideal voice that can sustain its unbroken line and, without hurrying or languishing, caress its last graceful turn. The differences between the first and second stanzas are few and are due not to the text, but rather to the composer's love of little changes in repetition. The alteration of the voice in m.21–22 and m.24–26, a third higher or lower than in the first stanza, brings slight adjustments in spacing of the chords of the accompaniment, as well as one harmonic change (m.22) and the addition of the seventh in m.25. The three-measure coda gently sinks through the darker subdominant to a delayed D chord, all members below middle C (original key, D).

Vergebliches Ständchen (Op. 84, No. 4)

THE LISTING OF *Five Romances and Songs* of Op. 84 as "for one or two voices" was suggested by the poems, all of which are semi-dramatic scenes between two persons. Since there is no difference in the range of the voices and in only No. 5 are there a few measures of a second part cued in, the songs are almost invariably presented by one voice. The text of No. 4 is a Rhenish folk song, freely extended by Aug. von Zuccalmaglio. The ardent suitor pleads with the maiden at her window to open the door and let him in. The dutiful daughter remembers her mother's counsel, and, even though he begs pitifully, she is only amused and teasingly tells him to go home to bed—to sleep. The bounding tune and spirited accompaniment are repeated for the second stanza. With the lover's second turn in the dialogue, however, his wretchedness in the cold night is caricatured by the melody in the minor, a busier, more independent accompaniment breaking out in a rough three-measure interlude which delays the maiden's final entry. Otherwise, her melody is as before, but the accompaniment bounces in novel two-part writing, finally stamping out a full and hearty cadence and roguishly continuing with its longest "solo" stretch, all of five measures, which is over in the twinkling of an eye.

Von ewiger Liebe (Op. 43, No. 1)

AT THE VERY opening of his great song year, 1868, Brahms made this setting of a text by the Bohemian Wenzig. Dark and silent is the night as the lovers return from the village. They have talked of many things. He asks if she is not distressed at, even ashamed of, her love for him. Should they part, would not her love pass as quickly as it had come? The maiden swears that their bonds are stronger than iron or steel, that their love shall be eternal. This is a big song in every way. The form is complex, A A B C C', but logically shaped by the divisions of the poem. The description of the scene and entry of the lovers is a repeated stanza, the introduction serving again as interlude (m.21–24) and bridge (m.41–45) to the large second division, in which the lover's anxiety prompts new music, a restless triplet figuration in the right hand opposing a sturdy, assertive voice and bass

in quarters and eighths. The extension of this accompaniment rises to great strength (m.68–73) and then softens (m.74–79) to prepare for the entry of the maiden in major, new measure, 6/8, and tempo, *Ziemlich langsam*. As she sings of constancy, the music mounts from *dolce, pp,* to a modest, but intense *mf* on the dominant, the close of the first half of this division. An interlude on the dominant brings the fifth stanza (m.99), whose first phrase is new and whose last phrase is extended and intensified into one of the most glorious cadences in song literature. A part of its grandeur comes from the conflict of 6/8 and 3/4 (m.113) and the repetition of the spiritual key note of the song, *"ewig"* (eternal).

THESE SONGS have illustrated Brahms' power of seizing upon the central mood of the poem, whether it be one of deep seriousness or open gaiety; he can strike a tune for sunny love accepted or read the heart of the lover rejected. The popular *Minnelied* and *Ständchen* must be passed by. More hesitatingly foregone is a moment with *Feldeinsamkeit,* whose arching theme is as ample as the bow of the sky, which in this song yields such quiet and peace. The grasp revealed in Brahms' last work, *Vier ernste Gesänge,* is so great, spiritually and physically, that all except a few are barred from this holy of holies. Approaching it, but from afar, and within more human scope, is Op. 96, No. 1.

Der Tod, das ist die kühle Nacht (Op. 96, No. 1)

THIS, LIKE THE third one of the *Serious Songs,* is an apostrophe to Death. The mood of Heine's poem is one of resignation and welcoming, devoid of the bitterness so poignantly expressed by the son of Sirach in the first half of *O Tod, wie bitter.* The night is near, and in peaceful dream is heard the nightingale's song of love. A lulling 6/8, *molto lento,* is set in motion by the tonic chord in $^6_4$ position, soon anchored by a tonic pedal; for six measures over tonic and dominant pedals, quieting harmonies shift.

The value of the rests in separating lines (m.4, m.6) or thought within the line (m.8) is most poetic. With m.6 the harmonies move into more obscure worlds, and above the pedal on D (original key, C), its third avoided, a peaceful other-worldly feeling is given by the B-flat in the cadence of the voice, soon reaching the light of G major (m.13). The second stanza reflects the dream

hat   mich   mud'   ge _ macht

of tree and nightingale, the left hand filling in arpeggio figures, always rising from tonic or dominant (m.14 23); the voice mounts, its melody uninterrupted by rests; when the arpeggio motion is lost, when phrases of the voice are shortened in span and broken by silence, when the harmonies are truly seraphic— even here the bass has but moved from dominant to the tonic, where with gentle insistence the low bourdon C sounds to the end.

CHAPTER X

Hugo Wolf

THERE is great pathos in the story of Hugo Wolf (1860–1903). For a time he would compose literally like one possessed, only to have his mind and spirit suddenly become so clouded that there was no invention in him. Most of the last five years of his life were spent in an asylum; earlier, there had been a lapse of five years with nothing written from 1891–96. His fate seems more tragic than that of Schumann, whose melancholia left him with no desire to create. There were occasional rifts in the night that had settled upon Wolf, and once in revolt he cried: "Heaven gives a man genius full and complete, or else no genius at all. The devil has given me everything by halves."[1]

In truth, nature granted all or nothing to Wolf in his composing. The wind blew hot or cold; there was no temperate zone. And as one might expect for a creator of a new kind of song, much of the criticism regarding him is extravagantly for or bitterly against his music and methods. Critics are very human, and he who writes "Save Beethoven from his friends," holding that "many of the master's works fell far short of his high-water mark," can let his enthusiasm for Grieg make the "rough places plain."[2] The candidate, who charged that his opponent's thinking was merely a rearranging of his prejudices, struck at a common failing. Yet we are most grateful to that keen scholar, and brilliant and provocative writer, Ernest Newman, whose great enthusiasm for Wolf led him to challenge all comers with the

---

[1] From a letter to Wette, dated August 13, 1891, quoted by R. Rolland, *Musicians of Today,* 183.

[2] H. T. Finck, *Musical Progress* (Philadelphia, 1923) and H. T. Finck, *Grieg and his Music* (New York, 1909).

Mörike lieder, "which in their totality are beyond any other fifty-three of one man's songs in the quality and variety of the life they touch."[3]

Few indeed are those for whom Wolf tops the list, but we must not spend our space in favorable and unfavorable comparisons. Let us rather recall the advantageous place of Wolf in time and milieu. In his early teens he came under the spell of Wagner; later he made pilgrimages to Bayreuth, and, although he was no servile imitator, the mark of Wagner left its deep impress. As a young critic Wolf lashed out against Brahms, who, he charged, could not "exult."[4] Wolf was essentially self-taught, and from his vantage point in time he could examine in detail the lieder of Schubert, Schumann, and Brahms. To his poetic mind none of them had been fair to the poet. They had all erred, even Schumann whom he admired most, in an undue emphasis of the music. In every form in which words and music are joined, each generation hopes to reach a solution satisfactory for that day. In the field of opera, Wagner's reforms in favor of the drama had focused a new light on text and declamation. It was not a conscious attempt on the part of Wolf to parallel in the world of song what his idol Wagner had wrought in the music-drama; Wolf's whole temperament was attuned for this mission. To Humperdinck he wrote: "Poetry is the true source of my music." He gave it first place, and more truly and more fully than any of his predecessors he permitted the poem to shape the song, not only in the large, but particularly in the small details.

After his earliest work, Wolf never roved among the poets. He settled on one, and, with a terrific concentration, he pored over the poet's verses; he came to know all the quirks of rhythm and structure; he was able in spirit to vibrate sympathetically with the poet's moods; with no preconceived musical plan or idea, Wolf let the poem call the "tune." In such a fashion, fifty-

[3] E. N. Newman, *Hugo Wolf*, 211.
[4] *Ibid.*, 36.

three poems of the Swabian pastor, Eduard Mörike, were set in 1888; nor did Wolf return to the same poet, for the musician had taken all that could be illumined by his art. Thus he moved on to another poet's world, becoming so wholly absorbed in the newness of its idiom and emotional atmosphere that when songs appeared they were quite unlike the music which the earlier poet had inspired. His two hundred mature lieder are clustered within four of the years from 1888–97. This strange concentration began with fifty-three settings from Mörike and closed with three sonnets from Michelangelo, written only two months before Brahms wrote his last songs, the *Vier ernste Gesänge*. From Goethe, Wolf set fifty-one poems. His *Spanisches Liederbuch* contains thirty-four folk-song poems, translated into German by Heyse and Geibel. The last large collection of songs is the *Italienisches Liederbuch,* the poems translated by Paul Heyse; divided into two parts of twenty-two and twenty-four songs, the first was dated 1890–91, the latter, 1896, those fateful five years of silence intervening.

The Musical Times, London, April 1, 1903, in its obituary of eight lines and one word, reflects something of the neglect and scorn which Wolf had frequently encountered, but its phrase, "He wrote songs wholesale," is the "most unkindest cut of all." Two hundred and forty-four lieder are published, many two or three pages in length. Certainly, Wolf worked at white heat when the spirit was on him, but 244 songs is far short of even two gross. Further, Wolf worked only with the details of one song at a time. If ever there was a "retailer" of songs, it was he. Each poet and each poem commanded an individual pattern. Even the principles of true declamation, certainly the cornerstone of his art, refused to crystallize into a pattern that repeated itself mechanically.

Most binding or, as it appears, most natural for Wolf was the matching of one syllable with one tone, as in the old syllabic chant. The accented syllable is often higher in pitch than the unaccented, but Wolf was too much of a musician to demand that the curve of his melody literally represent a graph of word accents. The more subtle stresses within the poetic line were reflected in the lengths of notes. The flow and rhythm of poetry is freer than that of metered music, and rhythmic feet of verse and melody cannot keep in step for long without one or the other yielding. Yet Wolf does not chafe against the bar line, nervously jockeying back and forth with changes of metric signature. There are surprisingly few of these changes, the most common being in a final vocal cadence, where one measure of 2/4 is inserted in the 4/4. There is a strong predominance of duple measure in Wolf, 4/4 the most frequent. One is scarcely aware of this in studying the songs, for the patterns within the measures are varied, the melodies flexible, and the harmonies fresh.

If the voice line tends to be more broken and melodically less conventional than that of earlier writers, a greater responsibility must be placed on the accompaniment in bringing logic to the design. Wolf's admiration for Wagner's music-drama led him to adopt some of the elements of the Bayreuth master's style. Like Franz, Wolf unifies many songs by the repetition of a short motive; by transposition and variation some of the dangers of such a unity in the span of a song are lessened, and usually the method appears less obvious in Wolf. That it does so is largely due to the more involved texture of Wolf's music. The harmonies are often bold; accidentals are plentiful, and at times the chromatic wavering is puzzling; not only is the accompaniment frequently quite independent of the voice line, but several melodic strands may be found within the piano part. Since the piano has no declamation of words to follow, it is free to underline mood and develop atmosphere suggested by the text. Modulation is free; more than one of Wolf's songs begins in one key and ends in another.[5] Wolf's use of motives, a declamatory voice

[5] E. N. Newman, *Music Critic's Holiday* (New York, 1925), 172. Jadassohn advised Breitkopf und Härtel not to publish Wolf's lieder as they have "nothing in common with music, except they contain tones and rhythms."

line, bold chromatic harmonies shot through with contrapuntal lines, and an increased weight, both tonal and emotional, allotted to the instrument—these may have stemmed from Wagner, but the younger man wrote thus, not in imitation of one he admired, but because it was the way he thought and felt.

That there was a strong current of emotion back of his music-making was not always perceived by his contemporaries, who were often baffled by his unconventionalities or wrapped up in the analytical delights of his declamation. Wolf did not compose in a cold, calculating fashion. The poem had been read and studied as poetry. Often before retiring, Wolf would reread some poem; on awakening in the morning, the music for it might be fashioned in his head; he would hurriedly write it down, and seldom did he rescore. In a letter he says that one of his songs "sounds so terribly strange that it frightens me. As yet there has been nothing like it. Heaven help the poor folk who are condemned to hear it some day!"[6] Wolf did not cater to his audience, singers, or publishers. He made no concessions to anyone. He would accept the publication of his songs only in albums—not a selection of a few songs from each of his "cycles," but all fifty-three Mörike or all fifty-one Goethe, and each of these only in its original key. Schott, who finally took over his songs in 1891, sent the composer in October, 1895, a check for royalties covering five years. It amounted to eighty-six marks and thirty-five pfennigs, or an average of less than forty cents a month.[7] How long it was before Schott got his money back we do not know, but sales have never been large. Wolf has been much honored, but the bulk of his work remains unsung. Perhaps a dozen songs are in repertoire, and occasionally a venturesome spirit makes some of the others live for a season. But the singers' common attitude may be represented by this phrase from a writer in *Music and Letters,* who found Wolf's songs "erratic, and inclined to fatigue both mind and body, and it may

[6] Rolland, *Musicians of Today,* 180.
[7] *Ibid.,* 187.

be asked whether they are worth it."[8] If Wolf were here he might quote from Pope:

> *Praise from a friend, or censure from a foe,*
> *Are lost on hearers that our merits know.*[9]

Verborgenheit

WE TEND TO accept as beautiful that which is much like what has pleased us before; a touch of the unusual is intriguing, but too much of it is baffling. The early acceptance of *Verborgenheit* was due to some similarities between its music and that of known composers, Brahms in particular; that the song still retains its hold is due to the high satisfaction that it continues to bring. Melodically, harmonically, and structurally, it is convincing and emotionally moving. Over a double pedal, tonic and dominant, a gentle rocking in eighth notes dips to the raised fourth and second to return to the fifth and third of the tonic chord. At the slow tempo, this introduction evokes a mellow, somewhat pathetic feeling that is continued as the accompaniment maintains the figure, the voice reinforcing the pull of the raised fourth and second in the first and fourth measures of its first phrase. Otherwise, the melody moves in simple dignity, the accompaniment weaving about it, here above, there below, and again with it. In m.7, voice and accompaniment exchange the pattern of m.3, the voice continuing with an intensifying variation to a broad, satisfying cadence in the tonic. A new idea enters with the second stanza, m.11. In place of the plea to be left alone to brood upon the joys and pains of a love that once had been, the anguished one confides that grief and sorrow bring tears that dim the sun's light; yet often in dreams there has flashed a brilliant joy, penetrating even the darkness of his breast. Wolf has pictured this repressed, yet nervous, spirit with an off-beat entry of the voice. Phrases that begin in a short and exclamatory way soon press

[8] *M&L*, Vol. XI (1930), 52.
[9] A. Pope, *The Iliad of Homer*, x, 293–94.

forward in a continuing and mounting line. The accompaniment moves in relentless eighths and is chromatically restless, modulating from relative minor to its fifth, then to the parallel tonic minor, blooming forth in the cadence of the second stanza on the V_7 in the key of G-flat (original key, E-flat). Now in m.20, as earlier at m.17, expectations are denied, and the music starts in a new key, leading once again toward the parallel tonic minor.

The insistence of the diminished seventh on A-natural, m.23–25, the broken angular phrases, and the dynamic surges at last lead from the repeated height of G-flat magnificently up a third to B-flat in the piano, a G-natural in the voice, supported by a huge tonic $^6_4$, whose noontide brilliance fades within the measure to a *pp* re-entry of the first stanza in exact repetition. Most astonishing, for one who is upheld as a model in scrupulous care of the poet's every word, is the breaking of the phrase *"und die helle Freude zücket // durch die Schwere"* in m.23. Wolf, even as Schubert, Schumann, and Brahms before him, allowed the sweep of the musical idea to dominate the scene, even breaking a poet's phrase in two. With the musician's license, one might suspect that the exact repetition of the first stanza was made to round out the musical form, ABCA. It is thus, however, in Mörike's poem.

Gesang Weyla's

ALTHOUGH Mörike did not include this eight-line poem in his novel, *Maler Nolten,* the subject is related to the fantastic interlude, *The Last King of Orplid,* inserted in the romance. Mörike imagined a fabulous island between America and Asia, which was under the special protection of the river goddess Weyla. Wolf wrote that he imagined her "sitting on a rocky edge in the moonlight, holding her harp in her hands."[10] Throughout its nineteen measures, on every quarter within the 4/4 measure, he scored a chord rolled up from the bottom. In only two measures,

---

[10] Newman, *Hugo Wolf,* 182. Wolf told Kauffman that he imagined her "sitting on a rocky ledge in the moonlight."

m.12–13, does the piano part rise above purely harmonic support, but this simple pattern is richly colored, its basic D-flat softly solemn. The voice of Weyla begins as a priestess intoning a noble hymn of adoration to Orplid, whose shores are kept ever young by the sun and mist; before her deity, the sun-god Sur, kings bow and are but vassals. With this last, the voice descends chromatically from tonic to fourth and then mounts a seventh, the accompaniment also rising in parallel motion to a tonic $^6_4$; without break, the voice sweeps downward through the chord in a sumptuous close.

Vor dei-ner Gott-heit beu - gen sich Kö - ni - ge,

Anakreon's Grab

GOETHE RECALLS not the old Ionian poet's verse steeped in wine and love, but rather the quiet and peace where Anakreon now sleeps; Goethe writes not as an older Greek did for the poet's epitaph: "O Vine, grow lush and long above the tomb of Anakreon!"[11] Rather the rose and laurel, the turtledove and cricket, and spring and summer surround his resting place. Wolf is at one with Goethe as he echoes the mood in a slow, soothing 12/8 measure; the soft lapping of the triplet figure, as at the end of m.3, is a magical bit of color. The accompaniment is modestly scored, mostly in three and four voices, with little counterplay in the inner parts. The harmonies are thoroughly romantic, with

11 W. Durant, *The Life of Greece* (New York, 1939), 149.

Wo die Ro-se hier blüht, wo Re - ben um Lor-beer sich schlin-gen

not a single touch of the modes that the Golden Age of Greece might have suggested. Measures 8–11 modulate through color-ful keys to the darker side, cadencing in the subdominant. The introduction is repeated at this new level, m.13, and modified for a return to the tonic, with the entrance of the voice whose melody is new, but as lovely and natural as was the old. The ac-companiment is the same as before, except for the final measure where the home key is sustained. A gentle, wavering epilogue closes with an echoing figure in the tenor, followed by the bass's chord of finality. Classic in restraint are the dynamics, the *mf* of m.9 being the high, and *p* to *ppp* its normal range.

Er ist's

ONE OF THE canons of Wolf's criticism was that the true test of the greatness of a composer was his ability to exult. This setting of Mörike's greeting to spring is Wolf in his highest spirits. Swinging back and forth in gay abandon, the accompaniment gains such momentum that when the ten short lines of the poem are over, the piano cannot stop, but must expend twenty-one measures in gradually dropping from the *fff* close of the voice to the *ppp* ending of the epilogue; and, even then, Wolf feels the need of a cushion of a whole measure's rest, with a *fermata* above it, to break the motion. The voice part is agile and bounds around in its gay tune. Exciting harmonically are: the unanimous drop of a half step at m.7, the width of the key excursion to C-sharp (m.11; original key, G); and, the dainty echoing of *"Horch!"* by the arpeggiated chord (m.20), which, through the phrase, simulates the harplike tone heard in the distance. The climax is cunningly contrived, the rise to its dynamic fullness not even hinted at in the first half of the song, which is impetuous in motion, but restrained in dynamics.

AN EARTHY WISDOM, a love of simple things, and the enjoyment of life are motives which frequently appear in the poems of the Spanish and Italian songs. The subjects which attracted Wolf are greatly varied, although from the beginning he was drawn less to the highly subjective and seemed generally more convincing in grief than joy. Yet there is playfulness and humor, as well as anger and scorn, in these poems. Wolf's style in these latter songs—there are eighty in the two collections—is simpler in both melody and accompaniment. The Tristan-like harmonies that were frequent earlier now rarely appear. Most of the songs are short, twenty measures often being sufficient; but they seem less compressed than some of the earlier songs of equal length. Wolf placed *Auch kleine Dinge* first in the *Italian Songs.*

Auch kleine Dinge

THE POEM, translated by Paul Heyse from a popular song in Tommaseo's collection of Tuscan songs, bids one reflect on the worth, goodness, and perfume of "even little things," such as a pearl, an olive, and a rose. "Slowly, very tenderly, always *pp*," Wolf has written. As if hesitant to intrude, the right hand's "N" figure of sixteenths appears only on the even quarters, the chords of the left hand only on the odd quarters until the fourth measure of the introduction, when, with a little run upward, the right hand settles into a fluttering sixteenth-note figure, maintained until the music of the introduction returns as an epilogue. The left hand has a single-line scale that steps downward, first diatonically and then chromatically. We note its repetition, commencing in m.9 and again in m.17, and realize that this is a varied strophic design: introduction, A A'B A", epilogue. The melody for each stanza is modified, and m.13–16 are contrasting material. The last phrase is extended by an added measure in 2/4. It is such a little song, but it is as lovely a gem as the pearl, as full of substance as an olive, and as sweet as a rose.

The *Spanish Songs* are divided into sacred and secular songs. The most frequently sung of the first is *Nun wandre, Maria,* a Christmas song in which Joseph tries to inspire Mary with courage on the weary journey to Bethlehem. A gently jogging bass that settles down into plodding even quarters in the cadences (m.9–10, 33–34) is pictorial, while the right hand weaves throughout a garland of thirds, the restrained voice line serenely going its way. Of the secular songs, the scene, *Auf dem grünen Balcon,* is colorful and gay. In a lilting accompaniment of 12/8, the left hand strums a guitar, the right hand toying with a sinuous single-line figure spiced by an occasional "Spanish" triplet. The voice has its own melodic line, reflecting the Señorita whose eyes say "yes," but whose finger warns "no." Delightful variations are found in its pattern, which follows A B (m.8) A'B'C (m.30), with its interesting key and melodic variation of A.

Three of the most frequently heard of Wolf's songs are: (1) *Fussreise* ("Tramping") with its simple, steady, marching melody, but faintly suggesting a folk tune; (2) *Der Gärtner* ("The Gardner"), in which Wolf has picked out as the motive the prancing horse of the princess, who rides down the adoring gardner's path—the song's light gaiety is irresistible—and (3) Dedicated to his father was Wolf's setting of Kerner's *Zur Ruh! Zur Ruh!* ("To Rest!"), one of his noblest songs. Its descending motive brings a solemn peace, broken by enharmonic modulation to the second stanza (m.17), where the music gropes upward toward the light, which the poet visions for the body freed of earthly pains. Its goal reached (m.30) in a broad climax, the theme of resignation returns as coda and sinks deeper and deeper to its resting place.

CHAPTER XI

Strauss

I n the critical studies of Strauss (1864–1949), the songs are almost entirely ignored. The symphonic poems and operas, which are generously covered by the critics, represent the composer as a dramatic artist, one who is able not only to conceive his subjects in broad and telling strokes, but also to intensify the sweep of his "alfresco" generalization with fine and impressive details of expression. All of Strauss's orchestral masterpieces were composed in the last century, but after these his interests centered in the theater. Such an approach to music is, by its very nature, not conducive to song writing. Earlier, we noted that no successful opera composer has been an important contributor to song. Strauss, by virtue of a dozen or more of his some 140 lieder, comes nearer to refuting this statement than any other composer. Yet I would hold with Oskar Bie in *Das Deutsche Lied* that*"Er ist keine Liednatur,"* Strauss is not a song man;[1] his was a temperament not disposed to the making of songs.

If some good lieder happened to issue from him, it was—as he himself explained to Siegmund von Hausegger in 1893—the fortunate meeting with a poem that exactly matched an already existing musical idea. "If I happen on a poem which approximately corresponds with the musical idea that came to me, the new opus is ready in a moment. But if—as unfortunately happens very often—I do not find the right poem, I nevertheless yield to the creative impulse and set to music any random poem that happens to be at all suitable for a musical setting—but the process is slow, the result is artificial, the melody has a viscid

[1] Bie, *Das deutsche Lied*, 257.

flow, and I have to draw on all my command of technical resources in order to achieve something that will stand the test of strict self-criticism."[2] This method of writing recounts an approach to song composition that is certainly unorthodox, and it is small wonder that the large majority of the songs, despite all their charm and ingenuity, fail to thoroughly move or convince. I do not suppose we should complain because Strauss occasionally dashed off a song during the intermissions of an opera he was conducting. Great songs have been written in less congenial settings. Witness Schubert's *Hark! Hark! the Lark*. There is no telling when the inspiration may strike, but, in the case of Strauss, we may wonder if it was the Muse or the publisher calling. Strauss was always a keen businessman, and his attitude toward the song undoubtedly at times was like that of the composer whom Horatio Parker once met on his way down town to "cash an anthem."

The Strauss songs are scattered all along the way. Although they offer dubious confirmation of the antipathy between opera and song, one notes the infrequent issues of songs in this century, with a pause of sixteen years between Op. 56, in 1903, and Op. 66. His first collection of songs, Op. 10, begins with *Zueignung,* and its eighth and closing song is *Allerseelen,* both high flights for an eighteen-year-old lad. Higher still were the songs of Op. 27, written ten years later. Indeed, what stronger motive for the making of inspired lieder could the composer ask than the fruition of his love dreams? These songs were dedicated "To my beloved Pauline, 10 Sept. 1894," the day of Strauss's marriage. Pauline de Ahna had played the role of Freihold in Strauss's opera *Guntram.* Earlier, she had sung the role of Elizabeth at Bayreuth. Strauss loved her and her voice, and she loved the composer and his music; after their marriage, she devoted herself to introducing her husband's lieder. There are later songs of importance, as *Traum durch die Dämmerung,* coming in the time of *Till Eulenspiegel.* The most productive period for

[2] H. T. Finck, *Richard Strauss,* 287.

songs, from 1899 to 1901, includes six different collections total-
ing thirty-one numbers. One questions the sincerity of the writer
more often in the later songs. These charming trifles occasionally appear overdone, a little heavy-handed; where a serious tone
is employed, the quality of nobility, when striving for an elemental simplicity, trembles on the edge of the commonplace; where
it strives for grandeur, one has varied response—as when listening to the "Transformation" theme in *Tod und Verklärung*—
now it seems truly great, and again it seems inflated, merely pre-
tentious. The spiritual resources of the bank are not equal to the
notes that have been drawn on it.

Strauss could write in a broad, flowing line, and be suave
and full of glittering, sensuous charm. Even though his natural
mode of thought was symphonic, the songs appear less the ex-
pansion of short motives than of longer melodic themes. Too
frequently the melodic line is erratic; skips are many and of
awkward widths, often resulting from harmonic, rather than
melodic, urge. The range is often excessive, though the difficulties seem to arise less from the width than from the sustained
heights that he particularly demands when writing for soprano.
He expects his singer not only to be agile, but flexible; and he has
scored tellingly in both *bel canto* and coloratura.

Even when the voice part is lacking in distinction per se, it
takes its place along with the accompaniment, which in Strauss
almost invariably commands the chief interest; the accompaniment is the principal agent in the expression of the moods behind the text. His "lust for ink" is revealed in elaborate scoring,
thick harmonies, rapid modulations, here and there bold polyphonic interweaving, and, again, swirling arpeggios of a simple
but extended harmonic pattern. The singer usually feels, however, that, as involved and active as the accompaniment may be,
it is more helpful than distracting. Despite all the bustle and assertiveness, the voice shines through. Eight of the songs were
originally composed with orchestra accompaniment, and eight
more were transcribed by the composer; friends have provided

more transcriptions, such as the one for *Ständchen* by Mottl. This yearning for orchestra seems natural in a composer whose chief fame rests on symphonic poems. Yet the song accompaniments are conceived for their medium; they are pianistic, but their richness, warmth, and frequent elaborateness suggest the orchestra.

Zueignung (Op. 10, No. 1)

THE SUBJECT of the first of Strauss's published songs is one that would have appealed to Wagner, the hero of the young composer. Von Gilm's poem with its refrain, *"Habe Dank,"* is a glowing tribute to the redeeming power of love. Strauss has marked its last stanza *"mit Weihe"* (with consecration), and the voice and accompaniment mount with sacred force to a great climax, increasing from m.25, with the word *"heilig,"* through to the end, m.30. This last division enters—as have the phrases at m.5, 14, 16, and 23—after an eighth-note rest. Here, however, the right hand anticipates the voice, doubling its line even in the drop of the seventh, expressive of the word *"sank"*; the accompaniment expands the phrase leading to a voluminous tonic, $^6_4$, the voice shouting its thanks. This time its short refrain phrase, which twice before had mounted only a minor third to the flatted seventh of I, now soars a major sixth to the third of the key, kept ringing as well in the ecstatic upward sweep of the accompaniment. The song is hearty, even lusty. Why should the lover celebrate his redemption in sackcloth and ashes? The contrast of the triplet figuration with the syncopated voice line vibrates; within its basic stanza form, one notes the compression preceding the second *"Habe Dank,"* which now appears in a new place within the measure; note, too, the extension of the succeeding interlude (m.19–20) and the triumphant climax of the last stanza (m.25–30).

Morgen (Op. 27, No. 4)

THERE IS A note of quiet confidence in the song of the loved one, who thinks of the morrow when lovers will meet and slowly go down the sun-drenched path to the shore and the deep-blue waves. Silently they will gaze into each other's eyes, and a great joy will descend upon them. This sentiment of the German-Scotch poet Mackay drew from Strauss one of his purest and most sustained cantabile melodies. In great tranquillity the theme rises in single tones reinforced by an alto voice at cadence points; the left hand in ascending triplets fills in the harmonic support, its motion giving impetus to the first half of the measure. As the broken chord stops, its impulse is carried over into the single tone of the melody, which seems strangely suspended and ethereal. Two measures before this sixteen-measure idea closes, the voice enters with an independent melody, half-recitative.

Und mor-gen wird die Son-ne wie - - der schei-nen,

As the cadence of its first declaimed phrase closes, the accompaniment begins again its long-spun melody, unchanged until the last half of m.30, which parallels m.15 of the statement. Here, with suspensive close and sustained chords, the coda begins. The voice has gone beyond its quiet declamation, mounting to the climax in a rising and arching phrase beginning *"und zu dem Strand"* (m.24). The voice is silent this time as the piano turns the cadence deceptively to a I_9 with lowered seventh. There follows the simple recitative line, the full and rich but ever *pp* chords of the piano stretching outward, but drawing back for the suspended cadence with which the voice closes. The five-measure epilogue is the extension of the first two measures of the song, now mounting slowly to the suspended $^6_4$ position of the tonic chord.

Traum durch die Dämmerung (Op. 29, No. 1)

THE BROAD MEADOWS, a jasmine bush, the gray of twilight with stars appearing. The lover dreamily returning to his beloved in the gloaming. Strauss paints this landscape of the poet Bierbaum in delicate, softly trembling colors. The pattern of the first measure is repeated exactly through four measures; its lulling motion of triplets and eighths above, with dotted eighths and sixteenth below, is broken only three times in the song. The first break occurs in the rich modulation to D-flat (original key, F-sharp), when the bass marches, in even tread, to the new tonic (m.12–13). Again, at the climax—a relative term, for the whole song moves in a dream world whose dynamics never exceed *piano*—in m.23, a rhythmic intensification fills the first half of the bar, the effect further heightened by the short silence of the voice. The last four measures erase the waving motion and suspend the tonic chord well above the center of the keyboard, perhaps Strauss's translation of "a velvety band of soft blue."

Although the tonic key is quietly insisted upon, the three-

geh' ich hin zu der schön - - - - sten Frau

measure phrase at the close of the first section unobtrusively moves a major third higher as the D-sharp enharmonically becomes E-flat, giving easy entrance to the second key, B-flat. A contrasting idea, *"weit über Wiesen,"* entering in m.10, moves directly up a small third to D-flat (third key), where, again by a simple enharmonic change, the original tonic is regained, the key movement having traced the tonic chord. The first two measures of the return, both of key and the A idea, are now at the dominant level. Measure 17, which repeats m.5, leads to an extended phrase and climax in the home key. The coda, m.26–33, repeats the opening phrases of the last section. In the last phrase, the voice steadily rises through the octave to the fifth, which it peacefully sustains for two whole measures. The preceding notation looks strangely restless, but the mood is one of gentle tranquillity.

Ständchen (Op. 17, No. 2)

SOME REGARD THIS as a romantic *salon* piece.[3] The composer was a bit disgruntled at its popularity, perhaps believing that some song of more involved texture, illustrating a deeper philosophy, would better represent him. But contrapuntal ingenuities and athletic modulations have never been enough to save a score. *Ständchen* still holds its place in the affections of singers, accompanists, and audiences alike, for it has the true ring of the inspired spontaneous idea, put down at white heat with nothing lost in the telling. It glows rather than gushes; it whispers rather than shouts; but its ecstasy is no less real. It may be flashy, but its downright honesty is disarming.

"Awake, arise, but softly my love, that no one from slumber awaken!" And the lover waits in the garden in the mysterious shadows of the linden trees. The nightingale, he says, must dream of our kisses, and the roses, when they awaken, shall glow with the thrilling bliss of the night. For the poet von Schack's opening phrase, *"Wach auf"* (awake), the voice lightly bounds

[3] Bie, *Das deutsche Lied,* 258.

the octave, which it repeats, and thence skips to the tonic a fourth above. In the cadencing phrase, *"um Keinen von Schlummer zu wecken,"* the voice seems to tiptoe about. The last four measures of the stanza are in 9/8 and have the feeling of a refrain. The second stanza modifies, without good reason, its seventh measure and then convincingly condenses, by two measures, the phrase beginning *"zu mir in den Garten zu schlüpfen."* Again, the cadence of the refrain fills to the full its last measure. New material is then introduced; the accompaniment, however, continues its original descending arpeggiate figure, now drifting below center, perhaps in response to the "mysterious shadows under the linden." A cadence in G-sharp (original key, F-sharp) is followed by a gesture of return to the first division, the piano introducing twice the phrase of m.11, only to have the voice soar (*"hoch glüh'n"*) to an extended climax (marked but *mf*) and luxuriously expand its final cadence. The piano's epilogue is the refrain idea, with melody doubled and the bass more active in its arpeggios. The last two measures are made of the original figure capped by a rolled tonic chord, high, then low, *pp, una corda.*

●

CHAPTER XII

Contrast of German and French Song

L ET us introduce the French school by broadly opposing its qualities to those of the German school. This chapter, yielding frankly to the dangers of oversimplification of a very involved problem, is Janus-like: from its vantage point it looks back over the chapters on German composers and peers forward into the section on French song. Even though the subject of the Art Song focuses our attention on the nineteenth century, there are surprisingly sharp differences of character and ideals within such a short span and within each country. Such crises as the defeat of Napoleon (1815), the July Revolution (1830), and the Franco-Prussian War (1870–71)—and these are but a few of the fateful moments in this seething period of French history— reflect the jagged course toward freedom. Music, which had been centered in the court and theater and bound by aristocratic and stylistic traditions, was freed by native French composers, who gradually won an appreciative audience in the public concert hall.

Although Germany won the war of 1870–71, France was the artistic victor. Disaster roused her from smugness and apathy, and she stubbornly set about freeing herself from foreign influences. Germany had experienced her national awakening much earlier. Weber's *Der Freischütz,* whose *première* in 1821 was deliberately set for the anniversary of the Battle of Waterloo, is the cornerstone of German romantic opera. This opera and the lied are the two richest musical fruits of the "Wars of Liberation" in Germany. Despite the fact that the unification of the German people proceeded slowly, and that it was not until 1871 that Wilhelm I was proclaimed German emperor, there had been through these years a national artistic solidarity. A galaxy of tremendously great native composers arose, in part made possible by Germany's musical heritage, which had spread deeper, wider, and longer among the people than had France's inheritance.

Rising from this heritage—even as late as the nineteenth century—are art songs which were colored by the folk song and folk poetry. On the German side, Mendelssohn illustrated frequently the *volkstümliches* style, as in *Es ist bestimmt in Gottes Rath*. All the most important creators of song through Brahms used voice melodies that seemed to arise from ancestral memories. Always simple and sincere, frequently rather sturdy and serious, the deep-rooted German folk tone crops out again and again. In contrast, the strain of French folk song that appears in the romances, chansons, and *pastourelles* in the eighteenth century is generally light and gay, even coy. The nineteenth-century hands of J. B. Weckerlin and Julien Tiersot bedeck *bergerettes* of the eighteenth century and *Chants de la vieille France,* but French composers of the last century rarely expressed their true selves in such terms. When occasionally they simulate the older folk style, they recapture the tone of *Jardin d'amour* more easily than that of *L'Amour de moi*. What we think of as nineteenth-century Art Song centers in the latter half of the period. When, however, we think of the German lied, we think instinctively in terms of the first half of the century. Naturally this difference in the season of flowering brings contrast, the French school availing itself of many of the technical skills that romanticism had already won.

The contrast between the two schools can be more readily caught, if we draw up a balance sheet, listing in condensed outline the characteristics, grouped under such headings as "temperament," "rhythm," and "melody." The statements will appear all too rigid; there are many half-truths and oversimplifications in such a method. Frequently, the opposite of what is listed is also true. Style traits are seldom simple, but exceptions do *not* prove the rule.

General Characterizations

I. TEMPERAMENT

German	French
Sentimental, romantic	Rational "front," masking sentiment
Frank, bald, hearty	Hidden, subtle, discreet
Confiding in all	Half-revealing, half-concealing
Lone working, scarcely aware of their public	Knowing men, loving and requiring their approval
Independent, free	Strongly aware of artistic tradition
Deliberate, methodical	Dexterous and cunning; paradoxically: orderly, yet capricious
Creating, then explaining	Theorizing, then creating
Introspective, contemplative of the soul	Keenly observant; much impressed by the world about
Idealistic (as the artist feels)[1]	Realistic (as the artist sees)
"Half-poetical, half-philosophical"[2]	Poetic, vividly pictorial

II. GOAL

German	French
Eternally seeking to penetrate beyond this world, to explain philosophies and beliefs, to promote great thoughts and noble emotions	Satisfied with beauty itself as a goal; content to bring joy and pleasure, both emotional and intellectual; avoiding pretensions that bring boredom
With "axes to grind," resulting in occasional confusion	Defining the art work itself in clarity
Lavish	Simple
Romantically excessive	Economical
Dealing with soul states	Interested in formal charm
Warm, broad	Elegant, precious
Nourished by beer	Excited by champagne

III. ROMANTIC SUBJECT—LOVE

German	French
Devoted, pure (Minnesinger)	Sensuous (troubadour)[3]

[1] D. Ferguson, *Evolution of Musical Thought* (New York, 1936), 324.
[2] Carlyle of Schiller.
[3] See E. J. Dent regarding the Mediterranean temperament in *Terpander* (New York, 1927), 47.

Spiritual, mystic	Voluptuous, but not vulgar; *carpe diem* attitude
If unsuccessful: crushed, bitter, brooding	If unsuccessful: repressed, not vocal; or, tossing failure off with a flash of wit or irony
Personal	Objective

Traits of the Song

I. RHYTHM

March of the music dominating, even subordinating, the text and its rhythm	Keenly sensitive to poetic rhythm; pliable, even fluid; whimsical
Seldom of first interest; seldom eccentric or astonishing	Strongly appreciative of "measure," developed from ballet

II. MELODY

German song may give impression of a wider, more expansive vocal range than that of French; yet the German compass is smaller; Schubert, Schumann, Brahms, and Wolf have an average range of about a minor tenth; Strauss's range is seldom less than an octave and a fourth and his average a half step beyond this	The feeling that French song is content with a small compass may come from respect for a normal *tessitura* and frequent recitative-like phrases, freely modeled on the poetic text; actually, the average range is an octave and a fourth; Debussy exceeds this, while Chausson is the least demanding of the "great," averaging a minor tenth
Although later-period songs frequently illustrate unexpected melodic intervals, German melody in the large is natural, warm, and spontaneous	The long-dominant opera casts its shadow on French song, resulting frequently in facile, supple, sweet melodies (Bachelet's *Chère Nuit*); at the other extreme are melodies that appear studied, subtle, recherché.
Mostly diatonic	More chromatic; dashes of Eastern and whole-tone scales

III. HARMONY

Fairly orthodox	Avoiding the usual, scorning the obvious
Frequently thick, lush	Often thin, delicate, exquisite
Climax often through I_4^6	Climax seldom through I_4^6

134

IV. FORM

It is the nature of romanticists to rebel against authority. The romantic phase in the evolution of an art, in Hegel's philosophy, is marked by the predominance of the Idea over the Form through which it is expressed.

Not content with a mere formal scheme, as were the earlier Italians, the German romanticists find a form that grows out of the idea to be expressed	The rational attitude of the French demands that the artist understand what he seeks to express and know the means by which he is to make it clear; native architectural skill is so strong that no matter how great the freedom and individualism, there remains a balanced, logical design
Seldom complex	Concise

CHAPTER XIII

French Song

No nation has been able to keep up to "concert pitch" in any single field of art. The history of secular song in France illustrates this fact. From the twelfth to the sixteenth centuries there was no other nation more active, none more creatively significant, in cultivating the secular song. Then France fell behind and did not resume her leadership until the late nineteenth century. The common French term for secular song is *chanson,* but its meaning has changed with the years. Troubadour, trouvère, Machaut, Dufay, Jannequin—successive symbols of the twelfth to the sixteenth centuries—all wrote chansons, but the music varies from a simple tune to involved polyphony. In the seventeenth century, there is a sharp falling away from this long-sustained excellence; the earlier strength and artistic daring are replaced by grace and gallantry. The chanson loses its high artistic calling and becomes the *chanson populaire,* the *air de cour.* These court airs reflect the decadent taste of the day. The poet's slight fancies, centering about love, treated now sentimentally and again maliciously, were handled with an airy, naïve grace; often their apparent simplicity masked many artificialities of pattern and phrase. Although the text had always played a significant part in the earlier chanson, in this period it suddenly became extravagantly important.

In his *Dictionnaire de Musique,* Jean Jacques Rousseau writes that a chanson is "a short lyric poem, to which one adds an air to be sung on such intimate occasions as at table, with friends, mistress, or even alone, to relieve temporarily the ennui, if one is rich, and to help one to bear more easily misery and toil, if one is poor." The music was simple and direct, easy to recall; the melody was often sung alone, but if supported by a lute, or later a harp, the harmonies were quite elementary and harmless. There were many varieties of these *airs de cour,* such as *bergerettes, brunettes, parodies, pastorales, romances, rondes,* and *vaudevilles.* As the fashion changed, one after another came to the fore and passed. The romance entered late (eighteenth century), but lasted long, its popularity undiminished through the first half of the nineteenth century.

Even the great poets of the period contributed their share to the form, and "a good little bit of a poet,"[1] like Pierre Jean de Béranger (1780–1857), became a great poet of the French chanson. He was a man so loved and so representative of the best French sentiments that manuscript copies of his poetry were handed about, prompting Robert Louis Stevenson to write that Béranger "was the only poet of modern times who could have altogether dispensed with printing."[2] It was only on the eve of the Revolution that composers began to claim and receive credit for their part in the success of the romance. Just as the poetry was contributed by the great and near-great, the musical settings were composed by professors at the Conservatory (such as Auguste-Mathieu Panseron (1796–1859), winner of the *Grand Prix de Rome* in 1813) and tunesmiths (such as Luise Puget who had an immense vogue in the period of Louis Philippe).[3] Characteristic are Henri Romagnesi's *La jeune Orpheline,* Garat's *Dans le printemps de mes années,* Jean Jacques Rousseau's *Le Rosier,* and Hippolyte Monpou's *L'Andalouse.*

Of the several million romances which flooded the years 1775–1850, the one that has remained most constantly in circulation and has not tarnished is *Plaisir d'Amour* by Schwarzendorf. A strange name for a French citizen, but such this Bavarian became, changing his name, however, to Martini.

---

[1] "Beranger," *Encyclopaedia Britannica* (11th ed.), III, 762c.
[2] *Ibid.,* 762a.
[3] A. Lavignac, "Histoire," *Encyclopédie de la Musique,* 1646.

Small wonder that the collections of Italian songs of the eighteenth century frequently include *Piacer d'amor,* the Italian translation of the beginning words of Jean Pierre de Florian's delicate verse; and the same collections often credited the music to the famous Padre Martini. The real composer soon found that his unreal name of Martini had been adapted by the French into Jean Paul Égide Martini (1741–1816). He is just another in that long line of foreign artists who were absorbed by the French and created French styles. Witness, to mention a few in the world of music, Lulli, Cherubini, Meyerbeer, and Franck. Martini was among the first composers of romances to score his accompaniment in detail. Already a popular figure through his military band music, when Martini turned his hand to romances, the public recognized the musician as well as the poet; gradually the tables were turned, and the poet was later slighted fully as much as the musician had been earlier.

Plaisir d'Amour tells how Sylvie has sworn to love the poet Florian, as long as the waters flow in the brook. Alas, the stream still flows, but she has changed: "The pleasure of love endures for a moment, but the sorrow of love lasts a lifetime." The first two lines are used as a refrain, reappearing between the two quatrains and at the ending. The design is A, B (m.15–22), ending in the dominant and interlude returning to tonic, and A. The second stanza, which reveals the faithlessness of Sylvie, is in the parallel minor, its first four-measure phrase answered by one of three. The left hand has an important melodic pattern in even eighths, while the right hand syncopates. The third line, m.42–45, goes to the relative major, the final line of the quatrain returning to the minor. The refrain enters again in m.52, concluding an AB (m.35–51) A design. This forms a very neat pattern, more extended and subtle than the usual strophic design accorded romances. Note the interest of the introduction, interludes, and coda, forming a pattern of ABCBcA.

Berlioz

DESPITE THE apparent gusto with which the French public acclaimed the romances, there were stirrings of dissatisfaction with things as they were—not only in music, but in the whole world of art. Although there were rumblings before, the romantic revolution in France may be said to have broken on February 25, 1830, with the production of Victor Hugo's drama, *Hernani*. It was not by chance that among those present, prepared to overcome opposition, were the poet Théophile Gautier and the musician Hector Berlioz.[4] Berlioz moved more freely in literary than in musical circles; almost all of his music springs from romantic literature. It was in this same year of revolutions that Berlioz had composed the *Symphonie Fantastique,* and two years earlier he had begun his *Huit Scènes de Faust.* One would not expect a composer of such a strong orchestral and dramatic bias to be drawn to the song. He was, however; and his penetration of the text, the justness of his declamation, the suppleness of his melody, and the expressiveness of his harmony contributed a new kind of French song. That this new song was native French no one denies. It is what Albert Bertelin[5] terms the *lied artistique,* which is none other than the art song. The adjective *artistique* is not necessary, since the French took the term *Lied* over into their vocabulary, as we have done. The term chanson from this time on most frequently means a song leaning to the popular side. Later, the term most used for the art song is *mélodie.*

Most of the difficulties that have always militated against frequent performances of Berlioz's larger works are present in reduced proportions in the songs. By disposition, he rebelled against current techniques. He loathed conventions and had a horror of the commonplace. Yet his own technique was not al-

---

[4] W. H. Hadow, *Studies in Modern Music,* I, 71–72.
[5] *Traité de Composition Musicale* (Paris, 1931), III, 184.

ways able to bring order out of his giant fancies. Too much of the deep emotional urge which Berlioz felt was lost in the scoring. He was least bound by the customary limitations of song in *La Captive,* Op. 12. This work is like a small symphonic poem, with transformations of the principal theme and the accompaniment originally conceived for orchestra. Many of the songs composed with piano accompaniment appeared in later versions with orchestra. Berlioz not only did not play the pianoforte, but he had no sympathy for it, and it is surprising to find the accompaniments as playable as they are.

The most frequently sung of his solo songs are the Nos. 1, 2, and 4 from Op. 7, *Les Nuits d'Été,* settings of six love poems by Théophile Gautier. When this work was published in 1841, Berlioz touched up his scoring of 1833–34. The orchestral versions of the accompaniments date from 1856, except that of *L'Absence,* which was reset in 1843. The *Villanelle,* No. 1, is gay and fresh. The light, high, repeated chords of the opening stanza by the end of the second phrase are in a key but a half-step higher, and this is representative of modulations and harmonizations which, though abrupt, give a lilting and joyous swing to this out-of-doors song. Strophic in form, as are most of his songs, the repetitions are varied; in both the second and third stanzas, the accompaniment is fuller with harmonies changed; there are bits of imitation, and even the voice part is modified. *Le Spectre de la Rose,* the second of this opus, one notes is for a different voice. There is a sweep to this longer song; its accompaniment figures are many, but are all called forth by the text. Indeed, the setting is like a *scena,* the voice closing with recitative-like phrases, with the accompaniment in a single line, a third below or above. *L'Absence* is *the* song of the set, the best of Berlioz. What French song of the first half of the nineteenth century catches more of the overtones of the forlorn lover! Gautier's poem found a natural response in Berlioz, who was one of the most tragically lonesome of men. One trait of this song which distinguishes it from so many of its fellows is its avoidance of any restless seeking for effect. Strophic in form, there are a few harmonic changes in repetition, but nothing like the strivings to give variety found in such a successful song as *Villanelle*.

L'Absence is direct, deep, tender, and passionate. Was the trumpet figure at the opening suggested by the call to the loved one to return? "O return, my well-beloved! As a flower far from the sun the flower of my life is closed when far from your glowing smile. O bitter fate, what vast spaces of country and towns, valleys and mountains, separate our hearts and our kisses. *Reviens, ma bien-aimée*." Some point the finger of scorn at the

resolution of the seventh of V_2^4 in m.3 to the tonic, a natural pianistic judgment.

Berlioz's orchestration has the seventh sounded by the oboe and second clarinet, which melodically carry the normal resolution a half-step down. Far more significant is the color in m.16–20, where the voice moves in simple recitative line, accompanied by the strangely hollow, descending octaves in the accompaniment. Note the amplification in its return in the second strophe (m.41–47), the added melodic line, and the *ascending* motion of the octaves leading to the climax, a third higher than before, but marked, with unusual restraint, only *forte*. The ending of each stanza, m.26 and m.51, is strangely on the V_7 of the relative minor, intensified the second time by the movement in the bass. Berlioz sustains this harmonic goal and then marks a *fermata* over a sixteenth rest. Directly, and in this he is a modernist avoiding conventional transition, the dominant of the home key begins the call to the beloved. With its third appearance (m.51), the voice is marked *ppp sotto voce ed estinto*. The tonic chord of its first and fourth measures is reinforced on the second quarter of each measure by a thin wraith of the same harmony, an octave above and below. The two final lines bring again the glorious diatonic upward-sweeping phrase and chordal-minded reply with cadence.

This song is a fine illustration of what Berlioz believed were the prevailing characteristics of his music, for in it are the "passionate expression, inward warmth, rhythmical animation, and unexpected turns."[6]

Gounod

LIKE ANY talented Frenchman of his day, Charles François Gounod (1818–93) knew that the greatest glory and rewards came to the composer of operas. *Faust* was only one of many of his stage works, which were complemented by a considerable amount of religious music, whose blending of lyric and dramatic styles—though earth-bound—gave great joy, within and without the churches, beyond the turn of the century. These dramatic and religious works defined a French style which has persisted to this day. Gounod's four volumes of songs reveal the same traits. His style is refined and harmonious. His melodies are clear and spontaneous. They flow with gentle grace along easy tonal ways; they are sweet, even saccharine; and when we apply this word, we should recall that saccharine has no food value. His is an art essentially feminine. His harmonies are warm. The sensuous, even voluptuous ecstasies which he frequently poured out are due largely to his never-too-harsh dissonances, pushed forward by a driving rhythmic pattern, coupled with a mounting sequence. His accompaniments seldom add more than sup-

[6] H. Berlioz, *Memoirs of Hector Berlioz* (tr. by E. N. Newman) (New York, 1935), 488. From a postscript to *"Lettre a M.—,"* dated May 25, 1858.

port to the voice. The design is almost invariably strophic, here and there modified in repetitions. He seldom plumbed the depths of the poetry he set. He matched phrase to phrase, rather than word to tone. His interpretation, therefore, is broad and flowing.

As winner of the *Grand Prix de Rome* in 1839, Gounod set forth for Italy. In his *Mémoires* he wrote that almost immediately after arrival at the Villa Medici he composed several songs, including *Le Vallon* and *Le Soir* (1840).[7] The music of the latter he adapted ten years later for the *Ode de Sapho* in Act I of the opera of the same name. *Le Soir* ("Evening") remains to this day as admired as any of Gounod's songs. The poem by Lamartine tells how, in the evening silence, one watches the night advancing. Venus, the evening star, casts her mysterious light about, shines on his troubled brow, and softly touches his eyes. Troubled, he asks the ray if it brings light to his soul. Does it come to reveal the divine mystery of the world? "Do you come to unveil the future to a tired heart which implores thee? O heavenly beam, art thou the dawn of the day which will never end?" A gentle melody, swung along on repeated chords in eighths—this motion maintained throughout—moves to the darker side of the key (subdominant, m.7), but directly turns homeward. The voice begins the melody of the introduction, but after three measures leads it in new paths, cadencing, however, on the tonic (m.17). The mid-division of the song, B, of a simple strophic form made up of three periods, ABC, is a major third lower, modulating back to the dominant of the home key (m. 25). Immediately, a seventh is added, and the last period affirms the home key, rising to a climax, perhaps too extravagant for the sentiment of the text. Rapidly it descends from these heights into the quiet of the mysterious star-filled night.

The opening of *Le Vallon* ("The Valley") has depth and color. *Au Printemps* ("To the Spring") with its light arpeggiated accompaniment, gives a sparkling background to a delightful, flowing melody. This melodic style reaches a peak in

[7] C. F. Gounod, *Memoirs of an Artist* (Chicago, 1895), 82.

Sérénade, the poem by Victor Hugo. Here the accompaniment swings in a purposeful monotony from tonic to dominant. After the short stanza, the refrain in a delicate buoyant bit of coloratura bids the loved one to sing, smile, and slumber. The song has no depth, but its surface beauty and elegance offer much charm.

The influence of Gounod spread far, but was most marked in Jules Massenet (1842–1912), whose style, however, was his own. Most popular is *Ouvre tes yeux bleux* ("Open Thy Blue Eyes"). The poem by Paul Robiquet introduces the lover who, in bright and arching song, tells his darling to wake, for day is here. The birds are singing, the sky is roseate. There is great artistry with the change of pace in the poet's second line, just half the length of the first. But not always does Massenet break the animated upward swing of the arpeggios for succeeding "half-lengths." The reply of the blue-eyed one brings a new melody, supported now by repeated chords in eighths, while the maid chides the lover for looking on the earth and its beauty when he might find love and light in her heart. The climax brings a unifying return of the first phrase of the first stanza, capped now by an assertive cadence. Clear as crystal, glittering in its open enthusiasm, this represents only one facet of a great French charmer.

Saint-Saëns

CHARLES CAMILLE SAINT-SAËNS (1835–1921) reminds one of the dilettanti of the Renaissance because of his lively curiosity and great breadth of culture. He was one of the most brilliant men who ever worked in music. This virtuoso composer's damning facility outran his power of creating valid, musical ideas, and his ingenuity often made palaces out of straw. Most of these have toppled over, but in their day his symphonies and chamber music, and his own championship of a French school of instru-mental music, attracted composers to develop this sphere that they had so long neglected. Nearly one hundred songs are scat-tered through his long career, but, with the exception of Op. 26, he failed to give them opus numbers. The results deny that he considered a song a "no-account thing," although strangely enough he honored an *Élevation* for harmonium and an *Étude* for the left hand with opus numbers. The Op. 26 contains six settings of poems by Armand Renaud, and the title, *Mélodies persanes,* is probably the first use of *mélodie* to signify the Art Song. Although Eastern subjects in French art had entered many years before these songs were composed (1870), the East had lost little of its attraction. Composers were inspired by the Nile (*Le Nil* by Xavier Leroux), the slave (*L'Esclave* by Lalo), Persian roses (*Les Roses d'Ispahan* by Fauré), and Brahma (*Chant Hindou* by Bemberg). Most frequently sung of Saint-Saëns' songs is *La Cloche.*

La Cloche

THE POEM BY Victor Hugo is an apostrophe to the bell, which though often vibrating in resounding tone, now sleeps in silence in its high, dark tower. The poet feels a kinship in spirit, for he, too, though lonely and silent, cries out in love as the bell clangs in the sky. Pictorially responding to the text, Saint-Saëns first sounds alone—deep down in the bass—the tonic octave which is a symbol of the great bell. There is no other bass for twenty-five measures, this pedal point being sounded each of the first five measures and then tolled only every third measure. The right hand sustains a sober pace with its three-voiced chords, while the simple, restrained melody of the voice adds to the mood of solemn loneliness. The first long division of this song consists of three periods (8+8+6), ending in the key a major third lower. A measure of transition sets up a syncopation on the old dominant, and the voice, as it sings of a soul that has a kinship with the great bell, strides restlessly in the parallel minor. The accompaniment, pulsing in even eighths, is here and there broken by a jagged pattern in the bass (m.32, m.36). With the line *"Sens-tu par cet instinct vague et plein de douceur"* ("Feelest thou by that instinct faint and full of sweetness"), the left hand swings above to tardily sing a duo with the voice. The key of the dominant is reached (m.43), and with m.51 the final division pushes forward with increasing tension. Triplets move with syncopation in the right hand, while the left hand steadily marches on in quarters; its tenor anticipates the soprano and sets up a jangle of dissonance. The mounting climax breaks at m.64, and it is a long, falling action from there to the end, Saint-Saëns—with no real poetic reason—repeating the last two lines of Hugo. This last division is the most conventional and the least convincing of the song. The design is what the French call *lied continu* ("continuous song"), their parallel for the German *durchkomponiert* ("throughout-composed").

CHAPTER XIV

Gabriel Fauré

To come to Fauré (1845–1924) in the history of French song is to enter the promised land. Berlioz and Gounod had seen it from afar and, in a few moments of cosmic consciousness, had true visions of it, but Fauré dwelt within its borders. He was born in the right time and by temperament and training was destined to free not only French song but French music from bondage. What his sensitive spirit could not accept were the sentimental excesses of romanticism. Fauré was one of the few Frenchmen able to appreciate Wagner without succumbing to his style. Nor was it merely the German brand of romanticism that Fauré rejected. He could not stomach the phantasmagoria of the French school. His training in the École Niedermeyer under Saint-Saëns had strengthened his natural love of order. This led him to state his ideas with great precision. His native aristocratic refinement kept him from cheap and easy techniques; his honest independence made him true to himself. He seemed little concerned with charming the public, whom he approached by the intimate channels of songs, piano pieces, and chamber music.

Although Fauré ate not of the ripe fruits of romanticism, he tasted and relished an offshoot of the movement that eventuated in symbolism. Some poets were attempting to free verse from conventional shackles of form and meter. They were tired of the exact and limited meanings of words and sought fresh approaches through symbols and indirect allusions; they found pleasure in the sound or music of words, independent of meaning. Fauré, too, wanted to free music from those traditions, tonal and formal, which he found too obvious. All of his songs are settings of verse of his time. The romantic poets, Hugo and Gautier, he never returned to after Op. 6. Fauré's name is naturally paired with that of the most original lyricist of the latter half of the nineteenth century, Paul Verlaine (1844–96), in the same way that one couples Schumann's name with that of Heine.

The first eight opus numbers are given to twenty *mélodies,* all loosely dated about 1865. Fauré kept returning to song for almost sixty years, his Op. 118, *L'Horizon chimérique,* having been composed in 1922, two years before his death. He wrote about 100 *mélodies,* most of the later songs in cycles. The three collections, each of twenty *mélodies (Edition J. Hamelle),* represent very loosely the three styles. With Fauré, as with Beethoven, one finds throwbacks in the last period, as well as "throwforwards" in the first. Despite his long career, the highly individual style of Fauré is recognizable all through the years. Let us review some of the characteristic features of his style.

An important clue to the character of a song writer is to be found in the poems he sets. Fauré was attracted to the short poems of the symbolists, to verse that was fresh in pattern and thought. He avoided long, sharply defined scenes and rarely chose a tense dramatic situation. He loved mood pieces with a touch of sentiment, delicately, even mysteriously handled. Irony and humor are out of his sphere; he can join the poet in lightness and gaiety, but he tends to be wistful, and many are the poems tinged with melancholy. Naturally, one truly sensitive to this subtle and delicately fibered verse could never set it in a pompous or inflated fashion. Fauré wedded it to a music elusive and tender. He seems to be communing with the poet, and their voices seldom rise above an intimate conversational level. There is no shouting; there is no tumult. It is a poetry and music devoid of exaggeration. Those who do not like it call it pallid.

Melody

NEITHER THE JUICY and voluptuous sweep of Massenet, nor the tender but obvious symmetrical phrases of Gounod are duplicated in Fauré. His melodic line is more hesitant, less obvious. His melodic courses had not been charted by others, and since they make their own way and create new contours, his position became not unlike that of Brahms, whose melodies were earlier condemned as unvocal. Brahms, however, had a persuasive strength and firmness, and a chordal-mindedness that soon made people recognize his melodies as only an extension of romantic practices. Fauré's melodies are less easily caught. They are vocal, not extreme in range, preponderantly conjunct in motion, little rising-scale passages of three or four notes appearing frequently. Yet Fauré is not easy to sing. The patterns and their meaning are sometimes difficult to grasp. There is line, but its continuity sometimes baffles one: for now clearly it is the supreme factor, riding on top, only a phrase later to be submerged and quite secondary to the piano. Rarely is the text drawn out or hurried to fit a preconceived melodic line. Rather the text calls the tune, whose motion and rhythm are fashioned out of the verse.

Harmony

THE ACADEMIC GRAMMAR of chords, in regard to both their spacing and their progression, was frequently violated by Fauré. We are so accustomed to unusual resolutions, or lack of resolution, from later impressionistic practice, that we find it difficult to believe how fully Fauré anticipated them. The difference between Fauré and later composers in employing these new harmonic freedoms is one of degree. Fauré, despite his daring, had a strong classical conscience which kept him from undue emphasis of any one method. We find chains of sevenths and ninths, unexpected modulations to distant keys, and—just as unconventional —returns to the home key without a long cadence formula affirming the fact. The final goal is often reached before we are quite aware of it. Small wonder that our sense of tonality is occasionally disturbed. We are a bit like a dweller on the Texas plains, accustomed to wide open spaces and an unbroken horizon, who is suddenly moved to a mountain valley. All the traditional gauges for light, color, and distance are upset. Romantic standards were bent by Fauré and his followers. Sequences are few. Imitations are not frequent, but there is a considerable amount of contrapuntal interest, seldom obvious. There is a return to the medieval modes, nor were they something foreign to this composer, whose duties at the great Parisian church, *La Madeleine,* led to facile improvisation on Gregorian themes. The modal flavor most frequently found in the songs is that of the Lydian, with its characteristic tritone, F-B-natural.

Form

Songs of Fauré are short, the average length of sixty *mélodies* being about fifty-one measures. The early songs are longer and generally strophic. Later he tended to become more precise and sparing. Composite or modified strophic, ternary, and through-composed—each design is employed in response to the music that the poem has called forth. There is nothing hard or unyielding about these designs with Fauré. They all seem flexible, and often a return of an idea is one of the most colorful and exciting parts of the song.

Accompaniment

While the vocalist is challenged by a far-from-commonplace melodic line, the pianist faces his problems in accompaniment figures, chord spacings, and progressions that demand constant alertness. Frequently the melody is supported by a chordal accompaniment, whose very appearance on the page, however, disowns connections with the *Volkstümliches Lied*. The prosaic support of block chords is frequently disguised by broken patterns of arpeggios, often scored very thinly and, again, though light and fleeting, spread rather wide. The unity of many of the songs, particularly the later ones, is largely secured by the exact or varied repetition of a single figure. There is no emphasis on countermelodies in the usual sense of the term. The accompaniment is often a mood poem, and scarcely ever is it based on exterior or pictorial figures drawn from the text. Its highest function is to create the proper atmosphere; it is often content with brushing in a background for the voice, occasionally doubling or countering. Independent interludes are few; introduction and epilogue, when present, are rather short and not weighed down with meanings beyond the body of the song.

Lydia

COMPOSED ABOUT 1865, introduced in 1873 at a concert of *La Société Nationale de Musique*—that organization which gave many Fauré works their *premières*—*Lydia* has maintained its position as one of the master's most loved songs. His collaboration with the poet Leconte de Lisle brought several masterpieces. There was a strong sensuous strain in Fauré, which responded to this thoroughly pagan tribute to Lydia, fair and rosy, a cascade of golden hair rippling over her white neck. "Countless delights from thy beauty flow, O goddess young and fair! Forget the sad tomorrows, let us take today with its love and joy."

Two measures of serene tonic chords set pace and key before the voice starts its mounting pattern of the first phrase, its second measure like the first, but commencing a tone higher and touching the augmented fourth from the tonic, characteristic color of the Lydian mode. Succeeding phrases of the stanza are tonal, a cadence on V in m.10, the third phrase closing in the minor of ii (m.14). The final phrases are given added charm by the graceful, falling triplets of m.16 and the wistful minor sixth in both m.17 and m.18. The top line of the accompaniment has faithfully followed the voice, the block chords sounding anything but prosaic because of the unorthodox harmonization. Excluding the introduction, there are only four measures of the stanza without accidentals, yet, in the voice part, only four notes are changed. The music is repeated for the second stanza. The coda weaves a garland for Lydia, with the delicate march of thirds upward through four measures in the left hand. An octave-jumping figure of the right hand lightly descends to the tonic.

Après un Rêve

THE BEST KNOWN of Fauré's compositions is this early setting (about 1865) of a poem by Romain Bussine, a professor of singing at the Paris Conservatory and the first president of *La Société Nationale de Musique*. The poem relates the dream of a lover who, carried to the gates of Heaven with his beloved, and shown the splendors of paradise, awakens to the sadness of life, and cries out: "Bring back my dreams, O night, return my radiant one, return mysterious night!" It is this uninhibited stream of yearning melody that won the public. It is a compelling melody: wider in range, more full-blooded in climax than most of Fauré's. The pair of triplets on the last two quarters of the measure is a marked feature, appearing eleven times with only one pattern repeated (m.7). Its charming turns are occasionally vocalized on a single vowel, a true melisma. The voice is supported throughout by block chords in eighth-note motion in the right hand, while a strong, directive bass line often fills the measure with one note. Over its substantial foundation, the right-hand harmonies move from one chord of tension to another, occasionally reaching consonant triads. The design is a much modified strophic, the repetition beginning in m.17; but after a cut and then an amplification of the pattern, the last division—from *"Hèlas!"* (m.31) to the end—is new. As the climax mounts, the bass presses forward in quarters and then summons the close by a sustained dominant pedal, which sinks in parallel octaves with the voice to the tonic.

Les Roses d'Ispahan

LECONTE DE LISLE's fancy of Lydia is matched by Leilah, of whom he sings in *Les Roses d'Ispahan*. The moss roses of Persia, the jasmine, and the orange blossoms have a perfume less sweet than the breath of Leilah. Her voice sounds lovelier than the rippling of waters or the singing of birds. But, with their flight, her kisses have ceased, and there is now no more fragrance in the flowers. "Oh let young love return ... and once more perfume the orange blossoms, the Persian roses in their mossy sheaths." This charming fantasy was set by Fauré in 1884, with a graceful, languorously swinging music. The design of A^1 A^2 (m.22) B (m.44) A^3 (m.59) contains slight modifications of materials. One of the most interesting is the progressive shortening of the introduction from seven measures to five (m.22–26) and before the last entry of A compressed to four (m.59–62). The syncopated rocking of the bass—the first note of its figure frequently forming a pedal as in m.1–14—often supports an active alto in the right hand. Its dotted motion of m.4–5 is carried upward in m.14–15 to a second division of the strophe. Here the accompaniment is in even movement, while the voice line is filled with most interesting rhythmic patterns. The compressed repetition of m.16 in m.17, beginning on the second eighth, paradoxically occupies more time, since the final note is extended for the word *"douce."*

Ont un par-fum moins frais, ont un-e o-deur moins dou-ce,

The phrase structure throughout is delightfully irregular, and the cadence (m.21–22) III $_4^6$–V$_6^7$–I is quite fresh. The repetition of A, beginning in m.22, closes with a new cadence in the key of the major third higher (m.41), but it enharmonically shifts back, and B (m.44) moves through the subdominant to its relative minor (m.52), where a tonic pedal upholds the voice's phrase in Aeolian mode. Home key and A (m.59) return with slight changes. The coda is drawn from the basic introductory figure, but lazily flats the seventh in its second measure, only to peace-fully settle down to an extended and enriched plagal cadence.

Clair de Lune

THE FIRST OF SEVENTEEN poems from Verlaine which Fauré set was chosen from *Fêtes Galantes* (1869). These poems evoke the scenes and moods captured by Watteau, whose canvases picture masked gallants and ladies making love and music. In *Clair de Lune,* Verlaine dreams: "Your soul is like a landscape rare, where masked figures go singing, dancing, and playing the lute. Through all their gaiety there runs a strain of melancholy, and their songs mingle with the moonlight, sad and beautiful, where-in the birds dream, and the tall slender fountains between the statues sob in ecstasy." This is one of the rare occasions when Fauré made use of local color. To summon the period of Louis

XIV, he chose a *menuet,* or so he calls this engaging music, which the piano plays, seemingly indifferent to the voice wending its own way. The voice part is almost without repetition, only one phrase returning, and that directly (m.28–34). The "accompaniment," however, is astonishingly economical, based on three motives, which appear and reappear, relieved by episodes. The

form, with such an instrumental piece as the foreground, is unique, but by broad grouping it can be classed as a rondo: AB (m.17, relative major) AC (m.38, major third lower) A, coda. Modal tendencies in m.2 (flatted seventh), the tritone of Lydian (m.40–41), the unexpected key (m.38), the perversity of Fauré in setting *sur le mode mineur* (m.27) in the major, and the color of the final cadence VI_4^6–I—these are a few of the delights.

Prison

THIS POEM WAS WRITTEN by Verlaine, while awaiting trial in the *Prison de Carmes,* Brussels, for wounding a boy who had brought him great trouble.[1] In the summer of 1873 this is what the poet saw from the window of his cell while remorse and despair tortured him: "High o'er the roofs the sky is so blue, so calm. A treetop gently sways, a distant bell softly tolls, a bird sings its plaint. *Mon Dieu,* how bare and still the life! That faint murmur comes from the city. What hast thou done, O thou, there, forever weeping—tell me what hast thou done with thy youth?" The repressed anguish of Verlaine, Fauré has set with a music

[1] "Rimbaud," *Encyclopaedia Britannica* (11th ed.), XXVIII, 1123d.

infinitely sad, rising, indeed, to as great a tension as he ever reached, but with no histrionics. There is a solemn tread of the quarter-note movement in the 3/4 measure and a certain monotony in the three-measure phrases that close suspensively on the dominant and on the last of the measure. Is that doubled octave sounding there the distant bell? The voice carries the fourth phrase into the succeeding measure (m.14) and with a strange new harmony which prefigures the rising tension of the next three phrases, each of which in sequence mounts a half-step. The last six measures of superb harmony, rising over a tonic pedal, seem naturally to yearn for a growing climax, but Fauré has commanded *pp,* as the voice fades away in memory of misspent youth. The cadence falls from VI_6–I; the voice, doubled by the alto and tenor of the accompaniment, falls from the sixth to the dominant.

La Bonne Chanson

GENERALLY REGARDED as the high creative point of the careers of both poet and musician is *La Bonne Chanson.* Verlaine had lost his heart to the sixteen-year-old Mathilde Mauté, and, in the greatest happiness and sincerity he ever knew, he poured forth twenty-one poems from a heart that was like "a nightingale singing in the night." Fauré chose nine of these and wove them together with common or cyclic motives. This greatest of French song cycles has been called the *"Dichterliebe"* of France. It has the warmth and spontaneity of the Schumann cycle, but its unity and design spring from, and rival Beethoven's *An die ferne Geliebte.* Only one of the motives appears in the first song, *Une Sainte en son auréole;* the suppleness with which this theme is maintained and modified, interlaced with other voice parts of the accompaniment and supporting a graceful, fluid melody, illustrates the lyric freedom of Fauré's counterpoint. The voice moves within its small ninth, one syllable to a note, its phrases delicately matched to the verse. The three-measure phrase of the introduction is twice repeated before trying its theme a minor third higher (m.9). It returns to tonic and balances, before proceeding to a new idea with an insistent offbeat tone (m.22), that may be the "golden note of the horn heard in distant woods." The rich and unusual harmonic colors which result from separate voice leadings are further enriched by the scale begun by the voice (m.34) and, a measure later, imitated and carried up diatonically an octave and a fifth before its Phrygian modal line is cadenced in the home key (m.39). A new figure of balancing (m.49) offers interesting cross relations in its lulling two-measure pattern. The return (m.70) of the "horn" in distant key (sharped fifth) drifts sequentially back home. The augmented fourth in the melodic line (Lydian) of the final cadence is older, indeed, than the era of Charlemagne. The name which haunted Verlaine was—Mathilde. It was of her that he thought as he wrote: "A Saint in her aureole, a lady in her tower, all that human word contains of grace and love,—the golden note of the horn heard in distant woods, joined to the proud tenderness of the noble ladies of yesteryear, the whiteness of the swan, the blush of the maiden, pearly tints white and rosy, a sweet patrician accord,—I see and hear all these things in her name, Carlovingian."

CHAPTER XV

Franck

ONE of the strongest and clearest of the currents forming modern French music is that which flowed from César Franck (1822–90) and his pupils. A difficulty which all forward-looking French composers faced is most glaringly illustrated by the indifference and opposition which Franck's colleagues at the Paris Conservatory accorded to this man and his music. The upholders of tradition, as the Conservatory and Academy felt themselves to be, were fighting a losing battle. The very forms which the pupils of the Conservatory were taught to stuff according to the rules were revivified by Franck and filled with living ideas. Undoubtedly his greatest importance lies in the warm and fluid treatment of harmony and design in larger instrumental forms. Yet he was devoted to whatever work was in hand and gave it the best he could summon. But even an artist whose life and works are motivated by the highest aesthetic and religious ideals cannot always rouse himself to vital works. In his songs written as early as 1842, there is nothing distinguished; and, quite unlike the early works of such men as Fauré and Debussy, there are few anticipations of the composer's final style.

There are turns which we associate with Gounod, and, even as late as 1871, the popular *Le Mariage des Roses* has more than a suggestion of the easy-swinging, not too-deeply-probing sentiment of the host of white-kid-gloved French composers. Franck was not truly one of them, and there are redeeming points in this song. His pure and simple soul was devoid of poses and artifices. His was a world of tone which he tried to make ring true. The overtones that the musicians were trying to catch in painting and poetry and then incorporate in their music—these troubled Franck not at all. I do not think we can charge off the bad and mediocre songs to the choice of second-rate poems, which for some reason had appealed to him and then had failed to inspire him.[1] In theory, a good song results from fine poetry, which calls into being good music. But it is not always thus that the spark is set off, and the union of the two is often of unequal values, as, indeed, is true in life, where frequently one finds the spark set off between two strangely unequal beings. Now the poetry of neither the *Nocturne* nor *La Procession* rises much above the level of other poems set by Franck, but somehow they brought the spark of life, resulting in the best songs which Franck wrote.

The more original poetic fancy is that of Charles Brizieux in *La Procession*.

La Procession

IN THIS WORK, the poet pictures a priest carrying the Host and leading his assembly of the faithful across the fields. This is no brilliant scene such as the Venetian, Gentile Bellini, made memorable when he painted another Corpus Christi day procession before San Marco. Brizieux's poem calls up a humble scene: people of great faith, whose songs mingle with those of the birds, whose offerings of incense rise with the perfume of the wild flowers. "God is moving across the fields." This appealed to the devout organist of Ste Clotilde, and what was more natural than that he should recall a sequence proper to the day, the great hymn of Thomas Aquinas, *Lauda Sion, Salvatorem*.

Franck begins by preluding, as if on an organ, drifting back to repeat the first measure as the voice enters in free recitative. This continues as the piano theme is developed *fugato,* leading to sustained half-note chords, descending chromatically. Only after this first half of the song does Franck introduce the theme

[1] E. Blom, *Stepchildren of Music* (London, n.d.), 163.

of the liturgical chant, its melody outlined by the top voice of the accompaniment, starting in m.32. At the end of its first phrase, the accompaniment, freely joined by the voice (*"La foule autour"*), interpolates the earlier theme of its *fugato,* which in turn had been derived from the opening measure of the introduction. The church chant is resumed, the introductory theme once again interpolated (m.42–43). *Tremolandi* indicate the increasing tension of the drama and lead to a new figure of sixteenths in the accompaniment, which flows freely through various keys, finally to swell into the climax on the home dominant (m.62). Rapidly receding from this *ff,* the *Lauda Sion* returns in home key, *pp* (m.65), the voice interpolating this time its entering phrase. As the voice of the beholder in mystic adoration repeats the first line of the poem, the opening "organ" theme, *8va,* underlines the cadence in augmentation (m.72), directly closing by repetition of the last half of the phrase in its original note values.

Nocturne

THE SUBJECT OF L. de Fourcaud's poem may be less original in fancy than Brizieux's *La Procession.* There have been many apostrophes to the mystery of the night. But the touching appeal of the poet to the cool, blessed, regally solemn beauty of the transparent, starry night to bless his troubled soul with its peace echoed in Franck's heart; he was a mystic; he yearned for the infinite. The *Nocturne,* (written in 1884, four years earlier than *La Procession*) reveals Franck at his best. Indeed, the poem seems a reflection of the composer, who was blessed by serenity and nobility, only occasionally troubled by tender melancholy.

The song opens with a descending chromatic line over a dominant pedal, closing on the minor chord of the tonic. The first phrase of the voice begins to repeat the opening in the relative major, extending its phrase two measures and returning to home key with a haunting cadence, II_3^4–I. The strophic pattern is repeated for stanzas two and three, but to each is added a rhythmic intensification. In the second stanza, the eighth-note motion, which had appeared only in the topmost line, is doubled in the tenor. The interlude repeats the introduction, but now in triplet figuration, whose motion is continued in the bass of the third stanza while the right hand returns to the original pattern of two's. No interlude follows, although the final measure of the stanza introduces the sixteenth-note figure which intensifies the accompaniment of the final stanza. This, however, is a new theme, and in the major. As it rolls forward to its climax with the repetition of the stanza's salutation to the night (the last phrases beginning *"O grande nuit"*), the closing division of the stanza pattern returns, hesitating between the new major and its original minor. Thrice before the cadence had closed in a diatonic descending line to the tonic. Now, it resolutely lifts a seventh to the tonic, supported by a widening, arpeggiated, major tonic chord. Despite the marking of *molto diminuendo*

and rallentando, which pare down a climax marked only *f,* one finds himself gripped more by the immensity of the night than by the final plea to "let sleep flow to my eyes."

Duparc

IT WAS A STRANGE QUIRK of fate which struck down the two most gifted pupils of Franck. Chausson, when forty-four, while his

great gifts were still expanding, met his death in a bicycle acci-
dent on his estate. More regrettable still was the musical silence
of Henri Duparc (1848–1933), from 1885 to his death. A tragic
neurasthenia settled upon him, and he did not compose a note
in almost half a century. Duparc destroyed some and disowned
others of the few *mélodies* he had written, the complete, authen-
tic edition of *Rouart, Lerolle, et Cie.* containing only thirteen
songs. The earliest of these was *Chanson Triste,* written about
1868, as was *Soupir. L'invitation au voyage* and *La vague et la
cloche* were composed during the siege of Paris, 1870–71. These
mélodies nearly parallel those of Fauré, though none are later
than his *Les Roses d'Ispahan* (1884). These two composers have
been called "co-founders of the renascence of French song." In
Duparc, there is a sweep and fullness, an ardor that makes the
slender volume of his songs one of the most precious books of
French music. Certainly as magically fresh, expansive, and
spontaneous as any of his songs is *L'Invitation au voyage.*

L'Invitation au voyage

DUPARC chose only the first and last stanzas of Baudelaire's poem.
These two fourteen-line stanzas, in their leisurely span, dimly
bring into focus a journey of lovers to the land of their dreams.
There, they imagine themselves alone in that country where the
sun through the mist is like the loved one's eyes shining through
her tears. The ships, rocking on the tide, wander to the ends of
the earth to gratify her slightest desire. The setting sun bathes
the streams with hyacinth and gold; the world sleeps in a soft,
warm light. There, all is order, beauty, splendor, pleasure, and
peace. Thus is woven the poet's "spell," which Duparc has intensified by a delicate web of colorful harmony and a peaceful,
flowing melody. Deep below sounds a double pedal of tonic and
dominant, anchoring this "journey" for more than two-thirds
of the song. I know of no other song which depends so much
upon the sostenuto pedal for its realization.

A tremulous movement of sixths, in lulling sixteenth-note
motion, begins the voyage; the intervals of the chord shift and
shimmer as they support the long phrases of the voice. The mode

Mon en - fant, ma sœur,

wavers between minor and major. With m.32, a refrain in 9/8
drops the sixteenth-note motion and, over the retained double
pedal, sustains, *pp,* rich, wide-spaced chords, which descend as
the voice intones its detached phrases on tonic and dominant.
Directly in m.40 there begins a repetition of the music of the first
stanza, but it freely evolves. For the first time the double pedal is
absent (m.50), and the "cyclic" motive of the song, first stated
by the voice in m.11–14, now appears in the bass, the voice adding
a countermelody and moving upward toward the dominant. A
spacious 9/8 movement freely extends the last half of the strophic
design; delicate, high-pitched, arching arpeggios gradually move
back to the original tonic in the major, with added light suc-
cessively from the sixth (m.71), second, and fourth. The double
pedal returns with the refrain (m.75), though the chords, which
before were sustained, now are outlined in the right hand, while
the left adds the "cyclic" theme. The coda has the ritard scored
in a foolproof fashion, for, marked *a tempo,* Duparc has in successive measures reduced the flow of movement per unit from
the basic nine, to six, to four, to three, to one. With this last
appears the first marked rallentando, closed a measure later by
the simple major chord, with a three-octave hollow between the
hands.

Phidylé

DUPARC AND FAURÉ were never more alike than in the opening
of this love song. Its simplicity, its intimacy, the little modal
turn in m.4–6, the direction, *doux et sans nuances* (softly and
without nuances)—in these first ten measures we find common
means of expression of these apparently kindred spirits. With
the refrain, *"Repose,"* however, Duparc begins to explore a
world of his own making. He moves directly to a key a small
third lower; the movement is doubled to eighths; the harmony
is richly blurred, but for six whole measures secured by a tonic
pedal. The reply (m.14–16) to the relaxing phrases of the voice
is a cyclic motive, which is a favored device of Duparc for unifying his amply spaced song forms.

A second division begins with m.22, a running accompaniment in sixteenths (the clover and the humming bees) moving
quickly through E, B-flat, D, F-sharp, E-flat (original key, A-
flat). As in entering this section, so in leaving it, a measure in
triplet motion bridges to the eighths and an amplified return of
the refrain in home key. The extension (m.49–53) over the
dominant pedal, with an interesting syncopated figure in the
tenor which will return in the coda, leads to the third large
division of this lied-continu. Its opening measures remind one
of Wagner, to whom Duparc was strongly attracted. Rich, warm,

subtle, and vibrant, this section leads on to a huge I_4^6–V_7 cadence in m.67, which is deceptively resolved in "Tristan" fashion. The ninth in its "resolution" is the beginning of the cyclic theme, repeated two measures later at tonic level with new harmony and a new countermelody in the alto. The romantic glow of this last page, one of the longest and most important codas in modern song, is quite opposed to the beginning, marked *sans nuances*.

The music seems highly faithful to Leconte de Lisle's poem, which begins with the invitation of the soft grass, the mossy bank, the murmur of the streams, the scent of flowers, and the hum of bees, all of which invite slumber. Repose, Phidylé! The midday sun glints on the leaves. The birds skim over the hills seeking shade; the flowers droop. But when the sun has run his shining course and the air grows cool, your radiant smile and your thrilling kiss will make glad the waiting lover.

Soupir

OF THE SHORTER *mélodies* of Duparc, the most frequently sung are *Chanson triste* and *Soupir*. The former has a most graceful, sweeping, melodic line for the voice, supported throughout by arching arpeggiate patterns. These arpeggios frequently contain foreign tones, often an appoggiatura from above, whose delayed absorption into the rippling stream of the harmony gives great pleasure. Indeed, the song, though tender and intimate, has a buoyant swing which belies the title. The lover's griefs and fears are forgotten, his wounded heart healed. Quite opposed is the verse of Sully Prudhomme's *Soupir*, which sings of a constancy luxuriating in its woeful loss. "Never to see her or hear her; never to call her aloud, but always faithfully to await her and love her. To open my arms when weary with waiting, only to close them on nothingness! But always still to be offering them. Tears consuming, tears ceaselessly shed, yet ever shall I love her! Toujours!" The phrases are short; they grow weak and droop in their grief; the pattern of the first measure of the introduction is both rhythmically and harmonically the key to the song, and its varied repetition unifies the design.

Four-fifths of the measures of the song begin with the single tone of the bass, the "sighing" motive entering an eighth later, lightly enforcing its dissonance in even tread of eighths to the last of the measure, where its motion seems to be spent and its dissonance softened or resolved. The first division of the song closes in the parallel major. B (m.12–37) repeats its first part a minor third higher, beginning at m.22, leading, however, to some bars of chromatic drifting (m.29–35), which are quite "Franckian." The voice has quietly intoned the last two phrases of this section. The dominant of the home key makes ready the return of A, with repetition of both words and music. The voice adds *"toujours,"* the piano settling the suspensive I_4^6 by doubling its low tonic for the first time an octave below.

Chausson

IN A LETTER TO Paul Poujaud, Ernest Chausson (1855–99) complains that his composing is going badly. He seems unable to get beyond a certain spot. Exasperated, he strikes out blindly, holding that his malady came from writing songs, which he now detests. "Pretty harmonic scratchings but they intoxicate, enervate, and weaken one.... D'Indy and Franck make *mélodies* but they make other things too."[2] Chausson also made other things, and his *Poème, Concert,* and *Symphonie* have lasted much longer than most of the music of his day. It seems strange that, even in a moment of dejection, Chausson should have depreciated his songs, for it was first in them that he revealed his personal idiom. He lived in a world of shadows, the deepest those of Franck and Wagner, whom he reverenced. A refined gentleman of great wealth, serene and meditative by nature, he had slowly asserted himself. He never deliberately set out to write a new kind of music, but his sensitive spirit, while true to itself, reflected the idiom of his day; he played an important role in the

[2] P. Poujaud, *La Revue Musicale,* December, 1925, 174.

founding of French nationalism, as one might have expected of a disciple of Franck.

Of the nearly thirty-five songs which were composed early and late, few have held a constant place in repertoire. Perhaps singers have felt that they could find in Duparc and Debussy a purer crystallization of the moods in which Chausson is most successful. No one can deny the intimate charm of Chausson; his songs are rich in color and modulation, sensitive to the poet's lines which most frequently tend to a serene melancholy, not one of bitterness or revolt. *Lassitude* (Maeterlinck) or *Amour d'Antan* (Bouchor) might illustrate this facet of Chausson, but I prefer to spend a moment with the popular *Le Temps des Lilas* (Bouchor). And this, despite the fact that it is an excerpt from the Op. 19, *Poème de l'Amour et de la Mer,* for voice and orchestra. It is the sad, sweet essence of Chausson as he matches with haunting phrases the complaint of the lover who mourns a love that has faded. The springtime that warmed with its sun and blessed with its flowers cannot awaken this love. The time of lilacs and roses has passed.

The principal theme enters in the prelude, gently rocked by offbeat accompanying chords above. As the phrase is repeated, the voice tardily joins. How just the accent which does not overstress *"temps"!* A foreign key is freely taken with *"le vent a changé"* (the wind has changed). The principal theme has appeared in various changes, the syncopated accompaniment retained through the first division. The middle section (m.38–55) sweeps to new keys, the phrases no longer languorous, but pressing forward, supported by a pattern of even sixteenths, which rock back and forth with colorful dissonance. Home key and syncopated accompaniment return (m.55) with an eloquent question; the principal theme recurs (m.67), the voice even more hesitant in joining (a measure of 4/4). The little epilogue finds the basic motive stated for the first time in other than alto or tenor range, as if it were now singing for the voice which has been silenced by the thought that "our love is dead forever."

Le Colibri

Two of the most frequently sung *mélodies* of Chausson are in his Op. 2, published in 1882. *Les Papillons,* the third of the set, is fresh and clear, with only the wisp of a cloud in the last line to dull the quick, light fancy which Gautier's poem called forth. The accompaniment is a pianist's delight as the hands alternate and interlace to give a tonal paraphrase to the floating and fluttering of butterflies.

The seventh and last song of this opus, *Le Colibri,* is far less obvious in its picturing. Yet, such repetition and slight motion as in m.9, or the descending arpeggio figures of m.21–28, and the ninefold repetition of chord in m.29–30 are tonal paintings matching Leconte de Lisle's images. This romantic poem may be translated as follows: "At dawn when the sun touches his nest with a rosy glow, the hummingbird darts through the air like a shaft of light. He flies quickly to the spring where the bamboo murmurs like the sea. There he hovers over the fragrant flowers, and drinks too deeply of their sweetness. Upon your pure lips, my beloved, so also my soul would sip and die." The metric signature of 5/4 is unusual, but rarer still is the ease and naturalness with which Chausson moves in its frame. Melodically, the interval of the third, up or down, filled in or not, is most important. Its upward, curling circle (m.15–16) is repeated a minor third higher (m.17–18). With m.21, the theme of the introduction reappears, its first note lengthened to give strong contrast to the quicker movement of the first section. The four-measure introduction is extended, descending a half step a measure to the dominant, where the pattern is that of m.15. A returns (m.33), and the voice overreaches its previous high point to descend in its final ardent phrase.

CHAPTER XVI

Debussy

THE most fruitful reaction against the hearty, supercharged type of romanticism, illustrated in full color by Wagner, was that quietly championed by Achille Claude Debussy (1862–1918). At first drawn by the sensuous richness of Wagner, Debussy later came to hate his music with a bitter hatred. A revolt against its extravagances had been in the air for some time. Unlike Fauré, Debussy was not troubled by a classic conscience. There was only one commanding voice which he heard, and that was from within himself. His whole life was spent in trying to shape a new language which could reveal to others the fantasies that his sensitive spirit and giant imagination had dreamed. There are many contradictory qualities in Debussy. His temperance in dynamics, with scarcely ever an indulgence in forceful emphasis, seems strangely opposed to his license in harmony. His philosophy that the whole function of music centered in giving pleasure[1] apparently takes him back to the days when the composer was not expected to know anything other than music.

Yet Debussy was the friend of poets and painters, and his translations into tone of the new beauties and freedoms they were seeking led men to transfer to Debussy's music the term "impressionism," which they had derisively invented for Monet's painting. If Debussy was the "painter of dreams" as Rolland wrote, his "time-canvases" are vaguer and far less realistically

---

[1] L. Vallas, *Claude Debussy, His Life and Works*, 13. Compare his reply to Guiraud who asked him "What then is your rule?" Debussy replied, "My pleasure." *La Revue Musicale*, December, 1920.

pictorial than the works of Manet and Monet. Actually, his invention seemed to be stirred more by poets than by painters. With the exception of Rossetti (*Blessed Damozel*) and D'Annunzio (*Le Martyre de Saint-Sébastien,* written, however, in French verse), Debussy found his inspiration in French poets.

Limiting ourselves to the forty-seven published songs for voice and piano, we find his first associations were with Théodore de Banville and Paul Bourget. The verses chosen are graceful and dexterous, if not distinguished; they drew from Debussy music of the same stripe. Almost at the same time, he was naturally drawn to the "versified music" of Verlaine's poetry. As with Fauré, this forms the true core of his songs. Here is no hard realism, no exulting, no romanticism. Fluid in substance and form, his verse moved between mysticism and sensuality and woke echoes in this symbolist musician. Later came Baudelaire, Pierre Louÿs, and Mallarmé. Then, turning from his contemporaries, Debussy found fresh and refined inspiration in the rhythms and imagery of the fifteenth-century poets, Charles d'Orléans and Villon, and in an obscure seventeenth-century poet, Tristan l'Hermite. Whatever the mood and cut of the verse, Debussy, having been drawn to it, pondered it; then through his music he intensified the mood and clarified the meaning of the poem. The words were after all only the husks or outer coating of the images which were half-concealed; the sensitive musician divined the hidden secrets and revealed them in movement and tone.

His songs stretch over forty years, from the schoolboy's inspiration of 1876 (*Nuit d'Étoiles*) to the cry in 1916 of a master, broken in body and spirit, expressing his sorrow for the children bombed out of their homes (*Noël des enfants qui n'ont plus des maisons*). In the first half of his career, publishers were not much interested in his songs.[2] In 1882, he received only fifty francs for his first song, *Nuit d'Étoiles.*[3] Twice he offered to

[2] M. Dumesnil, *Claude Debussy, Master of Dreams,* 72.
[3] Vallas, *Claude Debussy, His Life and Works,* 73.

write a set of Verlaine songs for Hamelle, but received no response. Publisher or public, however, did not matter too greatly to Debussy, who was gradually finding the technical means for expressing the music he heard within him. Despite his lessons at the Conservatory, he was practically self-taught.

Two forces that helped him to find his way came through Mme Von Meck (the renowned patroness of Tchaikovsky) and Mme Vasnier. To the first, Debussy owed his acquaintance with some Russian music, later extended to Borodin and Moussorgsky. Jean Cocteau, writing how Debussy had fallen into the Russian snare, held that "Debussy played in French, but with a Russian pedal."[4] There is but little Russian in Debussy; Falla even finds him "Spanish."[5] What Moussorgsky did was to strengthen the Frenchman in his will to be himself. For four years, 1880–84, Debussy was the almost constant house guest of the Vasniers; M. Vasnier was an architect, whose library of art books and literature Debussy absorbed, and Mme Vasnier was a gifted soprano who sang her guest's songs in private and public.[6] Her generous gifts, sympathetic counsel, and encouragement of the new kind of music he was making, softened those trying years. In that period he moved away from the broad, flowing melody, à la Massenet.

Mandoline and other settings from Verlaine, originally dedicated to Mme Vasnier, are more irregular in phrase, following the text in free declamation. This is not yet the French recitative that Debussy described as moving quietly between little intervals, in tones of almost equal duration. "Melody," he once said, "is almost anti-lyric, and suitable for the chanson which confirms a fixed sentiment."[7] His *mélodies* may have occasional bits, like recitative, but the phrases generally have melodic line and

---

[4] J. Cocteau wrote: *"Debussy a joué en français, mais avec la pédale russe."* La Revue Musicale, February, 1921, 106.

[5] M. DeFalla, *La Revue Musicale,* December, 1920, 206–10.

[6] Dumesnil, *Claude Debussy, Master of Dreams,* 54–55; Vallas, *Claude Debussy, His Life and Works,* 16–17.

[7] L. Gilman, *A Guide to Pelléas et Mélisande* (New York, 1937), 51.

an identity of their own. Once in Vienna, some musicians thought to honor Debussy by counting the ways in which he had freed music; when, however, the speaker said that Debussy had suppressed melody, the composer, as unconventional in his speech as in his music, audibly protested: "But all my music strives to be, is melody."[8] His is a melody that "does not cadence every two bars"; it avoids routine accentuations as well as intervals, and it is frequently founded on other than the classic scale. Melody of such an unconventional cut demands an accompaniment that is far from traditional.

There are no dull parts for the accompanist in these songs. Patterns are new; few of the classic and romantic figures appear. It is often an involved fabric of tone; by its weight and richness, it gives a wonderful foundation for the voice and, at the same time, contributes its own pattern and illustration of the text. Its frequent busyness and independence tempt the pianist to drown the voice and upset the delicate equilibrium that the composer planned. The harmonies that voice and piano make are still fascinating, but we are not shocked and baffled, as were our fathers, by the flagrant violations of all established routines. Dissonance takes on a new meaning, and its goal is not necessarily consonance. Chords of the seventh in parallel motion, hesitantly used by Fauré, are widened up to thirteenths and extended in time; the tonal system is stretched, but never breaks down into atonality. And most important of all is the fact that these novel procedures are not an attempt to shock the natives, but result rather from a supersensitive feeling for color and atmosphere. His designs, too, come from within. He wanted his music free, "never stifled under an accumulation of redundant motives."[9] Although his song forms exhibit motives, repetition, and contrast, the unity we feel seems due less to these than to the natural flow of ideas and rhythms born of the poem.

[8] Vallas, *Claude Debussy, His Life and Works*, 215.
[9] O. Thompson, *Debussy, Man and Artist*, 103.

Beau Soir

Composed in 1878 when Debussy was a student at the Paris Conservatory, this song reveals many of the traits of the mature composer. Note the open texture of the arpeggiated accompaniment with the spacing between the notes carefully chosen; note, too, the relative parallelism of m.2 to m.1, the progression, however, strangely out of key and unpredictable, as is the next excursion in m.4 to the minor triad on the flatted third, which sets up a fine cross-relation between the last eighth of the measure in the bass and entry of the voice; characteristic are the whole-tone melodic line in m.10 and final cadence, moving from an augmented triad on the flatted third to the tonic.

All these are color devices frequently found later. The melody is suave, and its contours grateful to voice and ear. The B (m. 20) sets up a new melodic interest in the piano, repeated at a new level (m.23), leading to a rather full climax. The falling away from this climax emphasizes again the chord color of m.2, and as the piano in m.30 repeats an octave lower what it has said in m.28, we find the voice meditatively declaiming on a single tone. A V_9 is rolled up and sustained (m.32), over which the voice faintly rises a small third, giving an uncertain, groping effect. The opening measures return (m.35–37), but as the voice concludes the poet's broken last line, by rising to the dominant, a new color of augmented triad drifts upward to a tonic chord, reduced to its simplest terms in the last unusual measure. Bourget's poem describes how "when at sunset the streams turn rosy, and a warm breeze runs over the field of grain, the troubled heart longs to be happy and taste life fully, while one is young and the evening fair. For we shall all go, as the stream flowing, it to the sea—we to the tomb."

Mandoline

In the early years when Debussy lived with the Vasniers, he began his settings from Verlaine, *Mandoline* being the first of eighteen poems by this strange genius that Debussy put to music. At the beginning of the music notebook for Mme Vasnier, to whom this song was dedicated, Debussy had copied five settings from Verlaine's *Fêtes Galantes*. The scene of *Mandoline* is one like the eighteenth-century painter Watteau pictured; the serenaders "and their lovely companions exchange silly nothings 'neath the murmuring trees. There is Tircis, Aminte, and tiresome Clitandre; there is Damis who made many a tender verse for many a cruel maid. Their short jackets of silk, their long trailing robes, and their soft blue shadows whirl in ecstasy 'neath a moon of misty rose, while the mandolin jangles through the trembling breezes."

Debussy's is the first important setting of this poem; Fauré's was composed eight years afterward, and Szulc's still later. They all give a fanciful background of the plucked strings, but here the similarities cease, although Szulc followed the poetic liberty of Debussy in introducing a wordless refrain of "la-la's." Debussy sets a jangling tuning-motive of a pair of superimposed open fifths, directly repeated an octave higher. This alternation of low and high in a measure of 6/8 makes exciting rhythm and color. After five measures founded on the dominant, the tonic appears only to swing to an off-center "dominant," V being sharped (m.6). The "murmuring branches" bring a sliding in parallel fifths that delicately drop in cadence to the major key, a whole step lower than the beginning. This swings by m.16

Sous les ra-mu-res chan-teu - - - - - - - - - - - ses

to the original dominant, the extended cadence of "Clitandre" moving about the key in the weak part of m.19–20, the flatted seventh giving whole-tone color.

The next phrase is very suave, as m.24–25 coyly extend the preceding two measures with an arching line, closing on V of the new key, a major third above home tonality. Note the one "half-measure," 3/8, which was all that was needed to bring the open fifth arpeggio to its double pedal at the beginning of B (m.28). In the one interruption of the gay, swinging 6/8, the voice shortens to fours to fit the "jackets." The cadencing phrase of the section (m.35–39) brings new color as the piano doubles at the octave the ornamented three-note rise and fall of the voice. This phrase is the source of the coda. The way is prepared for the return by the accompaniment's tuning-motive, without, however, the spice of the second fifth (m.37), its added jangling entering with the voice in m.39. The first two phrases are as before, the cadence dropping again a whole step below the tonic, then sliding still farther with a "la" to the lilting coda (m.50) drawn from m.35. Sequentially extended are m.53–55; home key is maintained from m.56, where the melodic refrain figure is plucked out as on a big lute, repeating it at four different levels. The last measure is like the first, the single, suspensive tone of the dominant, and imagining his medium, Debussy demands a *sfp* which mysteriously fades away in the distance.

Romance

THIS TITLE was applied to two *mélodies,* dated 1891, probably composed earlier. The term has been retained for the piece beginning *"L'âme évaporée,"* while the same poet's verse, commencing *"Les feuilles s'ouvraient,"* is called *Les Cloches.* This latter's *ostinato* "bell-figure" is practically unbroken through the song, an unusual feature for this composer. Paul Bourget's poem, *Romance,* may be translated as: "Sweet spirit, now vanished, soul tender and yearning, fragrant breath of lilies gathered in the garden of your thoughts. Where, then, have the winds borne away this sweetness of lilies fair? Is there no perfume still remaining of the heavenly sweetness of those days when thou didst hold me in a charm unreal and dreamlike, woven of hope, faithful love, blessing and peace?"

The memory of lost sweetness, symbolized by the lily, pervades the poem, and its motive, the first four notes of the top part of the introduction, is woven through the song, except for the contrasting section B (m.14–21). The germinal motive is directly repeated, and its close is the beginning of its third appearance (m.2), falling to the alto on the third quarter. The voice begins in declamatory phrases, outlining the chord on II, supported by repetition of the first measure of the introduction an octave lower, thence moving to the relative minor. The voice in m.5 begins pleasant, sweeping phrases, broken by short returns to simpler recitative lines in m.10, 14–15. The "memory" motive returns in m.9, with new harmonization, and leads to contrasting idea and key (m.14–21). A movement of mellifluous thirds and sixths, in even eighth-note motion, swings a V $_9$ over a dominant pedal, the voice traversing two of the most sumptuous phrases in Debussy. Note his customary delicacy, as the voice reaches the heights (m.20) with a decrescendo. The last measure (m.21) of the section is like its opening, and Debussy does away with the conventional transition, moving "home" directly (m.22). As the voice proudly recalls days of faith and joy, for the first time it joins in the motive, now intensified in octaves in the accompaniment. Note the descending line of the bass beginning in m.23, the one measure of 2/4 meter (m.25), and, as the voice quietly ends on the neutral fifth, the prolonging of the suspense by the skip of an octave in alto to the second, resolving *pp* to the tonic in the final measure.

Ariettes Oubliées

THE COLLECTION of six *mélodies,* published in 1888 as *Ariettes, Paysages Belges, et Aquarelles,* was reissued in 1903 under the title *Ariettes Oubliées,* the heading of one group of Verlaine's poems in *Romances sans paroles.* Here the poet's words often "transform themselves into music, color, and shadow," the very stuff of which Debussy made his dreams. The first of these, *C'est l'extase langoureuse,* is an evening mood which murmurs of languorous ecstasy, of the weariness of love, of the sounds heard in the woods at eve, of all the little voices of nature, of the soul of earth lamenting—it is ours, is it not?—from which exhales softly through the evening hours this simple hymn.

The song flows smoothly, but out of its unified pattern three elements contribute most to the impression. The first is the harmonious color of chords of the ninth, lazily slipping up and down. When their luminous shadows are withdrawn and a common triad sounds (m.34–35), how simple and cool it becomes. A second impression of importance issues from the frequent fall of the major second. A few illustrations may be noted, as in the opening phrase (m.1–2), with its returns (m.12–13), and significantly, that series beginning in m.36, closing in the epilogue (m.48–49). The last of the mood agents we note is the chromatic

descending motive, first appearing in m.24. It has oriental color, and its descending line also contributes to the feeling of languor. Yet this motive, which dominates the last half of the song, has been accompanied by counterascending lines, which have helped to illustrate the "sweet plaints of fluttering petals falling" and "the hollow sound of rolling pebbles underneath the restless waters." Note, however, that all restlessness is gone in m.46–47, where only the descending figure sounds, lazily accompanied by parallel fifths, moving from I to the flatted sixth. A gentle syncopation is present most of the time, in a world which moves dreamily in a range from *p* to *ppp*. The climax (m.44) is marked *mf,* the only dynamic surge beyond *p*.

Green

THE USE OF English titles for *Green* and *Spleen,* the two *Aquarelles* ("Water Colors"), in Debussy's first published set of Verlaine's poems, was not strange for a French poet in England, familiar with her language. To carry out the color scheme, *Spleen* might have been called "Blue," for the title—coming from Baudelaire and used by other French poets—means a low-keyed mood, like the "blues," not necessarily malicious or spiteful. *Green* is a love song, full of sensuous pleasures. With an offering of fruit, flowers, and foliage, the lover gives his heart and prays his lady that his humble gifts may find favor in her lovely eyes. He is weary and would rest at her feet to dream of sweet moments, which will soothe and refresh. There are two delightful contradictions in the score. The metric signature is 6/8, but more than half of the measures are wholly or in part in 4/8, adding a subtle fluctuation to the joyous spirit of its movement. Far stranger is the denial of the key signature in the music of the opening division in A-flat minor, the home key—G-flat—not established until m.20, where it repeats the introductory measures at tonic level.

That Debussy liked the opening key-color is evidenced by the return of A at its original "false" level (m.40), despite the fact that the contrasting section, B (m.24–39), in the true dominant, had clearly pointed the way to G-flat, up to the very last chord of its final cadence. What a gorgeous cadencing phrase that is, as the voice freely mounts in one tonal kingdom *("Rêve des chers instants")* to descend in another! In the restatement of A, all goes as before up to m.49, where the voice drifts upward. The closing phrases quietly establish home key. Note the rise of the bass by fourths from m.51. The melodic line from m.50 is in simple declamation, the piano enveloping the final low-pitched dominant in the voice, but sinking below it in the final chord. The flow of movement in these exquisite, last measures has lost the lilt of the 6/8 and moves in even twos. Only once before had voice and piano joined for a full measure in twos, and that was motivated by the word *"fatigue"* (m.31). Glancing backward, we must briefly point to the swinging motive of root and fifth in opening phrase, occasional flashes of whole-tone color, its gayest pattern in m.26, repeated in augmentation by the voice a half-measure later.

Green is so fresh and lovely in color and movement, such a pleasure alike to singer and pianist, that it seems impossible that its design is largely made up of repetitions of two- or four-measure patterns. The only exceptions appear in terminal phrases: m.17–20, m.36–39, and the closing group.

Colloque Sentimental

As USUAL, we come to the end of the projected space of a chapter with many songs which should be reviewed. Tempting is the *Rondel* of the fifteenth-century poet Charles d'Orléans, in which old modal turns run along with impressionistic figures, closing in a burst of *ff*. Despite his harking back to old French poets, Debussy was never interested in matching their verse with "period" music. He enjoyed the imaginary Greek poetess[10] of the time of Sappho, which his friend Pierre Louÿs had created in the *Chansons de Bilitis*. Debussy set three of these in 1897. The first, *La Flûte de Pan,* is a fanciful blending of a slightly bent whole-tone scale, which frequently skips down in a pentatonic pattern.

10 W. H. Daly, *Debussy,* 37.

Its lyricism and humor represent the composer in an unusual mood. Far more intense is the second song of this set, *La Chevelure,* a dream of love that rises from unconventional recitative to ecstatic climax. A bright, galloping song is the setting of Verlaine's poem about the Belgian fair, where the hobbyhorses of the merry-go-round turn at a wild speed (*Chevaux de Bois*).

Let us recommend most heartily, as an expression of the mature Debussy, *Colloque Sentimental,* taken from the second set of *Fêtes Galantes* (1904). This is the strangest fancy of a conversation between two specters, whose words only the night can hear. Its harmony, its restrained and sensitive declamatory line, and its long syncopated pedal reveal the qualities which we associate with the best of *Pelléas et Mélisande.* The range of the voice, an octave and a small sixth, apparently denies the restrained pitch variation of French declamation. Debussy's is not a realistic approach; rather it is the artistic transference and extension of declamation into subtle melody. Note, however, within its idealized setting, how true are the short replies of *"Non"* and *"C'est possible,"* which are lower pitched than the preceding phrases. Note, too, that where the song reaches its nadir on the word *"noir,"* its whole phrase is symbolic of the loss of hope.

NOT AIMING TO EMBRACE a great host of composers, which would have necessitated a guidebook filled with the bare names of composers and titles, I have devoted the major space to what might be termed "four-starred items." However, it is always tempting to stop with a song of a smaller giant, one who wears fewer stars in his crown. On the way to Ravel, let us pause for a moment with Paladilhe and Hahn. Émile Paladilhe (1844–1926) is taken as representative of a large group of able French composers of the last half of the nineteenth century, who busied themselves mostly in the theater. One has only to review the section for this period in Lavignac's *Encyclopédie de la Musique* to observe how strong was this bias. Paladilhe, winner of the *Prix de Rome,* member of the Institute, may be represented by one song, *Psyché,* the poem by Pierre Corneille. It sings, in warm and pensive mood, of the lover who is jealous of all nature, for the sun kisses Psyché and the wind caresses her hair. There is a remarkable equality in melodic interest between the voice and accompaniment, the latter carrying its own line throughout. Most unusual is the emphasis of the interval of the seventh, which seems here a natural melodic choice. Note the ending of the middle section of this ABA design, where in m.25–28, over a dominant pedal, the voice and top line of the accompaniment curve in contrary motion. The rhythms of the text, so faithfully followed, give a flexible pattern to a melody, which, with all its skips, seems most grateful.

Reynaldo Hahn (1874–1946) may be taken as the symbol of a group of composers who followed Massenet's steps; fated by their facility and habit of obliging the public, such composers wrote too much of too little depth. There is a genius in their charm, although one is aware that their gracious compliments endure for only a season. Hahn's songs are generally sweet and simple, though occasionally he strikes a dramatic note, as in the troubled question, *"Qu'as-tu fait . . . de ta jeunesse?",* which Verlaine asks in a verse born while the poet was in prison. It was Hahn who titled this song *D'une prison.* Later, Hahn placed together his settings of seven of Verlaine's poems, calling the collection *Chansons Grises.* It is a sensitive title, which the composer took from the poet's *L'Art Poetique,* in which he voices his faith in symbolism.

> *Rien de plus cher que la chanson grise*
> *Où l'indécis au précis se joint.*

(There is nothing dearer than the gray song, in which are joined vagueness and definiteness.)

These paradoxical attributes are better represented in Fauré, but many would be more pleased with the easy grace of Hahn's setting of the verse from *La Bonne Chanson,* which begins *"La lune blanche."* Pale moonlight, sighing branches, the reflections of the willows in the dark pool—a deep peace under the moon. O my beloved let us dream! It is the enchanted hour. Hahn draws from the poet's last line the title: *L'heure exquise!* More than half of the song is made up of the repetition of the pattern of the first two measures. The rocking from tonic to relative minor, the unperturbed flow of eighths "infinitely soft and calm," the general emphasis of the lower part of the voice in simplest, recitative style—these have an almost mesmeric influence. When out of this "gray" background, the voice delicately lifts from the fifth to the third, as at the end of the first stanza (*"O bien aimée"*), or, as in the last phrase without accompaniment, skips upwards *pp* a seventh to this same third, one feels the mood and color true.

Ravel

Although the poetic trends toward shadows and subtleties were reflected in the songs of the most sensitive composers, there were always those who preferred the trite and obvious. There were others who rebelled against the fogs and mists of symbolism. We now know that Ravel's impressionism was no imitation of Debussy. However, Ravel was not satisfied even with his own brand and once wrote that he had "never been a slave to any one style of composing.[11] His love of clarity in line and structure found expression in works called neoclassic. His setting of popular Greek chansons might be termed Neo-Hellenic. The most interesting, if not fruitful, experiment that Ravel made in song was the setting of the prose of Jules Renard's *Histoires Naturelles.*

These little sketches of the Peacock, Cricket, Swan, Kingfisher, and Guinea Hen offer many opportunities for unforeseen rhythms and sentiments, which shift from irony and roguishness to sympathetic understanding. The feature, however, which is most revolutionary and which caused the *scandale* when these songs were first heard in 1907, is the treatment of the text in a conversational fashion. Mute *e's,* for example, which had always

[11] D. Ewen, *Book of Modern Composers* (New York, 1942), 89.

been given a musical value and sung in all seriousness, were ignored. Thus the style became light, direct, and natural, but it broke long-honored traditions, both of melody and prosody. There is no doubt that, in the compromise of joining melody and text, words tend to become stretched out and sonorous syllables frequently overemphasized from the point of view of the natural rhythm of speech. Ravel's melodic line took on a conversational tone; its broken patterns in the French of everyday, underlined by a strange harmonic comment in the accompaniment, brought a new style, light and ironic, which the composer tried once again in *L'Heure Espagnole*.

Poulenc

AT THE TURN of the first half of the twentieth century, Francis Poulenc is a commanding figure in the world of song. Although he has written a considerable amount of important instrumental music of cyclic proportions, to many he is at his best in the intimate province of song. His youth was surrounded by song, and at the age of fifteen, in 1914, he was familiar with the contributions of Fauré, Debussy, and Schumann to this field. Although he appears as the natural heir to Fauré and Debussy, Poulenc is not weighed down with memories of their music. Indeed, now, he experiences little pleasure in Fauré, whose refinements and sentiment he finds rather soft, not *aigu* (keen) and precise, qualities he holds to be fundamental characteristics of true, Gallic charm.

Poulenc's exuberance has extended beyond his youthful membership in *Les Six*. Attracted to a wide variety of subjects—tragic and gay—this Parisian is particularly successful in bitter and humorous satire. His music abounds in reflections of the current scene, with occasional snatches that are suggestive of the song and dance of the music hall. His philosophy, that music to be valid must be of the here-and-now, has led him to choose contemporary poets, with whom he can feel a oneness of spirit and thought. True, he has set some verse of the sixteenth-century Ronsard, but he does not think that it represents him at his best. Guillaume Apollinaire, though much older and never encountered by Poulenc, has most frequently stimulated the composer by his fantasy, now almost child like, again coarsely cynical. Poetry and song are inseparable to Poulenc, who believes that if he is not to betray the poetry, he must "translate into music not merely the literal meaning of the words, but also everything that is written between the lines. Each, poetry and music, should evoke the other."[12] Unlike many composers, who would like to destroy their early works, Poulenc believes that the most personal revelations are the earliest. To him, the *Ariettes Oubliées* are of the essence of Debussy, while some of his later songs are touched with Wagnerisms and the responsibilities of the composer to his large audience. Thus, Poulenc—true to his theory—feels that his first set of melodies, *Le Bestiaire,* is most representative. Paradoxically, however, he likes the 1948 set of *Caligrammes* better than the *Poèmes de Ronsard,* vintage of 1925.

Le Bestiaire, ou Cortége d'Orphée

THE THOROUGHLY ORIGINAL drolleries of Guillaume Apollinaire, in the "Book of Fables, or Attendants of Orpheus," were caught to life in the inimitable miniatures that form Poulenc's first set of melodies. Most young composers, full of their own importance, would not have considered wasting their genius on such trifles. But, as the French love to say, *"Chacun à son gout,"* and Poulenc could not resist the poet's blend of fancy and satire. Imagine a dromedary, a grasshopper, and a carp in a procession! Note the pearl of wisdom that concludes the fourth, the last measure of *La Sauterelle,* in which the poet expresses the pious hope that his verse, like the grasshopper which nourished St. John, may be a feast for the best of people. *Le Dromadaire,* which suggests the train of thoughts that would carry the ad-

12 R. Sabin, *Musical America,* November 15, 1949, 27.

venturer out into the world, produces the longest piece of the series, forty-three measures short. The heavy, measured step of the dromedary, the beautiful, blurred figure with its original fingering for the left hand, the waggish contrast and dry wit of the coda—these give a weight to the opening sketch unmatched by the diminutive followers in the strange medley. With such a subject as *L'Écrevisse* ("The Crab"), many a composer would have indulged in a crab canon, but Poulenc, marking *"ironique,"* scores the opening figure in inversion (m.9) and even breaks the last of that pattern.

"C"

Deservedly popular is *"C,"* by Louis Aragon, *the* poet of the French Resistance. In a strange, unpunctuated poem of fact and fancy, Aragon dreams of the town *Les Ponts-de-Cé* (near Angers), which the Germans occupied. Upon leaving, they had destroyed the bridges over the Loire. As the poet thinks of crossing these bridges, he recalls the old, ruined castle of the mad duke and the glories of happier days. A haunting monotony is produced by each line's ending with the sound of "C." The *première* of the song, by Bernac and Poulenc, in Brussels, while the Germans were still present, brought an ovation which was quite beyond the understanding of the enemy.

A plaintive introduction is sketched in single line by the left hand. The symmetrical phrases of the voice are supported by a constant eighth-note motion and harmonies whose upper line almost always reinforces the voice part. For the sweet sadness of the refrain phrase, *"De la Prairie,"* Poulenc, in French, indicates for the piano score, "touch lightly and sweetly," and for the voice, "infinitely soft."

In the set of four *Airs chantés,* all fresh and full of charm, *Air champêtre* bounds along with something of the measure and naturalness of an old chanson. The *Air vif* introduces a bit of gay *fioriture,* suggesting a twirling melody from an old *opéra comique.* From Apollinaire's *Caligrammes* (poems placed on

the page in pictorial forms), Poulenc chose seven which he set in 1948. At one pole of these is *L'Espionne,* soft, bathed with pedal, and with one of his loveliest of cadences (*"Mais la vois-tu"* to the final chord with its raised third). Worlds removed from this is the whirlwind, *Aussi bien que les cigales.* Poulenc likes best of his settings of Ronsard, *Ballet,* free in metric changes, fluid of modulation, intriguing in the dry, lutelike accompaniment. The first of this collection, *Attributs,* moves deftly among the gods and goddesses, especially gracious figures summoned by Zephyr and the nymphs. Following the cares and tears that belong to *Cythérée,* Poulenc closes with the contented swinging phrase of his introduction.

CHAPTER XVII

Russian Song

THE foundations of Russian song are in the chants of the Eastern church and in the astonishingly rich heritage of folk song. The country is immense; her peoples and their music are most varied. Her "billowy harvest fields," her great wooded and frozen stretches, her rivers and mountains—these have formed her peoples and colored their music. One recalls the volatile nature of the Slav, although we in the United States have overemphasized his morbidity and pessimism. We often forget that the nature that sinks low can rebound to heights which prosaic middlers can never experience. So, there is much Russian music that voices a wild gaiety, an unbuttoned jollity whose vigor and elemental disregard for conventions reveal a primitive strength and intensity. Russia's geographical position has been one of the most important factors in her rise in nationalism. She faces both east and west. Something of oriental colors and rhythms was soon absorbed and a veneer of western forms and methods imported. But we must recall that, though the Russian scanned the horizons both to the east and to the west, he most frequently cast his eyes down to the Russian earth and remained himself. Russia reveals herself most fully in her songs. There is no danger of our belittling her great gifts for instrumental color, but should we want to know her most intimate self, we must become familiar with her songs.

Anton Rubinstein and Peter Tchaikovsky frequently have been denied full membership in the company of Russian national composers. The question "When is a Russian composer not a Russian?" has been settled by some almost entirely on the basis of a steady, conscious cultivation of national subjects, illustrated by music inspired by the folk. Indeed, by such a standard, Rubinstein and Tchaikovsky are not nationalists. Yet the Western world first became aware of a new voice in the concert of nations through the music of these two. Rubinstein, through his superb piano performances, won audiences for his compositions, most of which soon faded. His pupil, Tchaikovsky, soon became the greatest representative of his country, and, though the genius of other Russians was tardily recognized, Tchaikovsky has never been displaced in the affections of the public at large. Both men have been heartily reviled.

Anton Rubinstein (1829–94) used to complain that his countrymen looked upon him as German and that the Germans regarded him as a Russian; the orthodox Jews treated him as a Christian, while the Christians considered him a Jew. They all agreed, however, that he was a great pianist, and most of them admired him as a composer. His large-scale works—and he was a prolific composer—are scarcely ever sounded now, and of his over 150 solo songs, a scant half-dozen are in general concert circulation. Rubinstein's great lyric gifts bubbled over in charming melodies; the distinction between a natural melody and one that is insipid and banal was not always sensed by the impetuous, hard-working composer; seldom did he criticize and revise his outpourings. His songs, in both style and text, are more German than Russian; indeed, he is one of the few foreigners included in H. J. Moser's *Das Deutsche Lied*. Naturally, Rubinstein chose some poems of Heine, and of the six songs of Op. 32 —all Heine poems—two are as nearly perfect as any others he wrote. The setting of *Du bist wie eine Blume* is "so fair, so sweet, so pure" that it still holds its place beside Schumann's and Liszt's, the other two most loved settings of this perfect lyric. Directly following, and the last of Op. 32, is *Der Asra*.

Der Asra

HEINE'S POEM IS ONE of the narratives in the collection *Romancero* (1846–52). It begins like a romance with a scene near a fountain, where, toward evening, the lovely daughter of the Sultan daily walks. There she sees a young slave, who each day grows paler. One evening she stops and asks him his name, his home, his race. And the slave replies: "My name is Mahomet; I come from Yemen and my tribe is the Asra, who when they love, must perish." There is a legend that Heine's cynicism is hidden behind the word "Asra," which in Arabic means "a fool." But Rubinstein was content with the romance and drama on the surface of the narrative. The melody has fine sweep and contrast; Rubinstein is almost always pleasing to the singer. What is surprising is the thin scoring for piano, especially from a pianist surpassed only by Liszt!

It is rather rare for Rubinstein to begin directly, without introduction. Perhaps it was the simplicity of the ballad style which he had in mind when he scored the first unison phrase, which dominates the song, reappearing in m.5–6, 9–10, 13–14, and in the coda, never once colored by harmony. Most interesting are the replies, that in m.3–4 swinging plaintively in repeated plagal cadence; its replying phrase moves to the relative major; the bass, as it swings from V to I, in opposite motion to that of m.3–4, is not joined by the voice and its supporting third below in the accompaniment. Thus is set up a pleasant dissonance, which, if called forth by the "plashing waters of the fountain," seems rather timid. Transitional phrases in a chain of sixth chords move from the home key (m.16) to the key of the submediant (m.21), where a rocking phrase leads to the recitative-like phrases of the Sultan's daughter. Note the effective thin scoring of m.25 and the pure recitative phrase preceding the dramatic entry of the slave. His reply is first proudly reinforced by the stamping of the descending eighths of the bass. Then comes the passionate avowal, whose impulsive triplets and intervals of the

augmented second give an oriental color. Its direction is relentlessly downward, a symbol of hopeless fate.

Of the less dramatic songs, *Der Traum,* Op. 8, No. 1, is much
admired for its gracious melody. A song of which Schumann
would have been proud is *Es blinkt der Thau,* Op. 72, No. 1.
Its accompaniment figure and even the modulations make one
think of Schumann's *Widmung,* but the coda is a quotation
from the composer's own *Gelb rollt mir zu Füssen.* The ending
of the latter song, *"das es ewig so bliebe,"* evidently awakened
the refrain of the earlier, *"O, wenn es doch immer bliebe,"* both
ecstatic wishes for abiding love.

Gelb rollt mir zu Füssen

THIS IS THE MOST FREQUENTLY sung of the twelve songs which
Friedrich von Bodenstedt adapted from the Persian of Mirza-
Schaffy. Although the stanzas are touched with oriental fantasy,
the opening lines, that sing of the dancing waves of the raging
Kura, are related to the fourth and final stanza, frequently
omitted, in which "the stream of my love rushes to the dark sea
of your eyes." There is no problem of the unity of the music;
the stanza form serves for all. Its pattern is rich, though the song
is squarely built in patterns of eight measures. Each pattern has
its own charm, but the song is unified by the figure of the introduction, which is extended for the stunning refrain. Its original form then returns and serves both as interlude and coda.
Open fifths and triplets add some local color.

Tchaikovsky

PITY IS AROUSED by the contemplation of the career of Peter
Tchaikovsky (1840–93), who was not only at war with himself,
but opposed by the forward-looking group of his countrymen.
He has been declared a "Russian foreigner" and a "cosmopoli-
tanized Russian."[1] Balakirev even dissuaded the singer Mme A.

A. Khvostova, to whom *Nur wer die Sehnsucht kennt* had been dedicated, from polluting real Russian songs by including the Tchaikovsky song on the same program.[2] His music made its way, however, and for long Tchaikovsky covered western Europe as the chief representative of Russia. He sold his music far and wide, for people were stirred by his intense emotionalism; there was great appeal, too, in his fervid melancholy, for, as Edgar Allan Poe has demonstrated, this is a motive common to all mankind. His music and his name came to us via Germany, and for years we followed the German spelling which begins with "Tsch," in order to insure a soft "c."

Tchaikovsky never considered his songs as being of great importance. His friend of student days, Laroche, tells us that Tchaikovsky despised short piano pieces and songs. Yet he "descended" to both and was far more successful in the latter. One discovers a broad range of poets and moods that are usually accorded a generalized musical interpretation. He liked his accents strong; the sweep of the melody is well supported with romantic harmonies, the accompaniment often having a melodic counter of its own. This independence is further illustrated in the importance of preludes, interludes, and epilogues. Undoubtedly the most frequently sung of "Russian" songs has been *Nur wer die Sehnsucht kennt.*

Nur wer die Sehnsucht kennt

NEVER AGAIN DID Tchaikovsky find a poem so fully expressing his own loneliness as did this great lyric from Goethe's *Wilhelm Meister*. It is the cry of one from whom all joys have fled, a cry of utter loneliness and longing for an understanding soul. "Only one who knows such longing can know the grief I suffer." There seems no bottom to the depths of this woe; it strikes sharply and

---

[1] E. H. C. Oliphant, "A Survey of Russian Song," *Musical Quarterly*, Vol. XII (1926), 218.

[2] H. Weinstock, *Tchaikovsky*, 171.

keenly with no ray of hope. This is what Goethe expressed, and, when you have Tchaikovsky and Goethe playing four-handed with the Woe stop drawn, you can be assured of an intense experience. From the beginning to the end, the harmony is filled in by chords in syncopation, with melodic interest either above or below. This agitation deepens the impression of the poignant harmonies. Beginning with the striking skips of a seventh downward and upward, answered by a closely bound diatonic phrase, the piano introduces the haunting theme, which the voice repeats, bending away from the tonic to cadence on V of the supertonic (m.16), an important key-color of the song. The piano again introduces a continuing theme, B (m.17), the voice repeating (m.21) and mounting sequentially; it then moves via the relative minor to the home key and modified repetition of the first strophe. Instead of following with B, new material begins with the voice and rises emphatically to the highest point (*"allein"*), thence dropping in pitch, but growing in intensity. This is aided by a thoroughly characteristic Tchaikovskian climax, with a scale counterpoint in octaves steadily rising through five measures to the *ff* goal in the piano, on II (m.43). A dramatic silence is followed by the voice, *pp,* singing a new melody to the theme of the introduction, repeated without change, its final tonic chord extended two measures, while, *pp,* the right hand sinks from 4–3 and then more deliberately from 6–5, both hands ending with the suspensive feeling of a $^6_4$ position.

Pilgrim's Song

EARLY IN 1878, Tchaikovsky wrote from Italy to his patroness Mme von Meck, asking her to suggest some poems of Tolstoy which she thought would make good songs. She sent him a marked copy of the poems of Alexey Tolstoy (1817–75), "one of the few Russian poets who wrote in a major key."[3] In the two sets of songs, Opera 38 and 47, he is the poet of eight of the thir-

[3] *Ibid.*

teen songs. Two of these are among Tchaikovsky's best: the striking *Don Juan's Serenade* and *At the Ball,* in the latter of which the musings of the lover are woven into the music of a valse. Even greater to many is *Pilgrim's Song,* also titled *Benediction.* This is Op. 47, No. 5, written in 1881. The introduction, in descending and halting line, might suggest a weary pilgrim, but such he is not in spirit, as he blesses all of nature and rapturously welcomes all men as brothers. The introduction closes on the dominant, its hesitant, sighing strain never to return.

Beginning in m.14, the accompaniment figure of a single note in the bass on the principal accents, followed by three ascending arpeggio chords in eighth-note motion, gives the background for the broad melody of the voice, A (m.15), ending in

relative minor (m.24). The middle section, B (m.27), closes likewise in the relative minor, only brightened in the final measure by the raised third. A returns (m.37) and leads to a refrain of true exaltation, the repeated chords of the accompaniment pulsing in triplets. The bass climbs resolutely in half steps from the tonic (m.52) to the dominant (m.56), whose pedal supports increasing tension to the climax (m.60), where at last a V_7 is reached. It ceases as the voice rises a sixth from the dominant to anticipate the mediant, which it sustains through the following measure. The epilogue of unusual length restates A, gradually receding from its heights, a last hint of the theme in the bass of the final cadence.

Rimski-Korsakov

THE SOARING AMBITIONS of the members of the "Big Five" of Russian nationalism may be illustrated by the naval officer, Rimski-Korsakov (1844–1908). Opera 2, 3, 4, 7, 8 are groups of songs. He brought to Balakirev his first song, which was a setting of Heine's lyric, *Lehn deine Wang' an meine Wang.'* His "teacher" liked it, yet he entirely rewrote the accompaniment, which Rimski-Korsakov let stand when it was published.[4] The pupil learned fast, however, and the succeeding songs are all his own. There is a directness and spontaneity in these early works which the later professor of composition and instrumentation at the St. Petersburg Conservatory, with all his skills, seldom matched. In one of the gatherings of the nationalists in 1867, Rimski-Korsakov heard S. I. Zotova sing,[5] and it was with her in mind that he composed music for Koltsov's artistic improvisation on the legend of *The Nightingale and the Rose,* sometimes titled *Eastern Romance.*

Eastern Romance

THIS Op. 2, No. 2 is dedicated to Mme Zotova. The nightingale is the rose's lover, in the usual Persian figure made familiar to us in the *Rubáiyát* of Omar Khayyám, and, for her, he pours out his songs day and night. The rose listens, but does not understand. In like manner, a poet, as he sings to his lyre, may pour out his heart to his loved one. The maid does not understand and only asks for whom the song is sung and why he is so sad. Rimski-Korsakov had a marvelous gift for surrounding a subject with an atmosphere of mysterious beauty. But no matter what the subject, he idealized it and made it softly glow in the warm colors that his harmonies created. There is no ordinary

---

[4] Calvocoressi and Abraham, *Masters of Russian Music,* 348.

[5] N. A. Rimsky-Korsakov, *My Musical Life,* 67. "Her singing pleased me greatly and gave me a desire to compose songs."

realism of the poet's lute or the song of the nightingale or the East where the scene is fancied. They seem to be fused and make a new intangible poetry.

The introduction repeats the open fifth of the lute in each measure. Over it a fanciful melody, such as no nightingale ever sang, descends in great leisure, its song generously sprinkled with oriental seconds and a tremulous rhythmic twirl at the end of its phrases. Having come to rest on the top of open fifths, the

voice alone sings down the scale, only lowering the second in the falling cadence. The replying phrase moves in Eastern scale, and before it closes, the piano begins its comment, halting on the dominant (m.24). In the few measures in the relative major, the voice is supported mostly by sustained, conservative four-part harmony. The short phrases swing back to the minor and close with a most haunting cadence, IV_7–I. The whole introduction returns. Not content to stop as before, it repeats the nucleus of its song in single line and closes with a most delicate, high-pitched major chord on the tonic. More than half of the song is given to the piano alone, and this long epilogue has tempted some singers to claim its topmost line, which they vocalize while the piano strums the accompanying chords.

In Silent Woods

THERE IS A CERTAIN likeness between this song and *The Nightingale and the Rose*. Offering greater contrast, but clearly of the same idiom are *The Hebrew Love-Song,* from Op. 7, and *On the*

195

Georgian Hills, from Op. 3. The songs from the Op. 40's and
later are more varied, but not poetically as rewarding as this
early setting of Nikitin's *In Silent Woods.* Its introduction is
divided into two sections, the first never appearing with the
voice. It returns, however, as the interlude between stanzas and,
again, as coda. Its pattern contrasts the quiet pace of the odd
measures with the dainty, syncopated treading of the even measures. The second part begins (m.8) with the dominating motive
of the accompaniment, a gently rocking theme and Rimski-
Korsakov's tremulous twirl, curling downward. The voice has
a simple and restrained melodic line. The light filigree is in the
accompaniment; note the layers of imitation in its cadence of
the voice's first phrase.

After the interlude in this delicate, modified strophic form,
the voice omits its first phrase, m.28–32, repeating m.16–20. The
succeeding four measures are new and are as lovely a pair of
phrases as you will find in Rimski-Korsakov. Although tonally

Could this night with its vis-sions of bliss On-ly last in e-ter-nal em-brace!

supported, the voice, as it gracefully descends in the octave range
of the song, has a Phrygian modal feeling. Its harmonic relation
is blurred by the reappearance of the introduction, at tonic level,
with a lowered seventh. The pattern is shortened, and the second
section is represented by echoes of the principal motive with
tonic pedal. The poem is woven of the nightingale's last note,
pale moonbeams, and stars which cast a magic light on the loved

one's face. "Could this night with its visions of bliss only last in eternal embrace."

Moussorgsky

IF RIMSKI-KORSAKOV appears too conservative, too idealistic, stylized, and external, one may find the antidote in the music of his onetime roommate, Modest Moussorgsky (1835–81), who is radical, realistic, free of formula, and full of conviction. Moussorgsky refused to accept any of the conventionalized ways of writing or extending a musical idea. He had to discover his own way, and, in his search for truth rather than beauty, he created a music so sincere, simple, and direct that sometimes we feel a little uncomfortable in its presence. Art for him was a means of communication with the people, and, as with Count Leo Tolstoy, "the people" meant all the people. Moussorgsky is not only unconventional in his music; he is equally unconventional in the subjects he chose to illustrate. He pierces deep below the surface of things and wrenches our hearts with the whining cry of *The Orphan* for bread; he depicts a solider, in *After the Battle,* lying dead, a prey for greedy crows, while his widow stills her child with promises of a cake she will bake soon for father's homecoming. Nearly every one of the forty-odd songs is a vivid emotional experience. The composer was occasionally impelled to change a poet's line, not in order to fit a preconceived musical pattern, but to square it with logic and truth as he perceived them. He became his own poet, as in the cycle of children's songs, *The Nursery.* To allow the poet's glimpses of life and nature— from tragic horror to wild burlesque—to be illustrated faithfully in music, Moussorgsky treated each song as unique; each had to be accorded its own solution. There was nothing sacred about current methods, and Moussorgsky's use of rhythm, melody, and harmony was so free as to be revolutionary.

The commanding force behind all this change and the core of Moussorgsky's artistic credo is his belief that music must be an exact reproduction of the words. Despite his dogged adherence to this ideal, like other great theorizers, in actual practice he rose above the literal realization of his goal. Moussorgsky dealt in music, not language. The problem of the transfer of a song from one language to another is always severe, but one can easily understand that the greatest of difficulties are faced when the poetry is Russian and the composer Moussorgsky. To convey the Russian atmosphere and to be faithful to the original meter and rhymes—these offer almost insurmountable problems. Yet the essence of Moussorgsky is in the exceptionally faithful matching of word and music. M. D. Calvocoressi, writing of the difficulties of translating *Boris,* recounts in *Musicians Gallery* that there should exist "as nearly as possible everywhere, the same reasons as in the original for his subtly devised rises and falls of pitch, variations in emphases and color, and so on—an impossible ideal, no doubt."[6] Many of the subtleties of the composer only the Russian can sense, but Moussorgsky is so frank and real that he speaks to all men.

Trepak

THIS IS THE FIRST in a cycle of four songs, poems by Koutousov, titled *Songs and Dances of Death.* They are dramatic scenes, in each of which grim Death stretches out his hand and triumphantly claims his victim. It may be a child rocked by its mother, who feels that the unwelcome guest is lulling her child to sleep (*Death's Lullaby*). Another time Death sings a *Serenade* under the window of a fever-stricken maid. In heroic guise, *Death the Commander* rides forth on the battlefield, and before him friend and foe alike march by and greet him as master. The last three songs, although they are laid on Russian earth by Moussorgsky, seem far more universal than the first of the series, the *Trepak,* which is most narrative, most truly a ballad, and the most national of the cycle. It centers in the Russian dance, the *Trepak,* which, however, is but the subtitle for *Death and the Peasant.* Still and dark is the forest. A drunken peasant passes, soon joined

6 M. D. Calvocoressi, *Musician's Gallery* (London, 1933), 311–12.

by Death, who sings and invites his guest to dance. The peasant has lost his path, the snow is blinding, and wearily he sinks down, while the howling storm sings to him and covers him with a blanket of white. Death lulls him to sleep, and bids him dream of the summer and the larks' songs which will come again.

Moussorgsky matched this narrative not only with music of a heightened declamatory style, but with folk song and dance and vivid pictorial representations. It is the genius of Moussorgsky which holds these different styles in hand and out of the four elements makes a unified song. The narrative naturally suggests the three large divisions: (1) background of nature and time (m.1–12); (2) the dance (m.13–119); (3) the song and epilogue (m.120–54). For each there is a characteristic theme, reappearing where the text suggests it. Least tangible is the declamatory line of the first section. How cold and creepy is the atmosphere, emphasized by open fifths at the beginning and ending, under-the-breath and low-pitched *tremolandi,* and furtive figures in the bass! How cunning and prophetic its line, for the essence of the first phrase of the "dance" (m.14–17) is found in m.1–5! This division, in which Death and Nature join forces to lead the weakened peasant into oblivion, is divided into ten sections, the principal theme (m.14–17) appearing in several variants. The most dramatic and pictorial is that where the tempest howls. The rhythmic variations are many; the phrasings of 3's and 5's relieve the basic 4's. The "dance" presses on in ruthless fashion; the voice is silent in only six measures of 106, the first blank appearing as an interlude (m.94–97), introducing the new triplet figuration of the bass.

The other two measures bridge to the tranquil lullaby, which Death sings. Here a true melodic counter appears in the right hand, while the left accompanies with a wide, broken-chord pattern. Interpolated after the first and second phrases of the voice in this lullaby is one of the most engaging patterns of the dance (m.22–23). This also forms the epilogue. The two-measure pattern succeeded by the bass alone drops from tonic to dominant in a gesture of exhaustion. After a delicate, lamenting measure, the dance phrase recurs. A measure of silence is followed by a cadence of III, V, I, every one of its chords devoid of a third. This is no tonal picture, such as Liszt called forth when he cut capers in *Todentanz,* nor has this song the beguiling sweetness of Death's invitation in *Valse Triste* by Sibelius. This is grimly realistic and leaves one with an overpowering consciousness of death, perhaps of the futility of life.

More filled with hopelessness and the shadows of night is the cycle of six songs of 1874, from the same poet, Koutousov. The songs of the cycle, *Without Sunlight,* are less extended, less realistic. The last of the set, *By the Water,* casts a spell, and we hear strange voices, though they are not those which seized him who had looked on the moonlight and shadows on the waters. He imagined a voice that—had it called him—he would have answered by plunging into the depths. This is a strangely beautiful song, its most striking technical feature, a tonic pedal point that persists through the entire song. For the first fifteen measures, the tonic alternates in the triplets of the left hand and, for the rest of the song, attracts to itself the seventh, the two moving in an *ostinato* pattern. The vague, unconventional harmony which the mesmeric pedal has supported closes without finding peace, the epilogue's melodic theme repeated in augmentation, rising only to the lowered seventh above the tonic.

This is the most exceptional use of pedal in Moussorgsky's songs. Most striking in the changes of metric signature is *With Nanny,* the first of the cycle *In the Nursery.* Moussorgsky follows the rhythms of his own text, in which the insatiable child asks his nurse, Nanny, to tell the story of the bogieman or that of the queen whose sneeze was so loud that all the windows were broken. The composer's attempt to follow the babblings of the child resulted in twenty-seven changes of the metric signature in the fifty-three measures of the song. The cycle offers richest rewards in the matching of the child's inflections with musical line and rhythm. This is the child's world, not translated, not seen from without or through the memory of an adult. Fairy tales, a beetle, a robin, and the pussy cat, playing on a hobby-horse and putting dolly to sleep, then saying prayers at bedtime —of such is the kingdom of children. Fourth, in this series of seven, is *The Doll's Cradle Song*.

The Doll's Cradle Song

THIS IS A REVELATION of the motherly instinct of a little girl, try-ing to put her dolly, Tiepa, to sleep. She sings crooningly at first, "Tiepa, bye-bye;" then, threateningly, she tells her dolly that if she is not quiet the bogieman will catch her and Brother Wolf will snatch her.[7] A moment later she sings a real lullaby, pictur-ing a wondrous land of freedom, where golden birds in silver nests are singing. According to conventional standards, how thoroughly uncalculated is this melody: But how sensitively measured it is to text and mood! The short phrases, their usually slight pitch-range, and the very monotony of repetition are in a child's sizes. The steady patter of eighths, which fills most of the song, is soothing. When the pattern is broken, as at m.5–6, the voice seems meant to accompany the affectionate tucking in of the doll. Where later (m.11) the movement is interrupted, "mother" puts her foot down with a rather gruff warning, but immediately comes back to the soothing of Tiepa. To the repeti-tion and variants in the voice of the principal motive (m.1), there is now added a rocking movement in sixes in the bass, its broken chord lightly touching and retouching the droning double pedal of tonic and dominant. The way the child-mother tiptoes out, stopping (*fermata*) at the end of almost every one of the last measures, is just another of those poetic-realistic truths Moussorg-sky was always revealing.

[7] W. W. Roberts, "Child Studies in Music," *Music and Letters*, Vol. IX (April, 1928). Compare the editorial in *Saturday Review of Literature* (June 26, 1948) in which the jingles of "Mother Goose" are revealed as full of terrifying experiences.

Little Star, So Bright

THIS IS THE MOST ADMIRED of the early songs of Moussorgsky. Composed in 1857 when he was seventeen, it was "lost" and only came to light in Paris in 1909 in a manuscript containing seventeen songs. It is one of his finest lyric songs. The text may be Moussorgsky's own; at least no credit was given another. The poet asks the little star, "Where is thy light? Has a storm cloud hidden it?" Where is the golden-haired maiden? Has she forsaken her brave hero? The star is hidden by a cloud; the maid lies asleep in her lonely grave. There is a subtle charm in the melody, which swings along with greater ease and continued impulse than might have been accorded the subject in later years. Indeed, the song has many of the traits of true folk song. The cadence of the single-voiced introduction wavers between the normal and lowered seventh. It is the latter which colors the first division in the Aeolian mode. Over chords arpeggiated as on balalaikas, the voice ornaments the simple melodic line in degreewise turns. An eerie harmonic cadence brings the division to a close on tonic and open fifth. Immediately the piano states B (m.11) in relative major, the voice repeating and extending the theme. A questioning phrase is repeated (m.15–16) with different harmonies, the section concluding suspensively. The prelude returns, its first half harmonized. The voice's phrase is a variant and compression of the beginning, with a new phrase

Now the star is   hid by the black cloud deep,

for the suspensive close on the dominant, which has not yet reached its goal when the piano enters (m.25), stating B. Beginning in the major, the pensive reply in the sedate plagal cadence closes on the minor chord of I. Again, the first preluding theme returns, overlaying its wavering rise to the tonic in echoing pattern and capped by a high-pitched, *ppp,* tonic minor chord.

The Orphan

COMPOSED IN 1868 and dedicated to Borodin's wife, this realistic street scene of the hungry and homeless child as he whines his plea to the passer-by, is what Moussorgsky described as a "living melody." Born of the words—the composer's own—the melody follows the speech inflections. There is a method in the song's continuity, for the separate phrase, usually of four measures, is repeated immediately and passes on to a new pattern. There is one "classical" return, that of the first "begging theme" at m.38, although this might well be considered as a bitter, realistic touch in the orphan's wail. The pace is dull and relentless. The flow of the phrases, once begun, is rarely broken by an actual rest in the voice part. The droop of the first phrases and the frequent cadence drop of a third or fourth spell a hopelessness. This may well have been born of experience and repeated in this instance, for, after the increased pressure in the repetition (m.38), followed by new themes that are more excited and insistent (m.45–54), the voice dejectedly sinks to the dominant, the piano resting on V. The whole business of living seems so heartlessly incomplete, a tonic chord is scarcely worth the effort.

Hopak[8]

THIS IS A WHIRLING, passionate dance song, composed in 1866. The text is a Russian translation by Mey from the banned

[8] *Musorgsky Reader* (ed. by Leyda and Bertenson), 75. Subtitle of Gopak: "Lute Player: The old man sings and dances."

Ukrainian play, *Haidamaks,* by the Cossack national poet, Shevtchenko. Moussorgsky captured the wild gaiety of the peasant woman, whose youthfulness rebels against her old, vodka-loving, red-bearded husband. Often before the children came, she, too, would step out and dance the Hopak at the tavern. "Alas, my fate is sad, for I am the wife of an old Cossack." The rhythm of this lively dance from "Little Russia" rules the song. There is an almost constant pumping in eighth-note motion and frequent emphasis and alternation of tonic and dominant. Often there seems to be a constant whirring sound of the tonic. The strumming of open fifths of the introduction is broken by explosive chords, high, then low. The voice sings a vigorous eleven-measure strophe, closing with a shout. An interlude from the last of the introduction leads to a varied repetition of the first strophe. Gathering energy, it is not interrupted by an interlude,

but followed directly by three different episodes. The first of these, B (m.36–47), is succeeded by the first half, or "broken" measure, which returns and rises by half steps at the close of the three-measure patterns of C (m.49–60). The next division is the most varied of all and softens the wild urge of the movement by a most unconventional pattern of accompaniment. Its last four-measure phrase (m.87–90) focuses the bass on the tonic, which sounds on through the rest of this exciting song. A further element of order in this wild whirl is brought by the return of the introduction (m.91–96), shortened and intensified by the vigorous cries of the voice, which concludes with an exact repetition of the first strophe. A single chord confirms the cadence.

This song was orchestrated by the composer for the contralto Mme D. M. Lenova. Today it is often sung by men, some of whom attempt greater realism by offering "sound-effects" of drunken hiccups. This added realism seems far less called for in this generalized mood picture and symmetrical musical form, than, for example, the scratching motions of the realistic actor, singing *The Song of the Flea*. This song of Mephistopheles, in the Auerbach's cellar scene from Goethe's *Faust,* is often parodied further by treating it as an extravagantly humorous story. So it appears, this tale of a king who had the royal tailor make breeches and all the rest of the trappings of a courtier, for a flea. On him and all his relations were bestowed orders galore. But the queen and all the court, though in misery, were forbidden to scratch. "But we, when bitten, know how to scratch and kick. Ha, ha, ha!" Sardonic chuckles close each verse, epitomizing the biting satire on man's vanity and submission. Composed in 1879, this was first sung by the contralto Lenova on a Crimean concert tour that summer, on which Moussorgsky was both accompanist and soloist. He came back in high spirits and with hopes "to press forward to new shores,"[9] or, as he had earlier expressed it, "to unknown shores." This, however, was impossible, for brandy had destroyed him, the most tragic loss to music in modern times.

THE BELIEF THAT a national school must be founded on a folk foundation weakened considerably in the last of the nineteenth century. The cry for nationalism grew fainter, though anyone who has been through two world wars knows all too well that ours is not yet "One World." Indeed, the universal language of music is still spoken in many dialects. The conscious cultivation of Russian music on the folk basis was far less practiced by the generation following the "Big Five." It is among those who fol-

[9] Calvocoressi and Abraham, *Masters of Russian Music,* 239.

lowed this right fork of the road that we find Rachmaninoff and Gretchaninoff, the two whose gifts in song seem richest.

Rachmaninoff

IT IS QUITE PROBABLE that our grandchildren may regard Rachmaninoff as the "Rubinstein" of our generation. They may revere him as one of the greatest pianists of all time, but from the large catalogue of his works they may keep alive only one concerto and a half-dozen songs. After his death in 1943, there was more than one evaluation of this composer that placed him as "a survival of an extinct romanticism."[10] Rachmaninoff certainly never belonged to the "moderns"; but he had far too many companions and too large an audience to be charged with having outlived his time. His best music is spontaneous, inspired, and eloquent; he spoke with dignity, though it never meant for him stiffness or aloofness. His very honesty made him unafraid of sentiment, and this he poured forth as he felt it, with richness and intensity. In the larger forms Rachmaninoff, like Rubinstein, tended to draw out his ideas unduly. He found it difficult to let go of a good theme while there remained still other interesting ways to ornament it. A song forces the composer to concentrate his materials. He must heed Walter Pater's famous counsel and remove all the surplusage.[11] Thus the composer who tends to be wordy may be saved from his besetting sin when he writes songs. One never feels, however, that the song cramped Rachmaninoff's style. His melodies are spacious, often long of line. His lyricism, encouraged by his habit of expressing himself on the keyboard, made it natural for him to extend the sentiment of the text in introductions, interludes, and epilogues of some length.

[10] "Topics of the Times," *The New York Times,* May 2, 1943.
[11] W. Pater, *Appreciations* (New York, 1889), 16.

The Songs of Grusia (Op. 4, No. 4)

THIS IS FROM his first collection of songs, most of them composed in student days at the Moscow Conservatory, where his teacher in free composition was Arenski. Rachmaninoff wrote that these were days when his hand could hardly keep pace with the ideas which bubbled up within him. His prize opera *Aleko* was written in fourteen days. One feels this ease and naturalness of expression in these early songs, two of which are frequently heard. They are *In the Silence of the Night* and *The Songs of Grusia,* both introduced into the concert repertoire of this and other countries by John McCormack, who sang them with the ardor and abandon proper to love songs. Whitman has defined music as "what awakes from you when you are reminded by the instruments."[12] In *The Songs of Grusia,* a man far from his native shores of Grusia (Georgia) pleads with a fair Circassian maid not to sing the old songs of his country, for they awaken within him memories of his youth, of moonlit nights, and of a love now past. The song was dedicated to Mlle Natalie Satin, who was soon to become the composer's wife.

Harmonies that drift downward every two beats, a tonic pedal that pulses in eighths except for its silence on the principal accents and above, a slender melody which moves in a two measure pattern, A, that, at the last, turns languidly about the tonic a whole step both below and above—such in part is the eight-measure introduction. A rolled chord sounds, and the first three phrases of the voice are an unconventional recitative. The voice continues by recalling the melody of the introduction and cadencing shortly on the dominant. A new theme, B, appears in m.17, directly repeated an octave lower. The voice continues in a new and intensified pattern which moves in a narrow range. Its accompaniment is woven of the motives from A. As in m.17, but now at the level of the subdominant, appears B in m.24–25. A new, rising, sequential pattern begins in m.27 and intensifies

12 W. Whitman, "A Song for Occupations" (stanza four).

its stirring climax by the repeated notes at the beginning of the figure and the sustained high note, during which the accompaniment lashes along in repeated sixteenth-note chords. The phrase that follows anticipates the recitative, which repeats the opening measures of the voice. The coda (m.39–50) is the most haunting part of the song, for, while the piano sounds more fully yet softer than before the theme of the introduction, the voice adds a countermelody above. The voice's line in those last four measures, as the theme repeatedly dips down to rise not quite as high, reminds one of the graceful flight of the goldfinch. The piano then extends and changes the harmonies of the first motive of A, the gentle pulse of the tonic pedal continuing to the last measure.

The Isle (Op. 14, No. 2)

RACHMANINOFF WAS FREQUENTLY DRAWN to poems of nature— to pieces about a lilac bush, a peaceful stream, or a harvest field. One of the most tranquil and intimate of such scenes is Balmont's paraphrase of Shelley, which pictures an island of dreams, where nature always smiles and all that grows is sweet. No storms arise and all is peaceful. The tender, dreamy, short phrases of the voice in its opening six-measure theme move about the dominant as a reciting tone. While this is completed rather lazily, the accompaniment has moved with great precision as the bass descends in even quarter-note tread, three octaves, joined most of the journey by the alto a tenth above. Only once is the diatonic scale broken, and that where, by the fall of a half step and further by a change of measure, the cadence is enriched. Having come full cycle at the beginning of m.7, the pattern is repeated, but in its second stanza the alto twice imitates the voice a measure later and a fifth below, before joining the march in tenths. A new chordal theme for the voice—rather rare for Rachmaninoff— skips down in key to arch upward through a chord of the lowered sixth. The accompaniment for these four measures of contrast is an undulating or wave pattern, whose triplet motion

At sun-ny noon or fra-grant night   'Tis ev-er peace a-mong its bow-ers,

stops with the return of A in shortened version. The little epilogue brings back the waving and chordal motives of B.

There are many other moods in Rachmaninoff. Deep sympathy is aroused by Khomyakov's poem *To the Children,* in
which the lonely parent recalls the children once in the nursery,
which now is silent. The swinging, yet broken figure in the compound duple measure is sensitively matched to the poet's line.
The refrain phrase, in Rosa Newmarch's translation, "The love
of the Father protect you," brings a cadence (m.9–10) whose
simple beauty is touching. At the opposite pole, there are "big"
songs which strike dramatic and even epic notes. Others are
brilliant and more obvious, like the popular *Floods of Spring,*
which rushes along like the waters, dancing and singing "Spring
is at hand." The accompaniment is especially rich and of a marvelous sonority. Note the increase of volume as the pattern of
the earlier arpeggio figures is exchanged for repeated chords,
doubled, and swinging over the deep foundation chords on the
first of the measure. A song without words, *Vocalise,* Op. 34,
No. 14, is dedicated to the coloratura Mme A. W. Neshdanova
of the Moscow Grand Theater. A lovely cantilena, in which the
voice is used as an instrument, has naturally suggested the substitution of a violin. This *Vocalise* and Ravel's *Étude en forme
de Habanera* inspired J. W. Hausserman, Jr., to write a wordless
four-movement *Concerto for Voice,* which received its *première*

in 1942 with Margot Rebeil and the Cincinnati Symphony Orchestra.

Gretchaninoff

ALTHOUGH RACHMANINOFF's sympathies in composing were strongly in favor of instruments, Gretchaninoff turned to the voice and voices most naturally. Rachmaninoff was not truly a pupil of Tchaikovsky, yet he once admitted that it was permissible to regard him as a disciple of that master. Gretchaninoff, however, stemmed from the Rimski-Korsakov side of the Russian school. The two younger men were more eclectic and cosmopolitan than their masters, and naturally so, since they exiled themselves, Rachmaninoff settling in New York, Gretchaninoff in Paris. The latter, with over 250 songs, is one of the most prolific song composers since Schubert. In his portfolio there are a few songs of real greatness.

Cradle Song (Op. 1, No. 5)

THIS IS A UNIVERSAL type of lullaby, but its international clichés are so beautifully ordered, its vocal line so ingratiating to singer and audience, that it has endeared itself to countless folk. More than half of the song gently moves above a tonic pedal, the harmonics alternating between tonic and dominant and colored by mellifluous sixths and thirds. This harmonic rocking, together with a ceaseless motion of eighth notes in four-measure patterns, produces a lulling effect. Actually it is not as simple as it seems, the harmonic fabric glinting with frequent, sweet dissonances, the voice encompassing an octave and a sixth. A four-measure, harmonic background introduction is freely repeated, while the voice adds a melody, its four-measure pattern immediately repeated over the supertonic inflected in closing cadence back to home key. The single bar of interlude is like that of m.8, drifting this time, however, to the relative minor, where a second eight-measure theme begins, closing in the tonic. A four-measure epilogue gently syncopates the fifth of the double pedal, the singer being left free to spin out the final tone *à piacere* (rare scoring in the world of Art Song). Note, however, that the last measure of the voice line is a rest, the piano adding only the tonic above its already sounding final chord.

Over the Steppe (Op. 5, No. 1)

THIS SONG DIVIDES itself exactly in half, the first division (m.1–20) suggesting the aching loneliness of a heart reflected in the boundless, dark stretches of the steppe. The latter half (m.21–40) suddenly breaks into ecstatic song, as, with thoughts of the loved one, nature smiles, the nightingale sings, and the sky becomes studded with stars. Gretchaninoff has pictured the bleak monotony of the desert by the syncopated repetition of the tonic, doubled at the octave in sixteen of the first twenty measures. Note the short span of each vocal phrase and its extension at the same pitch, as the piano echoes the dying fall of the voice. Of important color value is the raised sixth, first appearing in m.3. Adding to the sense of weariness are the twelve successive measures supported by a double pedal of root and fifth. With a *poco stringendo e crescendo,* the last four measures of the division rise to an ecstatic outburst in relative major (m.21). Following the languor and repression, this three-measure phrase, *ff,* seems

Vi - sions of thee,   my   be - lov - èd one,

marvelously big and free. Although settling back to short-spanned phrases, there is an eagerness and forward push in their freely modulating course. The method of extending the voice phrase in the piano is resumed, the thought of the nightingale in the homeland suggesting the trill. The last trilling extension breaks into a new triplet figuration, while the voice intones the same note, which had so wearily pulsed along in the first division of the song. Here, however, there is quiet and peace and a note of hope, as the phrase glides rather unexpectedly to a close on the parallel major, richly colored by an added major sixth in the undulating figuration in the right hand.

CHAPTER XVIII

Grieg and Dvořák

Of the nationalists of the last half of the nineteenth century, two contributors to song are distinguished by the ardor and the completeness with which their spirits and skills were identified with their peoples. There is no note of weariness or calculation in the music of Grieg and Dvořák. Even if the dew that was on their music has here and there been burned off by the sun of another day, there is much that is still fresh. Grieg may speak for himself, and Dvořák, also, who wrote: "I have dipped from the rich treasures of native folk song and sought to create a national art out of this hitherto unexplored expression of the folk-soul."[1] Both these nationalists were peasants at heart and spoke the dialect of their people with pride in their very provincialism. How big was their world? Grieg's compatriot Ibsen wrote: "The boundaries of my country stretch as far as my work has set minds afire."

Grieg (1843-1907)

Like most gifted Norwegians of his day, Grieg went to Leipzig for further study. The old popular stamp, "Made in Germany," never produced much of an impression on Grieg, who later, when Gade counseled him to make his next work less Norwegian, stubbornly replied: "On the contrary the next shall be more so."[2] It seems a little strange, then, to hear Grieg later claim his recent works as more cosmopolitan and affirm that in

[1] D. G. Mason (ed.), *Art of Music* (New York, 1915), III, 95.
[2] Finck, *Grieg and his Music*, 27f.

style and form he remained "a German romanticist of the Schumann school."[3] In moods of quiet lyricism in both his short piano pieces and his songs, there is a warmth and delicacy that is quite like Schumann. Yet so individual is Grieg that if Schumann had reviewed the *Lyrische Stücke* of this "Chopin of the North,"[4] as von Bülow described him, Schumann might have turned the phrase which he had used for the *Préludes* of the Pole thus: "In every piece we find written in pearls, 'This is by Edvard Grieg.' "[5] One element of the charm of this northern music is found in the melody, which springs from folk song.

Grieg's melody is seldom phlegmatic; it responds quickly to change of mood, that may rapidly shift from mysterious melancholy to a wild gaiety, from a smooth flow to angular jumps. Most frequently repeated is a cadence that falls from tonic to dominant via the leading tone. The melodies of the songs are conceived for voice, and the composer most frequently was inspired by his wife, Nina, who introduced many of his songs. One wonders what greater riches might have been added to the world of song had Schumann's Clara been a singer rather than a pianist. Grieg's melodies, simple and straight from the heart, commanded some fresh harmonies for support. But Grieg's harmonic innovations extended much further. In his blurring of mode and tonality, in his frequent use of foreign notes, unexpected progressions, and resolutions, he enriched harmony and brought new colors into the world. He was more content than most lyricists to move in a sphere which he could command. No symphonies, no operas! Most frequently his songs are strophic, and, even within their short spans, sequential repetitions often appear. He was drawn to many poets, most of them of the North, and it seems a great misfortune that most frequently his songs are heard in the color of a different language with the inevitable dilutions of translation.

[3] D. G. Mason (ed.), *Art of Music*, III, 95.
[4] "Grieg," *Encyclopaedia Britannica* (11th ed.), XII, 593d.
[5] Schumann, *Music and Musicians*, 138.

Jeg Elsker Dig
(Ich liebe dich; I love thee)

THIS MOST FREQUENTLY heard of Grieg's songs was composed in 1864. It is the third of four poems from Hans Christian Andersen, which Grieg joined as Op. 5, titled *The Heart's Melodies.* The composer found in this verse an avowal of his love for Nina Hagerup, to whom he had just become engaged, and this song, telling of the wonders and raptures of love, was for her. As in some other instances, the song seemed so short to the German translator that he added a second stanza, although the original had none, nor any sign of a repeat.[6] Something of the lover's ardor is expressed by the chromatics—eight meaningful alterations occur in the two and one-half bars of introduction—by the rising phrases, and by the insistent eighth-note pulse; something of the lover's reverential wonder is expressed in the dynamics, which only in the last phrase mount to a fortissimo. The harmonies are rich, the emphasis of the supertonic strong; the completion of the first division by the piano in m.9 brings a return of the idea, the voice now reinforced not only by the bass but by the top line of the accompaniment (m.11) as well. The cadence is extended by two measures; the coda, a recollection of the first vocal phrase, delays by a rest the final cadence.

En Svane
(Ein Schwan; A Swan)

THE STORY RUNS that the poet Ibsen used the legend of the swan, "who living had no note, when death approached, unlocked her silent throat," to conceal in part his love for one whose shyness kept her from revealing her love for him until too late.[7] This may explain the intensity of the climax reached in m.20–21, which the composer insisted should not recede from the $f\!f$ until

---

[6] A. Desmond, "Grieg's Songs," *Music and Letters*, Vol. XXII (1941), 338.
[7] *Ibid.*, 334.

the pause, after which there is tranquillity, resumed in the first gliding and balancing phrase, ever so slightly reminiscent of *Lohengrin's* "swan" motive. Chords of the seventh color nearly every measure. The two-measure phrase at the opening of the second division (m.11–21) is answered by the piano; this is repeated a third higher, and, once again, this phrase with its characteristic melodic skips and introduction of a triplet figure appears now both heightened and extended. Note the above-center range of the accompaniment and the dramatic increase of sonority as the piano skips from its highest pitch to the low, rich chords which underline the climax. The first four measures of the return are exactly like the beginning. Then, as if entering the new world of death, the music moves to a tonal region untouched before; it returns for the quiet cadence, its last measure as a sigh and marked lento. It is only in this final measure that this basic, melodic motive is supported by the dominant, which one may have inferred, but which Grieg has never stated before. The alto characteristically moves degreewise from the leading tone to the dominant. All the lines of the cadence sink to the final chord on the weakest beat of the measure.

Med En Vandlilje
(Mit einer Wasserlilie; With a Water-Lily)

WITH A LIGHT PLAYFULNESS, this setting of an Ibsen poem moves along, swinging like lilies in the sunshine as they wave on the water. Three of the stanzas are the same, and the contrasting material, used for stanza three and repeated for the succeeding verse, follows closely the features already familiar. The song always impresses one as being more contrasted because of the frequent changes of tempo and the suppleness of the dynamics. The song illustrates several devices of which Grieg was perhaps too fond. The idea is extended essentially by repetition at different levels. There is no relief from the pattern of the accompaniment, which doubles the voice in both the bass and the topmost line. In the play between the two, however, there is considerable charm, the piano echoing for Maria the close of phrase, as m.5–6, in somewhat the same way a greater master lingered over a phrase praising Sylvia. In the mid-division with its warnings, the contrast of mode (m.39) and chromatic descending phrase is furthered by the replies of the piano, which now completes (m.41–42, 45–46), now echoes (m.49, 52) the voice's phrase. Some might complain that the voice is too frequently interrupted, though here it seems appropriate. As the voice falls to the tonic, the accompaniment begins the succeeding stanza (m.19). The return (m.67) is the more welcome, since the composer has avoided the two-measure introductory phrase both before stanza four and here. A piquant final cadence is added to this concluding stanza.

Solveig's Lied
(Solveig's Lied; Solveig's Song)

THE TWO SONGS for Solveig, this one and the *Cradle Song,* were among the very first incidental music which Grieg scored for Ibsen's fantastic drama, *Peer Gynt.* Soon after Peer had built a hut in the northern woods for his tender, golden-locked Solveig, he set out for further adventures. The curtain for Act V discloses a sunlit opening before the little hut. Solveig, now a middle-aged woman, as she sits and spins on a summer's day, sings of the passing of the years and the constancy of her love. In the wordless refrain, we overhear the peasant gently "humming," as if lost in dreams. Grieg wrote that the "whole song must be in keeping with folk-music style."[8] In a letter to Frants Beyer (April, 1903) the composer, smarting from the charge that all of his songs were adapted from folk tunes, wrote: "You know that out of all my hundred-odd songs, only one, *Solveig's Song* has borrowed a tune—no more."[9] Elsewhere he speaks of

---

[8] J. Horton, "Ibsen, Grieg, and Peer Gynt," *Music and Letters,* Vol. XXVI (1945), 66.

[9] Desmond, "Grieg's Songs," *Music and Letters,* Vol. XXII (1941), 343.

the "sombre depth of our folk music" and its "unsuspected harmonic possibilities." The first phrase for voice is repeated with a different harmonization; the balancing division is extended in this same way, closing with ornamented cadence. The first phrase closed with a folkish "snap" (m.12), over a drone bass. The drifting chromaticism, with augmented sixth chords on the weak beats of m.19, is quite opposed to the continuous peasant drone of root and fifth in the refrain and to the simple alternation of the superimposed dominant and tonic harmonies. The refrain, in triple meter and major mode, begins with voice alone, as it smoothly swells and recedes (*messa di voce*) and swings softly into a lilting, but not too gay measure.

Kjerulf and Sinding

GRIEG'S COMMAND for the wordless refrain—not the singer's license, as in the close of Rimski-Korsakov's *Eastern Romance*—calls to mind a song by one of Grieg's forerunners, Halfdan Kjerulf, whose songs were much admired by the younger master. Both composers collaborated with Björnson, and each was inspired to write one of his best songs by a scene from one of the author's novels. Grieg set *The First Meeting* ("*Det förste möde*"), Op. 21, No. 1. Kjerulf took a lyric from the peasant novel, *Synnöve Solbakken,* which the author introduces this way: "She did not shed a tear, but sat very still, looking out into the waking landscape. Presently she began to hum softly to herself, then a little louder and finally, she sang in a clear voice, the following song: How thankful I am for the happy hours of childhood we spent together. . . ."[10] But like Solveig, Synnöve sits and waits. Kjerulf has followed the author's suggestion. *Synnöve's Song* begins with the voice half-humming and half-sighing. The pensive song of remembered happiness concluded,

---

[10] The lyric of eight stanzas closes Chap. 6. As the song took shape it followed "another which she had known since she was a child." From the English translation by Julie Sutter. (New York, 1895).

Synnöve resumes her humming, the epilogue repeating the tender introduction.

The wordless refrain enhances the exotic color of the last two songs, but it is the delicate glissando in the accompaniment of Christian Sinding's *Sylvelin* that contributes most to its strange beauty. A dozen times, or in more than half of its twenty-three measures, the soft, tinkling tones of an upward, delicate glissando bring a rather magical effect, as its last note is supported by a six-four chord each time, with but one exception (m.11); greater security is found in the open fifth at the beginning of the next measure; the intervening beat, the last in the compound duple measure, the right hand leisurely fills with the fifth and then mounts again to the fifth, three octaves above the tenor. The benediction that comes to him whose heart and soul are lifted by the thought of Sylvelin, appears in the last measure, where the expected fifth is replaced by the tonic with the raised third on either side. The cadence glints with a soft radiance.

Dvořák

As Grieg is the symbol of the northern musician who refused to submit to German methods, Dvořák is the fair representative of the central European minorities who followed their own ways. Unlike Grieg, this Czech peasant had the instinct and skill to make long flights, as witness a string of symphonies, operas, and chamber and choral works. His urge was to free himself from program or poem, but when a work issued from such a source, we find that the instinctive artist had chosen a subject that was suited to his temperament. For him, it was the musical idea, however, that mattered, though occasionally he was led astray and yielded too literally to a pictorial turn of the text. Few of his songs, about sixty in all, scattered from Op. 2 to Op. 99, represent him at his best. Dvořák has frequently been likened to Schubert—both were simple, elemental souls bubbling over with melodies whose source they never questioned. Gifted with an almost unerring sense of color, not too troubled by economical use of materials and tightness of structure, they made music that warms the hearts of men. Rather Schubertian in the alternation of themes and in the shifting of major and minor, as well as in the color and spacing of the allegro section, is *The Cuckoo,* Op. 7, No. 3. A Biblical paraphrase of "All ye that labor, come to me," Op. 31, No. 4 illustrates the influence of sustained folk melody that so frequently colored his expression; here, too, one may find Dvořák's daring use of modulation, rather unorthodox even in its appearance here (m.30–34).

Unorthodox, too, is Op. 82, No. 2, *Over her embroidery,* whose broad, folklike opening theme returns, after a more troubled and modulatory section, in a key a half step lower. There is nothing in the text to suggest this, and the key change is far more daring than that in the ninth of the *Biblical Songs* or in the sixth of the *Gypsy Songs.* The ending of the latter, a small third lower (no relative key), might have been prompted by the poet's thought that the gypsy's song can be as free as the birds if he scorns silks and gold. If the music of this song reminds you of Liszt and Brahms in their Hungarian fantasies, recall that all three employed gypsy themes. Though a strong nationalist, Dvořák drew from many Slavic sources. A more sentimental strain of folk influence is found in the Op. 73, settings of Czech folk poems. The first of these, *Good Night,* a serenade that has had considerable vogue, starts like a cross between *Hearts and Flowers* and the Russian *Dark Eyes,* but becomes better and more intricate.

There are two sets of songs already mentioned which rise far above the others, the Op. 55, *Gypsy Songs,* and Op. 99, *Biblical Songs.* In composing the seven songs of the first group, set in 1880 to poems by Heyduk, Dvořák thought in terms of the tenor voice. But good songs, although they are dedicated to Frau Amalie Joachim, Julius Stockhausen, or Gustav Walter, soon are appropriated by all. The note most frequently sounded in the *Gypsy Songs* is that of freedom, and the robust spirit of the folk song and dance color the majority of the themes.

Highly characteristic is the first, *I chant my song,* which impetuously rushes through its short, vigorous dance motive, descending by degrees to settle down and roll the tonic chord until the voice enters. The second half of the stanza offers a delightful change of pace as the nervous sextolets are replaced by leisurely flowing triplets, echoing between accompaniment and voice and streaming into the duple values of the broad cadence, which points all its fingers and raises its voice to greet the relative major. But it does not arrive, for the introduction reasserts itself in the original minor. The second stanza is interestingly varied, the third offering still other variants of the first phrase. The color of the major at its opening (m.29) leads to a new counter in the tenor, while the right hand actively (*tremolandi*) doubles the voice. A rather quiet lyric interlude comes in the cycle with the third and fourth songs. Thoroughly individual and having scarcely a single trait in common with the other songs is *Songs My Mother Taught Me.*

Songs My Mother Taught Me
(Als die alte Mutter; Když mne stará matka)

THIS MIGHT BE CALLED Dvořák's *"Diploma Song,"* his assurance of a place in the academy of "immortals." The song is widely sung and loved. It has a tender beauty, doubtlessly heightened in value by the sentiment of the text. The remembered songs recall the mother whose eyes were wet with tears as she sang these same melodies. Freely the song moves from the major to its relative minor in the introduction's gentle rocking of the melodic motive from the first measure of the voice part. Apparently settled in the minor, the song directly resumes the major with the voice's entry. In the four-measure phrase and its repetition a degree lower, the rising of the fourth and the drop of the octave (m.11) to the cadence with seventh colorations are haunting. A subtle agitation is set up as the accompaniment, in a gently syncopated 6/8, moves with and against the even duple measure of the voice. Despite the fullness with which the chords are scored, there is no feeling of thickness; and, as the verse is repeated, the deep tones of the bass that begin each measure seem richer still. Quite like the gypsy's skill of decoration is the voice's filling in of the fourth (m.31) that had been skipped to in the first stanza. The pianoforte employs a shortened and ornamented version of the introduction for the interlude and a novel arpeggiation of the right-hand chords (m.31). The extension of the latter half of the stanza with the full, fervent sweep dying away on the suspensive fifth, delicately anticipated from the third and then the second below, seems inevitable. The interlude serves as an epilogue and turns to the major in the final chord, which fades away suspended as if in mid-air.

Biblical Songs
(Biblische Lieder; Biblické Písně)

THESE TEN SONGS, dated March, 1894, were written during Dvořák's stay in the United States. There is a natural temptation to read into them the influence of Negro spirituals, which affected his expression in the *Symphony from the New World* and the *"American" String Quartet*. Actually the sixth song begins with the identical melodic line of *the Largo,* whose melody for English horn has been fitted with words and is probably more frequently sung than any of the composer's true songs. In the Op. 99, the Negro influence is slight, the spiritual interpretation of the text broad and frequently dramatic. Note the angularity of the opening phrase and the graphic illustration of the "lightnings" in the first song. Such pictorial music brings to mind the engravings of Doré, who seized upon a moment of the Biblical story and depicted it, episodic though it might be, as if it were the core of the Christian belief. The texts are from the Psalms, the greatest storehouse of religious song, and the simple, devout Czech set them without pondering on hidden depths. Yet the set is far more subtle and detailed than the earlier *Gypsy Songs.*

Certainly as frequently sung as any of the Op. 99 is the third one, *Hear my prayer, O Lord,* based on the first part of Psalm 55. David cries to the Lord to hear him. Had he the wings of a dove, he would fly far away and escape from the stormy wind and tempest. The sustained note of pleading in the first vocal phrase is symmetrically answered by the piano, their eight-measure division immediately repeated with slight variation. More filled with complaint and agitation is the succeeding section (m.22–29), whose angular melody and very free modulations are intensified in their free repetition after two measures of interlude. The home dominant is romantically reached, and a three-measure bridge, closing with a high, quiet trill on this dominant, leads to the psalmist's longing for the wings of a dove. The cantabile of the voice is supported by a delicate, high-pitched, fluttering figure, which broadens and joins the voice in a glorious, warm, romantic phrase falling to the tonic. Then, with a sharp suddenness, the escape from the storm and the tempest is rooted in nature's open-fifth at the beginning and closing of this short section (m.54–62). The drama is vivid with *tremolandi,* dissonances, *stringendo* and crescendo, and a hurtling chromatic scale. These are effects which he had learned in his days of apprenticeship in the theater orchestra. Dvořák did not compose these songs for church use, but should this one be so employed, I am sure he would have sanctioned a return of m. 5–21 as a more fitting close for a service of worship.

CHAPTER XIX

Elizabethans and Their Successors

E NGLAND's supremacy in music and poetry during the Elizabethan period was firmly founded on a wide and deep appreciation of these arts. The heights to which England then
rose she maintained for a season, but never again has she been
able to soar so high. We shall not be concerned here with the
long preparation that made possible this luxuriant blossoming.
The great wealth that had flowed from her new-found trade
brought both leisure and a sense of obligation for the cultivation
of good things. Nothing gave such an immediate satisfaction as
music, which was supported not only by the old "established"
families in their great houses, but by the *nouveaux riches* in their
recently built manor houses. This was a period of astonishingly
fine taste and practice, when the amateurs in the home not only
wrote their verses, but were able to take their parts in the madrigals and instrumental ensembles which were usually enjoyed
after supper.

It was the joining of the arts of poetry and music which made
the Art Song. Undoubtedly there was a stimulus that came to
poetry from music, but it seems extravagant for Garnett and
Gosse in their *Illustrated Record of English Literature* to at-
tribute much of Elizabethan lyric poetry to the necessity of finding words for the lute melodies of Tallis, Byrd, and Dowland.
"The poems so employed were obliged to be lucid, liquid, brief
and of a temper suited to the gayety or sadness of the instrument."[1] In truth, Englishmen had been joining words to music

[1] R. Garnett and E. Gosse, *English Literature, An Illustrated Record* (New York,
1904), II, 275.

for centuries, and the skills they had won made possible the madrigal, the most important secular music of the sixteenth century. It was from one facet of the madrigal that the English art song broke off. In the simplest type of madrigal, the chief melodic interest is in the topmost singing voice, the other voices supporting the treble. This kind of madrigal came to be called an ayre. Often during the informal singing in the home, a viol, recorder, or lute substituted for a voice. William Byrd even noted that his music was "apt for voices or viols."[2] The lute player had an advantage in that he could play all the lower voices and sing the treble. Thus a part song was changed into a "solo-song with instrumental accompaniment." This adaptation was made largely by John Dowland (1563–1626), whose lute and voice were heard and admired in many lands. Most of his eighty-seven ayres were printed in two versions, as part songs and as solo songs (the treble and adapted lute accompaniment).

Canon Edmund Horace Fellowes, who has revealed so fully the music of this period, holds that Dowland was "by far the earliest composer in the world to reach first-class rank in the realm of art-song."[3] Some might not share the Canon's enthusiasm, which led him to say that Dowland "stands among, perhaps, the first half-dozen of the world's song-writers." Simple, clear, supple of melody, and intriguing in the free play of rhythmic patterns, these short songs are matched to English verse of great beauty. *Awake, sweet love,* in its symmetry of phrase and form (AABB) and in its extension of cadence, is quite disserviced in the lugubrious tone and tempo of a certain recording. Next to the last of the twenty-one numbers in the *First Booke of Ayres* (1597) is *Come, Heavy Sleep.*

[2] Fellowes, *William Byrd*, 87.

[3] "Dowland," *Grove's Dictionary* (3rd ed.), II, 90. Evidently the Canon came to agree with Ernest Newman whom he quoted in the preface to *Forty Elizabethan Songs* (ed. by E. H. Fellowes, London, 1921). "And in one at least of the lutenist writers— Dowland—he meets with one of the half-dozen greatest song-composers of all time."

Come, Heavy Sleep

THE POET'S PLEADINGS that sleep come and possess his tired, thought-worn soul, Dowland has set to music of great dignity. Yet "the image of true Death" has not come, and there is a plaintive appeal in the melody of the first division, each of whose first two three-measure phrases has fallen suspensively on the dominant; the raised third (m.8) of relative minor, as our age might interpret the cadence of the succeeding short phrase, is enhanced by the free change of measure, which is further modified by the swing of the last cadencing phrase reflecting the agitation of the text ("cries" and "the mind's affright"). This song enjoyed the greater freedom of accent and measure characteristic of the age; and the harmonic color with which the second section (m.11) begins is unusual for modern ears and has great charm. Rhythmically, the second section begins with a quiet strength, mounting in sequence on the same motive (m.13) that closed the first division. The sequence reaches the

That liv-ing dies, that liv-ing dies, that liv-ing dies,

same harmonic goal (m.13) as in m.8, and the "lute" freely repeats the earlier cadence figure; the voice, however, quietly expands the note values, restoring to the song the feeling of streaming breadth which the very opening phrase suggests.

The poet's name is not given for that verse which Dowland

set with such depth. Indeed, not a single part-book of the Elizabethan period has been found with a poet's name attached to the verse. One of the strangest quirks of this age, so filled with great poetry, is that few settings of Shakespeare by his contemporaries have come down to us. As admired as any is Thomas Morley's setting of *It Was a Lover and His Lass*.

It Was a Lover and His Lass

THIS IS No. 6 in Morley's last work, twenty-one "little short songs to sing and play to the lute with the bass-viol," as he described *The First Booke of Ayres,* which appeared in 1600. The lyric is an interpolation, not forwarding the action of *As You Like It*. In Act V, scene 3, Touchstone the clown enters with the country wench, Audrey, whom he is to marry. Two of the banished Duke's pages enter, and Touchstone bids them sing. Shakespeare then has the First Page take off the singer most tellingly: "Shall we clap into 't roundly, without hawking or spitting, or saying we are hoarse, which are only the prologues to a bad voice?" The Second Page follows with "I' faith, i' faith; and both in a tune, like two gipsies on a horse." Then comes the song, and Morley has followed his own advice, offered in the great textbook of that day, *A Plaine and Easie Introduction to Practicall Musicke*: "In dittying or composing music to words, . . . possesse yourselfe wholely with that vaine wherewith you compose."[4] With a gay swing and a refrain of delightful nonsense syllables, suggesting its ballet or dance origin, the air goes its merry way. Not yet had the tyranny of accent by the bar line or bisymmetry of phrase dominated the composer. Morley let his music ride with the text, but with an ingenious touch when he repeated, "In Springtime, the only pretty ring time," he wavered a little on his own account. To crowd such music into

[4] T. Morley, *A Plaine and Easie Introduction to Musicke* (London, 1937), 180. Shakespeare Association Facsimile, No. 14.

the measures of the regular duple, which had gone before, would have denied it the natural freedom that two measures of "6/4" bring; thus is avoided the false accent of *"only."*

Canon Fellowes in his transcription of the whole *First Booke of Ayres* from the only known copy, which is in the Folger Library, has included the lute tablature with its exact transcription for piano in a volume of *The English School of Lutenist Song Writers* (Series 1, No. 16, Stainer and Bell). Between two phrases of seven measures each is a bar of interlude (in some editions omitted) ; a six-measure phrase follows; and a repeat ("In Springtime"), beginning on the tonic level, omits the first three measures of the second phrase and, within its four measures, breaks forth into two "6/4" measures, followed by the six-measure phrase ("When birds do sing"). The modal color is height-

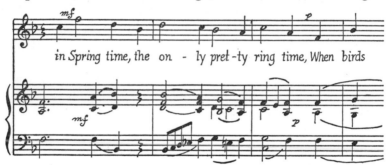

in Spring time, the on - ly pret -ty ring time, When birds

ened by the lowered seventh (m.3), which does not appear otherwise throughout the original voice part. The lift of the scale figure, as it bounces along in thirds (m.3), and the tripping down of "Hey ding-a-ding-a-ding" have made life gayer through three and one-half centuries.

Even earlier than Morley's and Dowland's first books of ayres (1600 and 1597) are some of the songs of their most illustrious contemporary, William Byrd (1542/3–1623). Unlike them, Byrd never scored for lute; nor had the virginal yet been chosen by composers to accompany the solo voice. Byrd used viols to support the singing voice, as in *My Sweet Little Darling.*

My Sweet Little Darling

THIS TENDER CRADLE SONG was written about 1581, at a time when the members of the Florentine Camerata were just beginning to grapple with problems that led to monody. Other than the prophetic work of the Spaniard Milan, almost a half-century earlier, this little song by Byrd is historically a "primitive." Artistically it is quite advanced, the simple melodic phrases molded on the text. Distinctive is the refrain phrase, "Sing lullaby, lulla," which appears after each line and, at the last, is extended with the sweet nothings a mother sings to her babe. Characteristic of its cadence is the soft English "knock" of the two even quarters, the viols either carrying on the phrase in their own way (m.9–10) or starting afresh (m.16–17). The text is not one to have drawn from this most inventive and daring Elizabethan other than pleasing melody and a simple but independent modal accompaniment. Just three measures from the close, however, Byrd introduces a new harmonic color, which, judged by his liking for underlaying the word and thought, might have portrayed for him the new world of sleep and dreams which the babe has just entered.

IT DOES NOT ALWAYS FOLLOW that the most poetic-minded solves best the problem of making music "framed to the life of the words."[5] The two poet-composers, Thomas Campion (1567–1620) and Henry Lawes (1596–1662), are ever interesting because of their theories and methods of joining verse and music. Campion wrote learned treatises on poetry and the *Art of composing Music;* to his own excellent lyrics, he composed many airs which were issued from 1601 to 1617. He appears now to have been like most of the great troubadours, whose contributions to poetry were greater than those to music. In his masques, it is the poetry that overshadows the music. Henry Lawes collab-

---

[5] W. Byrd's collection of 1611 of "Psalmes, Songs and Sonnets: some solemne, some joyfull, framed to the life of the words."

orated with Milton in the *Masque of Comus* (1634); here again the poetry lives on, while the music, which was equally admired, is now rarely sounded. Lawes's great concern in all his songs, he wrote, was "by giving each syllable its particular humour, to shape notes to the words and sense." How fully to the satisfaction of the poet he had done this is evidenced in these first lines from John Milton's sonnet, *To Mr. H. Lawes on His Aires*:

> *Harry whose tuneful and well measured songs*
> *First taught our English Musick how to span*
> *Words with just note and accent, not to scan*
> *With Midas ears, committing short and long;*

The resulting "recitative musick" resembled that of the Italians, but for his countrymen, who admired unduly the foreign music without understanding the words, he made a setting of the index of an Italian book. The resulting nonsense he titled *Tavola,* and this mock ayre appeared with serious companions in a collection of his songs.[6]

The return of Charles II from his enforced sojourn in French courts stimulated English composers to imitate French styles. A considerable amount of grafting of French and other foreign imports on English musical stock took place. Some English roots were weakened in the process, while others thrived. The sturdiest and healthiest composer of the Restoration, frequently hailed as "the greatest musical genius the English nation has produced," was Henry Purcell.

Henry Purcell

IN HIS PATHETICALLY short career (1659–95), Purcell wrote an immense amount of music, putting his stamp upon every form and medium his generation knew. Music for the theater, music for the church, odes of rejoicing or mourning for the state, songs, catches, sonatas for the home—to this astonishing variety of sub-

---

[6] In the essay opening the 1653 edition of "Ayres and Dialogues for One, Two, and Three Voyces."

jects he seemed always to attune himself readily, finding a music "that always rang true and characteristic of the country to which he belonged."

In the preface to the second edition of *Orpheus Britannicus,* the principal seventeenth-century collection of his "choicest songs," the editor noted that Purcell had "a peculiar genius to express the energy of English words"; in an age of considerable pomp and theatrical declamation Purcell appears faithful to the natural movement and accent of the words. This fidelity is most obvious in the recitatives, which appear occasionally even in the "single songs"; but Purcell is one who falls into a tune easily. He differs from countless followers in that his tunes are born of the words, and this results in flexible phrase structure with little of the rigid symmetry of period and repetition that we usually associate with a tune. This flexibility Purcell was able to suggest even in his treatment of the fashionable ground bass, the repetitions of its pattern bringing an obvious unity and continuity of structure. The relentless, square march of the bass Purcell often subtly relieved by rests or phrasing in the voice, that either at its beginning or its close, did not agree with the ground and might even suggest a modulation.

Most frequently sung of Purcell's melodies is Dido's lament, *When I am laid in earth.* Its haunting poignancy, strangely intimate—yet noble in its dignity—is founded on a ground bass. This is an aria from a dramatic piece. Paradoxically, the song, *O Solitude,* of somewhat similar mood, is two and one-half times as long and employs in the voice dramatic skips of the minor seventh and the diminished fifth. Its four-measure ground comes full cycle twenty-eight times, while the five-measure, chromatically descending "grief" motive of Dido has but nine repetitions. The aria is more concentrated and songlike than the song. Many of the 107 songs in volume 25 of the Purcell Society edition are quite short. Singers have chosen more frequently from the songs which are a part of the odes, operas, or masques. The jaunty *Nymphs and Shepherds* from *The Libertine* and

I attempt from love's sickness to fly from *The Indian Queen*
have remained favorites. This latter, from Act III of a play by
Howard and Dryden, expresses the distress of the Mexican
Queen Zempoalla, whose love for the emperor Montezuma
is not returned. Oddly enough the tune does not interpret or
intensify the verse of Sir Robert Howard other than to illustrate
the word "fly," on which the voice takes off for a solo flight, soon
halted by a cadence. But the twelve-measure refrain idea is so
fetching, the contrasting couplets so fresh and energetic, and
the whole structure (ABACA) so clear-cut that it is always
welcome.

In many respects the realization of one of Purcell's "single
songs," scored with only two lines—one for the voice, the other
for the thorough-bass—is more problematic than that of a Morley or Dowland air with its lute part entirely noted by the composer. As keyboard instruments rapidly took the place of the
lute, the accompanist was given considerable freedom in in-
terpreting the *basso continuo.* Even moderns who revere Purcell,
reading from the same score, arrive at strangely different music,
as witness W. H. Cummings and Arthur Somervell in their
versions of *The Knotting Song.*

The Knotting Song

THE FOUR STANZAS of Sir Charles Sedley's innocent verse picture the faithful swain waiting for some response from Phyllis;
the refrain does not vary, for each time Phyllis, "without frown
or smile, sat and knotted all the while." It is in the last line that
Purcell saw the chance for a motion picture with sound, and by
monotonous fourfold repetition of "and knotted," he gives a
humorous realism to the girl's occupation, that of twisting and
knotting threads to make lacelike fancywork. The sturdy English turn of the beginning phrase of four measures brings a five-
measure reply, closing in the dominant key. The refrain hesitantly returns to the tonic, and the repeated "knottings" stretch to

seven measures, the reply to the opening four-measure phrase. Purcell did not drop a stitch along the way. There is a most interesting pattern of motion woven by the voice and the bass, the movement in eighths alternating. The change to 3/4 meter in the refrain brings variety to the stanza form.

Dr. Thomas Augustine Arne

IT WAS THE GENIUS of Purcell that made his period a golden age in the history of English music. The Georgian period that followed (about 1720–80) was an age of silver, and its dominating figure in music, Thomas Augustine Arne (1710–78), has tarnished and lost much of the luster which then gave delight. There is no phrase of Arne's or his contemporaries that rings with the haunting, soul-searching depth of Purcell's Dido as she cries, "Remember me." The eighteenth century in England was marked by an elegant formality that satisfied aristocratic patrons, whose portraits were turned out in the grand style by Sir Joshua Reynolds, while Hogarth and Addison made fun of their foibles.

The music of Arne is thoroughly English and not an imitation of his contemporary, Handel, who, as Sir Charles Hubert Parry has keenly observed, adapted rather than invented the "English" style, leaving, of course, "the impress of his genius upon it."[7] In the same year that English citizen Handel died (1759), Oxford University granted to Arne the degree of Doctor of Music. Although many composers of rank have been honored with degrees, Arne is one of the exceptions whose name is usually prefaced by "Doctor." He is a rather paradoxical figure, who, though shallow and a bit of a tyrant and pedant, had a rich and seemingly inexhaustible store of splendid tunes. They bubbled over for every occasion, and like other eighteenth-century composers Arne was always busy with a new work. There was a stream of works for the theater—ballad operas, grand opera,

[7] C. H. H. Parry, *Style in Musical Art* (London, 1911), 160.

and much incidental music. In 1745, he was engaged as composer at Vauxhall Gardens, and, for this establishment, Ranelagh, and Marylebone Gardens, he wrote "shoals of songs," nearly twenty books of them; some of the best known collections are titled *Lyric Harmony, The Syren,* and *The Vocal Grove.* Simple, spontaneous, pert, and healthful, a few of these melodies have never been out of circulation.

Like Haydn, Arne contributed a song which became a nation's pride. For over two hundred years *Rule, Britannia!* has held its place in the hearts of Englishmen. Thoroughly English, too, are some settings of songs of Shakespeare. When *As You Like It* was revived in 1740, after forty years of neglect, Arne's music for *Under the Greenwood Tree* and *Blow, blow, thou Winter Wind* was introduced by Mr. Thomas Lowe. For *Love's Labor's Lost,* there were his settings of *When Daisies Pied* and *When Icicles Hang by the Wall.* Within the restrained octave range of the latter, the song of the owl, Arne does not resist the imitation suggested by the "To-whit, tu-whoo;" nor does he scorn the falling note of the cuckoo in *When Daisies Pied.* Unlike Daquin's more famous anacrustic *Coucou,* the Englishman's bird starts his call on the accent, the piano echoing. It is a delightful song. More distinguished is *Where the Bee Sucks,* the song of Ariel from Act V, scene 1 of *The Tempest.*

Where the Bee Sucks

THIS WAS "new set to musick by Mr. Arne" for the Drury Lane revival of January 31, 1746. Mrs. Clive (Kitty) first sang this inspired song. The second phrase, "In a cowslip's bell I lie," has a most genial nodding movement. Rather than "marred by awkward overlaying of *fioriture*" as one critic wrote,[8] the two measures of lifting sequence on "fly" are a capital inspiration. Ariel seems more earth-bound in the second division of the song, beginning "merrily," where for eight measures Arne rings

[8] D. G. Mason (ed.), *Art of Music,* V, 171.

rhythmic and tonal changes on tonic to dominant. Yet, somehow, this is so frank and alive and the cadence phrase so vigorous and final that we are quite won over.

Arne has an engaging vocal style. He knew the voice intimately; one of his first voice pupils was his sister Susanna, who as Mrs. Cibber, sang Polly in *The Beggar's Opera;* for her, Handel wrote the contralto solos in the *Messiah*. Arne sings the charms of Phyllis; her name, along with Chloe's, is recalled, as with lilting enthusiasm he rehearses the charms of *Polly Willis*. Most pleasing are the repeated notes in the buoyant, swinging cadence on the loved one's name. More famed and much more frequently praised is Molly, who was *The Lass with the Delicate Air*.

The Lass with the Delicate Air

THIS GAY TUNE, printed in the *Universal Magazine,* August, 1762, is by the Doctor's son, Michael Arne (1740–86), who was as versatile as his father, but less gifted. The verse of his day freely repeats the theme of the beautiful maid whose reserve or disdain causes anguished lovers to pine and sigh. Seldom are the tables turned, as in Stephen Storace's *A Sailor loved a Lass*. Most of the torment seems a pose, and like Michael Arne in this song, many musicians choose to reflect the sunshine of love rather than its shadows. A light-hearted, gay, sprightly sixteen-measure period closes with the dainty cadence, made in modern editions with detached eighths, illustrating the "del-i-cate air." A graceful, eight-measure florid refrain reinforces the sentiment and closes with a light, springing approach to the modified return of that precisely right cadence on "delicate air." This stanza, perfect in its way, is repeated for other sentiments, that, however, all lead at the appointed times to the title line, where the union of words and music is a bright spot in eighteenth-century English song.

This song has many companion pieces that continue to afford pleasure to singers and audiences alike. There is a light,

THE LASS WITH THE DELICATE AIR. *A new* SONG.

Young Mol—ly who lives at the foot of the hill, Where
fame ev'—ry vir—gin with en—vy does fil', Of beau—ty is
blefs'd with fo am—ple a fhare, That men call her the lafs with the
de--li - ate air: With the de————licate air, That men
call her the lafs with the de————li—cate air.

2.

One ev'ning laft May as I travers'd the grove,
In thoughtlefs retirement, not dreaming of
love;
I chanc'd to efpy the gay nymph I declare,
And really fhe'd got a moft delicate air.

3.

By a murmuring brook, on a green moffy bed,
A chaplet compofing, the fair one was laid;
Surpris'd and tranfported I could not forbear
With raptures to gaze on her delicate air.

4.

For that moment young Cupid felected a dart,
And pierc'd without pity my innocent heart;
And from thence how to gain the dear maid was
my care,
For a captive I fell to her delicate air.

5.

When fhe faw me, fhe blufh'd, & complain'd I
was rude,
And begg'd of all things, that I would not intrude;
I anfwer'd I could not tell how I came there,
But laid all the blame on her delicate air.

6.

Said her heart was the prize, which I fought to
obtain,
And hop'd that fhe'd give it to eafe my fond pain;
She neither rejected nor granted my prayer,
But fir'd all my foul with her delicate air.

7.

A thoufand times o'er, I've repeated my fuit,
But ftill the tormentor affects to be mute;
Then tell me ye fwains who have conquer'd the fair,
How to win the dear lafs with the delicate air.

As

airy grace in the dance pattern of Anthony Young's *Phyllis has such Charming Graces,* which appeared in Watt's *Musical Miscellany* of 1730. Much later was issued Thomas Brown's *Shepherd! Thy Demeanour Vary.* Here, too, the words and music are more closely joined than was customary in the period, and, though its melodic line is very active and generously decorated, the music is sincere and rewarding. "Dance and sing, be light and airy" bounds along in a most captivating fashion, with a two-measure repetition in the accompaniment to close the division. B is in the dominant, an eight-measure balance for A; a single measure of interlude now leads to C in the parallel tonic minor, reflecting the "dull looks and sighing." Its two lines of verse occupy only four measures and are directly followed by the return of A, much modified and introducing the buoyant "Fa-la-la's." There is an echo effect in the middle phrase and a resounding cadence in the dominant, with the third repetition of the "Fa-la-la" phrase. The first division is repeated, and then comes a gay codetta, the voice terracing upward to high-C, whence it cascades down and adds a crisp cadence.

Quite opposed to the gay, facile, and florid songs of the century are the earnest, simple melodies, such as George Monro's *My Lovely Celia.* A number of Monro's songs were published in the *Musical Miscellany* of 1731, the year of his death. *My Lovely Celia* is imbued with sentiment of the finest English kind, a little reserved, but full of heart. Although set to a continuous sixteen-measure period without repetition or veiled sequence, the poet's lines find their musical counterpart in phrases of two measures, with the exception of the last line, which ideally might have commanded an unbroken phrase. A somewhat similar melodic curve is to be found in all the phrases except the first and the last two. It is impossible to explain why such satisfaction should be found in the ornamented descent from dominant to tonic in the opening phrase, or why such beauty should result from the purely diatonic descending scale in m.13–14. In its simplicity, truth of sentiment, and sustained cantabile, it reminds one of Giordani's masterpiece, *Caro mio ben;* and, though quite dissimilar, it calls to mind that most familiar English love song, *Drink to me only with thine eyes.* (This beautiful tune by an unknown composer, to which Ben Jonson's poem *To Celia* (1616) is indelibly joined, has never been discovered in an earlier form than that of a glee published about 1770.)[9]

Thoroughly representative of the versatility of the eighteenth-century English song composers is Charles Dibdin (1745–1814), who won fame as poet-composer-singer-actor-producer. He is best remembered for some songs composed near the turn of the century for his own production of *The Oddities,* an entertainment comprised of varied musical numbers by one performer, usually himself. Especially admired were his sea songs, which recited the valor of the British sailor and made his life so appealing that the government granted the composer a pension. Dibdin might have joined in the wish to make the nation's songs and care not who made its laws. Healthy, hearty, richly gifted with the skill of turning an appropriate tune, Dibdin was a great favorite. Longest remembered of his over 1,400 songs is *Tom Bowling,* introduced at one of his entertainments and written to commemorate the death of his brother, Captain John Dibdin. Dibdin can not be charged with "prettiness." Quite occasionally careless in accent—as in this song where the first principal accent in the original fell on the word "a,"—and a little rough in harmony, he conveys a sense of strength and authority that is admirable in his sea songs. In the design of *Tom Bowling* (A8, B4, A6), the return is "extended" by repetition of the refrain line, "And now he's gone aloft," set to a new and illustrative music. Even more stalwart, free, and daring is *Blow high, blow low,* a true rondo introduced in *The Seraglio* in 1776.

James Hook (1746–1827) was an even more prolific song writer than Dibdin, whose ditties Hook outnumbered by about 600, this difference in quantity nearly equaling the total of songs by Schubert, his contemporary. For years, Hook was organist

9 W. Chappell, *Popular Music of the Olden Times,* II, 707.

at the Marylebone and later at Vauxhall Gardens, where every night he played concertos. That audiences were always craving new music in part accounts for the nearly 2,000 songs of this composer. Most praised through the years has been one sung first at Vauxhall in 1789; the poem by Leonard MacNally celebrated a lass, "a rose without a thorn," and it was she, *The Lass of Richmond Hill,* who became the poet's wife. It is with the same sweetness and light of the song that Hook's music wends its happy, tuneful way. Its eight-measure verse closes in the dominant, reaffirmed by a perky two-measure interlude. The refrain turns back in eight measures to the tonic on "Richmond Hill," followed by a nine-measure codetta that swings alternately from dominant to tonic. More admired now is *Mary of Allendale,* whose loveliness and pure beauty is as convincing as Monro's *My Lovely Celia.* There is strength in the repetition of the two-measure phrase beginning "fairer," and there is beauty and fervor as the melody overflows in a turn on the word "Mary," a third lower than the preceding phrase. This extended cadence is a "thing of beauty."

CHAPTER XX

Later English Song

THE last two composers have bridged us over into the nineteenth century, but before allowing its romantic tide to carry us along, let us look back on those eighteenth-century composers who generally were busy with music for the theater. The loosely organized masques, ballad operas, and various other types of dramatic productions were liberally dotted with lyric songs which frequently in their simple melodic flow and strophic design suggest folk songs. There was a tremendous output of ditties for performance at the various gardens, the crowded popular concerts of the day. The concerts, which began at five or six o'clock, lasted about four hours, songs and glees alternating with sonatas and concertos.

William Chappell's *Popular Music of the Olden Time* contains an essay on minstrelsy and generous examples of English balladry from the Saxon period to the close of the eighteenth century. One may well be confused by the loose usage of the term ballad, for to Englishmen it has meant different things in different periods, including any folk tune, traditional song, or popular ditty—the jogging verse and tune that narrates heroic, tragic, or commonplace deeds—and most recently the Victorian sentimental concert song. Certain elements of the drawing-room or parlor ballad had been present in English song for long years, but the strain of sentiment always present in romantic music became overstressed as the nineteenth century progressed. The typical sentimental strophic ballad that resulted was so popular that whole series of ballad concerts were not only artistically satisfying to the populace, but commercially profitable even for the publishers, who "plugged" their songs by royalties to every singer who programmed them. There were few composers from Bishop to Ronald who did not add their fair contribution to this movement, for these writers were, after all, a part of their race and time. Although native composers of large, serious works were seldom as favored as foreigners, the status of the English musician was gradually bettered during the nineteenth century.

The first English musician ever to be knighted was Henry Rowley Bishop, created Sir Henry by Queen Victoria in 1842. His operas, his professorships at Edinburgh and Oxford, his directorships and honors—all these are made faint by time, but one song of his has remained clear and bright. *Home, Sweet Home* was introduced in 1823 at Covent Garden in the opera *Clari, the Maid of Milan.* Its flowing melody and simple harmony are suggestive of folk song. Indeed, the composer had earlier introduced *Home, Sweet Home* as folk music when, lacking a Sicilian example for his collection of *National Melodies of All Countries,* he had written this tune to fill the place. This world-loved melody undoubtedly owes some of its preeminence to the sentiment of John Howard Payne's text, but had it not been joined to Bishop's tune it would never have sung its way into the hearts of generations. It had an earlier rival in Bishop's *My Pretty Jane,* or *The Bloom is on the Rye.* Far more involved is the delightful coloratura setting of Shakespeare's *Lo! Here the Gentle Lark.* In this, Bishop vies with the Italian opera composers of his day, introducing a flute obbligato and the customary emphasis on the decorative element. Behind all this elaborateness, however, is the simple line of a charming tune.

Charles Edward Horn (1786–1849) must have at least some mention here. After an active career in ballad, opera, and oratorio, he came to Boston, where he was director of the Handel and Haydn Society. Two of his songs, *Cherry Ripe* and *I've Been Roaming,* are frequently heard—and rightly so—as they are "full and fair ones"[1] and bubble over with good spirits.

[1] The phrase is from Horn's "Cherry Ripe."

As the Victorian age went its peaceful ways, a new national idol was set up beside Handel, as Mendelssohn became a sort of universal god of music, worshipped in many lands beside his own. A fair English reflection of his refined poetic manner is found in William Sterndale Bennett (1816–75), whose *May Dew,* in melodic line and accompaniment figure, reminds one of the favored devices in the *Songs Without Words.*

The most important single force in reasserting English independence and forwarding an English Renaissance in music was Sir Arthur Sullivan (1842–1900). One remembers him best for the Savoy operas, the long series of collaborations with Gilbert, which gave the world a host of songs still fresh and engaging. His success with incidental music for *The Tempest* led Sullivan in 1863–64 to write a number of Shakespeare songs, of which *Orpheus with his Lute* remains the most popular. The lyric is from the opening of Act III of *Henry VIII,* where Queen Katharine commands one of her wenches to take her lute and disperse with a song the troubles that sadden the Queen's soul. Sullivan's repetition of the lines is not a happy device for the poem, although the music is pleasant and singable. The second stanza is interestingly varied, extending with a codetta the last line of the verse, which had not fallen within the repetition. The epilogue employs the "lute" figure which has unified the accompaniment, now doubled at the fifteenth and scampering in elfish fashion to the simple cadence; this seems a bit facetious following the broad cadences of both the strophe and codetta. There were many other songs through his career, but one stands quite apart; it was by all odds the most popular song of the composer's generation. No English song since has received such wide acceptance.

The Lost Chord

THIS SONG WAS SKETCHED in 1877 at the bedside of the composer's dying brother, Frederick.[2] One can understand how, at such a

---

[2] H. Sullivan and N. Flower, *Sir Arthur Sullivan, His Life, Diaries, and Letters,* 113.

moment, the verses of Adelaide Procter, which had foiled the composer in an earlier attempt, came back to him with new meaning, demanding a new solution. "Death's bright Angel" did speak and in no subtle or esoteric fashion. The organist Sullivan simulates the instrument in the introduction; the voice chants meditatively above sustained chords and, then, in a mounting, improvised, but restrained way, concludes the stanza. The shortened introduction serves as interlude, and the first sixteen bars of the strophe are repeated with the accompaniment on a soft four-foot stop, as it were. The eighteen measures that follow begin *tranquillo,* but the gradual increase in speed and volume leads to a return of the opening period *grandioso.* The eighth-note motion that had helped build up the return does not appear again, the melody now supported by the forceful march of simple harmonies. Even if the more objective taste of today labels the song "banal" and "fatuous," there are a hundred ways in which the composer might have added grounds for these charges.

THE PASSING YEARS have made it easier to omit some composers of this period; for each of those that are selected as having moved in the main channel which English song was then cutting, it is most difficult to choose one characteristic work. Songs are individual, and the style of the composer is influenced by the poem he sets. Yet I choose to fire a few rifleshots, rather than point a shotgun and bring down a whole catalogue. Frederick Clay's masterpiece, *I'll sing thee Songs of Araby,* was one of the few songs to rival Sullivan's great favorite. Arthur Somervell is noted in preference to Cowen, although each had a great gift for charming melody; yet Somervell was more highly sensitive to verse, and his caterings to the banal drawing-room ballad style are less frequent and obvious. His cycle of twelve songs from Tennyson's *Maud* (1898) caught much of its longing and anguish; he portrays equally well the ecstasy of the poetic nocturne, *Come into the Garden, Maud,* at the close of Part I. Elgar's interest was in works larger than song, although the world knows him best through a trio of a military march, to which the words, "land of hope and glory," were joined; this has become a national song. He might have preferred to be remembered by *Where Corals Lie*. Although Elgar slighted song, there was a period when Cyril Scott found it his chief interest.

Lullaby

Scott's *Lullaby* is a setting of a little poem by Christina Rossetti. It has a fresh charm and a slight touch of strangeness, which Pater felt to be an important ingredient in beauty. The song is closely unified by a rocking figure, which swings for the first half of the song (twenty-two measures) over an unchanging pedal; yet this never becomes tonally monotonous, for the seventh, both in accompaniment and voice, is flatted, and the motion that swings the left hand up to the "high"-pitched chord of the measure on the third quarter brings contrast in tension and color. The chord on the lowered sixth, a principal color of

this song (m.17), is enharmonically notated. The first break in the motion of the eighths (m.29) is arresting; the resumption of the original figure and sequential return to home key is made reassuring by the first use of the natural leading tone in both voice and accompaniment. The voice tranquilly intones its last "lullabies," and, though the accompaniment is still attracted to the romantic seventh chord on the lowered sixth, the peace of the tonic chord is finally gained.

How the ballad may be transformed is illustrated by *The Unforeseen*. The remarkable use of a pedal and the growing acceptance of the seventh chord as a norm (four triads in 153 chords) can be found in *Night Song,* while the influence of French impressionism is marked in the setting of Christina Rossetti's *Tomorrow*. One of Scott's best fancies is the *Blackbird's Song* with its delightful, delicate, twirling figure of the blackbird in the accompaniment and a pleasant, arched flight for the voice with a highly effective, commanded, wide portamento in the cadence.

One of the gifts of the versatile Sir Landon Ronald was that of sensitive accompanying, whether with his orchestra or at the piano. He toured with Madame Melba, and to her was dedicated his most popular group of songs, *A Cycle of Life.* All five of these songs are typical of his deft scoring, where everything is grateful and counts for its full value. Most often sung has been *Down in the Forest,* a song of the spring whose tremulous stirrings are suggested in the soft dissonant seconds of the wavering accompaniment. The graceful and softer-hued songs of Roger Quilter have retained their attractiveness. His sensitive lyricism is illustrated in the setting of Tennyson's *Now Sleeps the Crimson Petal.*

Now Sleeps the Crimson Petal

EACH LINE OF THIS iambic pentameter verse is patterned with a measure of 5/4 followed by one of 3/4, the pause at the end of the line extended in the accompaniment. This metric oscillation springs from the composer's faithfulness to the poet's rhythms, resulting in fifteen changes of metric signature in the twenty-seven measures of the song, the introduction, interlude, and epilogue being sustained in 3/4. The interlude is none other than the introduction; although transferred an octave lower, it seems new. By the return of the first phrase, one might expect a strophic form, but new spontaneous melody flows along with the last verse. The "elision" of the last two lines with the voice, sustaining "slip" and repeating it on the accent, may not be the most accurate tonal translation of the text, but it is vocally right. With similar richness of invention, Quilter treats the two stanzas of William Blake's fanciful *Dream Valley,* and, with the poet, he tunes his merry note and fishes "for fancies as they pass." The melody of the second stanza is freely improvised upon the first; a triplet curls lazily where two eighths moved before; the final cadence finds its way back through the extension of the 4/4 measure, where the triplet in the voice is answered by the accompaniment. Again, as in m.11, the tonic chord is blurred by the added second, whose soft dissonance lingers and disappears only in the next to the last chord.

THE ENGLISH musical Renaissance did not slight song, and "to name the successful song composers," as Colles observed, "would be merely to recount most of the names of living English composers."[3] Though greatly admired by their countrymen, Mackenzie and Parry have roused little interest elsewhere. More frequently sung are the songs of their successors, such as Bantock, Bridge, and Ireland. Bantock's *Silent Strings* begins suggestively with a single line of melody that breaks after two measures into a six-voiced chord, in which two open fifths recall the tuning of strings. This chord pattern, repeated on different degrees, forms the principal accompaniment, sensitively broken when Samarcand and Avalon are mentioned. The climax that is reached in the final stanza brings a tremolo, followed by wide, sweeping arpeggio figures that end *pp,* sustaining the voice's long-held "song." After quiet lyricism, Helen Taylor's verse ends rapturously with "love shall quicken the silent strings into song." Mary E. Coleridge, the poet of Bridge's most popular song, *Love went a-riding,* begins exultantly and drops little from this level. The composer's fresh and vital symbol of the

[3] H. C. Colles, "Song," *Grove's Dictionary* (3rd ed.), 60c.

ride is given added spring by the mounting fifths supporting the first vocal phrase. The jolt of the dotted figure of the first section is softened in the even flow of the middle division (m.25–40). The transition to the return (m.51) reintroduces the first "galop" figure, and, as Love reveals that the horse he rides "has wings," the accompaniment scales up in distant key to trill, while the bass stamps downward to the home tonic and the repetition of A, with a brilliant close. The song has a natural strength and sincerity.

This manliness one finds, too, in John Ireland's most popular song, *Sea Fever*. John Masefield's lines have a strange and haunting beauty "of the lonely sea and sky," which Ireland has matched with a music that moves from the trough of one harmonic wave to another, frequently without the usual crests and transitions. Observe the nearly constant parallel motion, as in the first phrase, the aloofness of key and phrases that shift from tonal to modal to organum emphasis. The handling of the declamation is keen; the strophic repetition is direct with a rich new chromatic drift in the accompaniment of the final verse, closing with the gleam of the raised third of the last chord reached by a new pathway.

Vaughan Williams

W. H. HADOW's LISTING of the principal characteristics of English music as "strength, sanity, and tenderness,"[4] proves to be true in the case of Ralph Vaughan Williams. He has been attracted to fine verse, often noble, and steadfastly he has sought to reveal the musical meaning of the text.[5] Although strongly

---

[4] W. H. Hadow, *English Music* (New York, 1931), 174.

[5] H. C. Colles, *Essays and Lectures*, 105. Commenting on *Five Tudor Portraits*, Colles writes of the subtle problems which the composer faced in setting the lines of the sixteenth-century poet. "But the fact that all his life he has been setting to music English poetry and prose, the Bible and Bunyan, and George Herbert, Shakespeare (*Sir John in Love*) and modern poets, great and small, has given him an ease in that matter which rivals Henry Purcell's. The English language now holds no terrors for him, and his treatment of it is full of delight for the singers and the hearers."

influenced by the simple, elemental truth of folk music, he has never been content merely to make tunes. His melody issues from the words, not the lines. For him, as for the sensitive poet, each word has its own rhythm and its own melody. Yet the great poet, like the great song writer, can search for such detail and, at the same time, build the longer span which springs from the lyrical impetus of creation. William's early (1903) and very popular *Linden Lea* is in the style of a Dorset song and has all the air of the fresh out-of-doors. Squarely built in phrases of four measures, simple in design with rhythmic variation of the setting of the last line of the verse, it has the ring of rightness and distinction. There is always a lift, too, in the more resolute "I be free to go abroad" and the new harmony of the replying phrase. Most admired of his songs is *Silent Noon*.

Silent Noon

THIS IS THE NINETEENTH of the 101 sonnets by Dante Gabriel Rossetti, published as *The House of Life*. Each is "a moment's monument," in which the sensitive and imaginative poet-painter entered the world of the unseen. *Silent Noon* strikes deep into the hearts of two lovers, whose silent communion is at one with the "visible silence" of nature's noon. Can we discover how Vaughan Williams intensified by tone the magic mood of the "close-companioned inarticulate hour when two-fold silence was the song of love?"

Slow of tempo, with a quiet, sustained dignity, the music never mars the mood of peace. Here are no thick or strange harmonies, no awkward melodic progressions, no arresting dynamic bursts, for the general level is *p* to *pp*. Only twice is *f* reached, lasting for a single measure—yet the song gives a feeling of spaciousness and sonority. It is the noontide of love, not the restless morning or waning twilight. Sensitive is the key movement, which rises by thirds to the ending of line seven and then descends by thirds with a significant recitative setting of

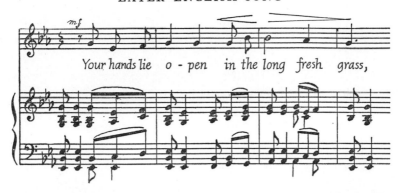

Your hands lie o - pen in the long fresh grass,

lines 9–10, picturing the suspended motion of the dragonfly. This melodically teeters within the octave and its fourth and shifts its mode. The voice then alone continues its pattern, broken on "sky"; and "so this winged" duplicates the voice's only other unaccompanied measure (m.45), leading to the home key (m.55) and return of A (m.61).

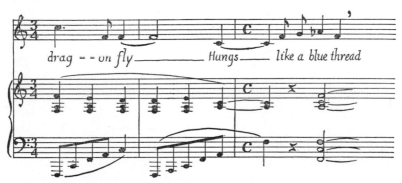

drag - - on fly_____ Hungs___ like a blue thread

Note in the graph below the natural truth of accent, which the composer discovered in the repeated iambic pentameter of the poet's lines; note the variety of phrase lengths, particularly the contrast of the 3's of A and the 4's of B.

In the analysis that follows, the italicized syllable is the composer's choice of principal accent and invites comparison with the poet's iambic pentameter. Measures of piano solo are placed between diagonals, e.g., /2/.

249

KEY		Phrase Length	Design
		/Introduction 3/	A
G	Your hands lie *open* in the *long* fresh *grass*	3	
	The finger *points* look through like *rosy blooms;*	3	
	Your *eyes* smile peace. The pasture *gleams* and glooms	2/1/1	
b-D	'Neath *bil*lowing *skies* that *scat*ter and a*mass.*	5	
B		/Interlude 4/	B
B-d#	*All* round our *nest,* far as the *eye* can *pass,*	4	
B-D#	Are *gold*en *king*-cup fields with *silver edge*	4	
..E	Where the *cow*-parsley *skirts* the hawthorn *hedge*	4	
E-C	'Tis visible *si*lence, still as the *hour*-glass.	6	
		/Interlude 4/	
A	Deep in the *sun*-searched growths the *dragon* fly	3	C
a	Hangs like a blue thread *loos*ened from the *sky,*—	4	
G	*So* this winged *hour* is *dropped* to us from *above.*	/1/8	A
	Oh! clasp we to our *hearts,* for *death*less *dower,*	4	
	This close-com*pan*ioned inar*tic*ulate *hour*	3	
	When *two*-fold *si*lence was the *song* of *love.*	6	
		/Epilogue 4/	

250

CHAPTER XXI

Song in the United States

WE shall not be concerned here with trying to isolate the ingredients which give the American flavor to music. Nor shall we be much concerned with biography, interesting as it frequently is. Seldom, however, are the man and his music one, and explanations of the man's music in terms of his native and acquired characteristics too often appear forced and lame. Why attempt to interpret the composer in terms of the physical stripe of the man? Very often, this may compel one toward exoticism and another to strong drink. Equally futile appears such "reasoning" as "being a merchant may have prevented his true growth." Another method that we shall not follow is the assignment of a composer to a particular type, with boundaries imposed. There are the experimentalists and the traditionalists, the daring and the staid, which youth might label "the quick and the dead." There have been many who, through training or inclination, have followed German or French traditions.

Naturally, in the early years of the Republic, there were no American traditions; the shaping of a nation and the building of homes made such demands on the creative forces of our forefathers that they were generally content to fall back upon the arts of the mother country. Undoubtedly too many of the succeeding generations continued to follow European traditions, but it could scarcely have been otherwise, for our population was steadily increased by immigrants. Although the young country absorbed many of these strains, it is too much to say that artistically we illustrated our national motto, *"E pluribus unum;"* American music is still not one, but many. Yet, with all the forces that pushed us toward a genial eclecticism and a harmless catholicity, there have been stronger countercurrents swirling about resolute individualists, who have listened to the voices from within rather than holding a conch shell to the ear to catch the overtones of European music. Such an individualist was William Billings, who, in the preface of his *New England Psalm Singer* (1770), signed his own declaration of independence. Its preamble states his rugged American individualism, maintaining that as he is "not confined to any rules of composition laid down by any that went before," in turn he grants freedom to others who would come after him. And he concludes: "So in fact I think it best for every composer to be his own Carver."[1]

Unfortunately, no solo songs have come down to us from this sturdy pioneer of American music. To his distinguished contemporary, Francis Hopkinson (1737–91), belongs the honor of having created the first American secular songs. Although full of honors—a signer of the Declaration of Independence, a delegate to the first Continental Congress, a moving and creative spirit in the poetry and music of Philadelphia—Hopkinson did not look lightly upon the honor that might accrue from his songs. We learn this from a letter to his friend George Washington, to whom he dedicated *Seven Songs,* the first published collection of American secular songs (1788). "However small the reputation may be that I shall derive from this work, I can not, I believe, be refused the credit of being the first native of the United States who has produced a Musical Composition."[2] There is something of the same humility and assurance earlier in the dedicatory letter, when he owns that "I can only say that it [the music] is such as a Lover not a Master of the Arts can furnish. I am neither a profess'd Poet nor a profess'd Musician; and yet venture to appear in these Characters united; for which, I confess, the Censure of Temerity may justly be brought against me."[3]

---

[1] See Chap. IX, 20.
[2] G. E. Hastings, *Life and Works of Francis Hopkinson,* 442.
[3] *Ibid.,* 441.

Something of the character of the music may be justly represented in a phrase of an advertisement in the *Pennsylvania Packet* of November 26, 1788: "These songs are composed in an easy, familiar style intended for the young Practicioners on the Harpsichord or Forte-Piano." We know, too, that the composer's daughters, as well as those of his friend Thomas Jefferson, found pleasure in them. The composer wrote: "If these Songs should not be so fortunate as to please the *young* Performers, for whom they are intended, they will at least not occasion much Trouble in learning to perform them; and this will I hope, be some Alleviation of their Disappointment."[4] Benjamin Franklin was particularly pleased with No. 5, beginning, "See down Maria's blushing Cheek," and Jefferson agreed with the poet-composer that the last of the collection (actually No. 8, added after the title page had been engraved), *The Traveller benighted and lost,* was "forcibly pathetic."[5]

On the shelves of Hopkinson's library, along with scientific, legal, and literary publications, were many scores of music. There, too, were manuscript volumes of his prose and verse. He set down in his own hand during 1759–60 some of his favorite music and scattered through its 206 pages a few compositions of his own, initialled "F.H." On page 63 appeared the first of these, the song *My Days have been so wondrous free,* the earliest secular American composition known, dating back to 1759. Almost all the verse which Hopkinson set was his own, and in this instance where he employed the innocuous lines of Thomas Parnell, the composer with poetic license substituted his own caption for Parnell's weak title, *Love and Innocence.*

The song is undoubtedly more exciting historically than musically; yet it has a certain charm and its frame and lilt are suggestive of the English songs popular in that day. Like them, it invited the harpsichordist to fill in the simple harmonies suggested by the given treble and bass. Highly acceptable was the

[4] *Ibid.,* 442.
[5] *Ibid.,* 444.

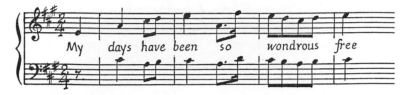

My days have been so wondrous free

cadence $I_4^6 V_7 I$, with which every important seam is affirmed. More novel was the continuity of the melody, with only a slight suspicion of repetition in its course. Fresh, too, was its rhythmic gait, a phrase of three measures responding to one of four, lending excitement as the succeeding phrase began before the cadence had filled its anticipated space (m. 14, 24, 34, 45). The excursion to the dominant is followed by a good climax as the voice mounts through the octave to descend in gay sixteenth-notes, followed by an already familiar cadence. The coda is a capital flight of fancy issuing from the sixteenth-note figure introduced in the last vocal phrase. It is difficult to understand why almost all arrangers have emasculated the song by substituting for the gay coda with its fresh ending, the cadence of the first half of the song. Evidently Francis Hopkinson did not care to purchase his unity in that fashion, and the cadence is "so wondrous free."

Although Mr. Sonneck felt that Hopkinson had not improved greatly as a composer during the thirty years between this song and his collection of *Seven Songs,*[6] some would judge the latter a bit more suave, though no more vital. *Beneath a weeping willow's shade* (No. 3) has a genial 6/8 motion with rounded cadences. Its melody has a relatively long span. The composer yields naturally to his own introduction of "Fond Echo," and the false re-entry at "The mockbird sat upon a bough" is echoed and completed by the bird's trillings in the harpsichord. Then the voice begins anew and extends and intensifies this C idea with a high note and scale fill-ins. *O'er the Hills* is a stirring huntsmen's song.

[6] O. G. Sonneck, *Francis Hopkinson,* 115.

To skip from the days before and after the Revolution to the late eighteen forties means that we must pass over the "growing pains" of American music. Music-making expanded with the country. The native musician as well as the newcomer won audiences from the meetinghouses of New England and the aristocratic *salons* of Virginia to the theaters of New Orleans and the halls of an ever extending frontier. Composers sharpened their craft on songs, operas, and symphonies evidencing some maturity. Would it seem to some, then, that we are turning back to America's musical childhood in choosing Stephen Collins Foster as the next in line of the most important creators of the Art Song in the United States? If so, let them rid their minds and hearts of any feeling of superiority and join with American people who have sung Foster's songs more often than those of any other composer. I have found no better expression of the cherished yet somewhat inexplicable place which Foster holds in the hearts of mankind than that of Bernard De Voto in an essay on "Stephen Foster's Songs," one of the sweets that fell from his full table of studies of the eighteen forties. "Art is mysterious, it is miraculous and undefined, but if that should chance to be art which a people take most closely to their bosoms and hold there most tenderly and longest, then Stephen Foster is incomparably the greatest American artist."[7]

Growing to high popularity in this period were minstrel shows, in which white actors caricatured the song, dance, and talk of the Negro. In somewhat the same degree that the white minstrels, beginning with the idea of an imitation of the darky, created a definite character that became the popular symbol of the Negro, Foster's music, resembling only slightly the "Ethiopian Melodies" they purported to be, came to represent, almost universally, Negro song and sentiment. Plaintive or gay, these melodies seem to have issued from the folk; they sing of simple and eternal things in such a direct, unstudied way that they may be classed as "the songs of the American people." *Old Folks at*

[7] B. DeVoto, "The Easy Chair," *Harper's*, Vol. 183 (1941), 109–12.

Home is just as American as a World Series, a piece of apple pie, or a skyscraper. And what a coincidence that its composer was born on the Fourth of July!

We need not stop long with the technical principles at the foundation of Foster's lyric style. Almost all of his tunes are hung on a simple frame of paired phrases and paired lines, swinging harmonically I–IV, I–V; I–IV, (V)–I. His tonal world circled in this orbit rather monotonously; beware the editings and arrangements of modern editions that spice his frugal harmonic fare. Strophic form is usual, and new music is rare for a second stanza, as in *Come where my love lies dreaming*. Although there are occasional exceptions to the harmonic and formal patterns, there is absolute constancy in the use of the major mode. This was a natural choice for the nonsense songs, such as *Camptown Races,* and inevitable in the war ballad, *We are coming Father Abraam;* but one would have expected now and again the minor mode to match the note of plaintive longing which is frequently the theme of Foster's verse.

The subject doubtlessly has helped to maintain *Old Folks at Home* among the world's most loved songs, for on the surface it seems like many another by the composer and his contemporaries. Obvious in its simplicity, monotonous in its repetition (just four measures of contrast in twenty-four), with only the melodic leap and syncopation of its second measure offering any marked difference of physiognomy from other Foster family portraits, its homely beauty lies too deep for analysis. *Old Folks at Home* is, in Milligan's phrase, "music and words in one syllable."[8] It is a bit difficult for us to understand now why the composer preferred to have this song first printed in 1852 as an "Ethiopian Melody, written and composed by E. P. Christy"; but Foster feared that prejudice against minstrel songs might injure his "reputation as a writer of another style of music."[9]

[8] H. V. Milligan, *Stephen Collins Foster,* 114.
[9] E. F. Morneweck, *Chronicles of Stephen Foster's Family,* 388–89.

Two years later there appeared an example of "another style of music," the tender love song, *Jeanie with the light brown hair*. To many, this is the peak of Foster's writing, rising both poetically and musically far above its companions. The melody, beginning on the sixth and moving with alluring curves through the dominant key, pauses a moment *on* the dominant before gently ascending the scale ad libitum to the fourth, thence to arch over to the sixth and with it to resume the haunting initial phrase. One familiar with Foster's paired phrases and paired lines would have expected the answering phrase long ago in m.7–8, but it first appears in the last two measures of the voice part. With unaccustomed extravagance, the succeeding epilogue introduces a new phrase, but closes by reaffirming the last vocal

Edward MacDowell

I PRESUME THAT every composer would appreciate most the honor of active remembrance, the repeated soundings of his music by succeeding generations. Foster has had his full share of this success, but as the writer of simple, heartfelt songs, he would be surprised that his fellow countrymen have erected to his honor on the campus of the University of Pittsburgh what has been described as "the most impressive memorial ever erected to a composer." Moreover, Foster was the first musician to be given a place in the Hall of Fame at New York University. The second musician in time to be thus honored was Edward MacDowell, frequently described as the first American composer to win international recognition. MacDowell and the composers who follow him in this chapter need no "explanations" such as were advanced for the amateur Hopkinson or the self-sufficient Foster, who feared that study might rob him of the common touch. All the later composers practiced their craft in and out of academic circles, trying to win enough skill to express whatever ideas came to them.

During MacDowell's long European apprenticeship he was

most influenced by Raff, but the pupil's music never sounded like anything other than his own. MacDowell's return to the United States after twelve years seemed to have strengthened his conviction that music must be judged as music, without any prejudice favoring the native composer. As he wrote Felix Mottl, he hated the "lumping together of American composers" as if they should not stand or fall on their own individual merits.[10] Despite his own admirable position, MacDowell was long held as the spearhead of the American school. The shouting has died down, and today performances of MacDowell's works are comparatively rare. His instrumental music has always held the favored position. This may have been partly due to the composer's feeling of restriction in matching music with poetry. Four pages of instrumental music might stem from a single line of poetry; but when faced with matching the syllables and inflections of that same line, MacDowell tended to become contractive rather than expansive. He preferred the land of his own dreams and frequently fashioned his own verse as a clue to a mood piece or as the text of a song.

Brander Matthews once said that MacDowell had "the sensitiveness of the poet and the poet's delicacy of perception as well."[11] Such gifts should have resulted in a larger proportion of great songs than we find among his forty-two. Was it the opposition, rather than the fusion of poet and composer, that hampered his free expression? Was it an instrumental bias that kept him from a free-throated vocal line? And may it not have been this same bias that paradoxically led him to suppress the piano part in his songs? Seldom does it rise to firm independence. In the eight most favored songs, introductions and epilogues are almost entirely absent, only seven measures thus scored in the eight songs. Another apparent contradiction of poet and composer was expressed by MacDowell to William

10 R. Aldrich, *Concert Life in New York* (New York, 1941), 461.
11 B. Matthews, "Commemorative Tribute to Edward MacDowell," reprinted from *Proceedings* of the Academy of Arts and Letters, Vol. IV (1922), 13.

Armstrong: "Words to me seem so paramount and as it were, apart in value from the musical setting, that while I cannot recall the melody of many of the songs I have written, the words of them are indelibly impressed upon my mind."[12]

Among ten sets of songs, Op. 47—consisting of eight songs —holds a place apart, primarily because No. 7 is *The Sea*. Huneker's opinion that this is "the strongest song of the sea since Schubert's *Am Meer*" was emphatically reaffirmed by H. T. Finck, and a whole chorus of "ayes" have seconded them. The agelong tragedy of the woman who cries in vain for the return of her lover lost at sea is voiced by William Dean Howells in simple, strong lines. MacDowell has matched them with a very direct music (thirty-five measures), clear in structure (ABA'). There is no prelude, interlude, or epilogue; yet the piano's share in the drama is great, for not only does it emphasize the composer's direction, "Broadly, with rhythmic swing," thereby portraying the relentless surge of the sea, but it suggests as well the inevitable tread of doom. Its full harmonies are rather thick and centered low, increasing in tension through both dissonance and motion at an early climax (m.8). Yet plain triads fill a third of the measures, and the simple division of the measure into two dotted quarters is maintained in all but ten bars. Every phrase is

---

[12] H. T. Finck, "Edward MacDowell-Musician and Composer," *Outlook*, Vol. 84 (1906), 988.

carefully marked concerning dynamics, and, in addition to gradations, there are six specific levels noted. The voice part, with a strangely impersonal regard for the lines, ignores the word "cries," but gradually responds to the tragic import, the octave emphasis in m.7–8 being bare and strong. MacDowell has caught the anguish of "in vain" with the delayed entry of the voice, the phrase repeated and supported by the chromatic ascending line of the bass, which had begun as early as m.6. The voice falls back into a modified repetition of the first stanza (m.21) and is again roused from its ballad-like opening phrases to a truer underlining of the text. The mark of genius is on the broken recitation of "far under, dead," and the close on the sustained mediant, gently lulled by tranquil chords, is supremely beautiful.

In the same set of songs is *Midsummer Lullaby,* a dreamlike fancy with romantic ancestry in Schumann's *Mondnacht.* The atmosphere verse *After Goethe* called forth from MacDowell an even more beautiful wonderland, some of whose beauties are these: the sweet and changing play of dissonance that seems scarcely to move as it drifts *sempre pp,* suggestive of shimmering heat; the voice caught in the accompaniment's web, but gently holding to its own narrow path; the pulsing motion of eighths begun by a measure of introduction and broken only at medial and final cadence; the strange mesmeric mood of verse and song that leads naturally to a repetition of all eight lines; and the codetta's haunting play with the flatted sixth that hovers above but finally settles on the dominant.

Entirely opposed to such quiet, trembling beauty is the passioned obviousness of *Thy Beaming Eyes.* The world loves this song for its impulsive sweep, although one notes that the composer, having begun with the rare command "loud," soon changes to "softly" and closes "soft as possible." *Merry Maiden Spring,* Op. 58, No. 3, is a light, gay, graceful song that refutes any charge of "stodgy accompaniment" or "failure to get going." Light of touch, too, and quite beguiling is the conversation of the bumblebee with the shy *Blue-Bell,* Op. 26. Of all the sets of MacDowell's songs, its title, *From an Old Garden,* is most similar to the choice of names for the collections of his piano lyrics beginning with *Woodland Sketches.*

Chadwick, Foote, and Nevin

THE CONTEMPORARIES of MacDowell who have more than a historic right to a place in a review of the Art Song are Chadwick, Foote, and Nevin. Following the death of George W. Chadwick (1854–1931), Henry Hadley, in a commemorative tribute before the American Academy of Arts and Letters, noted that the passing of Chadwick closed a definite period in our musical history, a period rich in achievement.[18] It would be profitable to explore the pioneer work of Chadwick and trace his healthy influence through example and precept, but we must be content with a few characterizations of several songs. The Op. 14 of 1885 begins with the setting of a verse of his favorite poet, Arlo Bates. *The Danza* is a gay dance tune of some span, yet simply and economically made. The accompaniment has a real lilt, which swings up to the second beat of the measure by a triplet, changed in the excitement of the second stanza to four sixteenths. Another delightful modification in the second stanza is the repetition of the line, "and her teeth were white as snow." This brings with it new music, which returns, however, to the pert refrain, "By Inez I was taught." The interlude now modulates enharmonically to the major third below, for the first division of the final stanza. The melody is now sung by the piano, the voice adding comments *sotto voce.* Soon the voice takes an alto a sixth below its former level, after which the accompaniment sinks back to its original role. There is a new twist given the final phrase, which sacrifices its former sauciness for greater brilliance.

[18] H. Hadley, "Commemorative Tribute to George W. Chadwick," American Academy of Arts and Letters, Pub. No. 77 (1932), 99.

In addition to the Creole Inez of *The Danza,* Chadwick was drawn to other exotic subjects, as witness *Bedouin Love Song, Egyptian Song* from *Ben Hur, Songs from the Persian,* and the favorite *Allah.* Someone has complained that this last is more Ethiopian than Mohammedan, but whatever its race—and it is of pure New England stock—its color is warm. Chadwick's setting of Longfellow's *Allah* has weight and majesty without awkward squareness. Contributing to its success is the movement of the triplets in the cadence of the first division. This graceful motion dominates the B division, which goes to new keys. The modulation back to home key seems at first a little perfunctory and tightly spaced, until we discover that the return of A is marked pianissimo and the melody is now supported by delicately arpeggiated chords. Four measures from the close the voice line arches a third above its former high, not to produce a climax, but to add a bit of lyric beauty.

Almost invariably coupled are the names of Chadwick and Foote, although they had little in common except period and place. Arthur Foote (1853–1937) was one of the few American composers of his day who did not have the German stamp of approval. His discipline under American teachers may not have made him as facile in contrapuntal technique as Chadwick, and natively Foote may have been less gifted with sharp wit and keen sense of color; but Foote knew the voice, and he loved the medium of song. He can be ingenious, but one of his greatest virtues is a simplicity that is sincere, thoroughly unaffected. *I'm wearin' awa'* and *Irish Folk Song* were both written in less time and more easily than almost any of the others, as the composer tells us, with an undertone of regret that the public should love them best.[14] Not that the public always chooses wisely, but in this instance these songs are representative of Foote's simple, homespun sentiment. The setting of Lady Nairn's Scottish poem required only an eight-measure span, repeated with slight intensifications for the second stanza. The warm, creamy melody

14 Finck, *Songs and Song Writers,* 233.

centers about the mediant, most frequently sustained on the second beat of the gently rolling 9/8 measure. The climax—for within its small limits there is this satisfaction—is pointed not only by mounting line, but by a break in the smooth roundness of the motion of threes. The emphasis by the unit of four (m.7), the rising pitch, and, for the first time, the doubling of the voice by the piano—these features produce within this small frame the high light of this Scottish mood-picture.

Some critics evidently have thought of Chadwick and Foote as moving musically with ease in aristocratic neighborhoods while Ethelbert Nevin lived on the other side of the railroad tracks. His traffic in sentiment is well known; almost everyone has admired it at some time or other. I can recall the day when the top of my Parnassus was occupied not by Apollo playing to the muses, but by myself whistling or singing Nevin's *Rosary* to my own accompaniment. This song occupies a place in the United States like that of Sullivan's *Lost Chord* in England; each has been the country's best seller.

From the day in February, 1898, when *The Rosary* had its first public performance, it has been a part of the American scene. This song is genuine; Nevin did not write down to catch the public's ear, nor did he suppress the warm, rich sentiment that welled up within him as he was moved by the verse of Robert Cameron Rogers. Love, "memories that bless and burn," absence, loss with resignation—the poem is crowded with sentiment, a perfect vehicle for Nevin's impulsive melody, warm harmonies, and impassioned climaxes. One admires the natural change to 3/4 for the last line of each stanza. But note that each time the repeated sixth (m.6, 14, 21) progresses to a different music, which seems the only right underlining of the poet's lines, varying in length and mood. The countermelody in the accompaniment of the third stanza, wishfully and revealingly marked vibrato, lends new interest during its four measures. The piano then stresses each syllable of the next phrase and wholeheartedly joins in the stirring climax. Rivaling this song in popularity is Nevin's setting of Kingsley's *Oh! that we two were Maying*. Its accompaniment glides along in sixteenth-note motion with an occasional shadow of alto in the right-hand thumb. The "coda" brings an unexpected cadence with coloration of a flatted third and added sixth. The tender sentiment in Nevin's songs for and about children is sincere, inspired by the verse of Riley, Field, and Stevenson.

Horatio W. Parker

IF ONE TRACES the ascending line of parentage of present-day American composers, it is almost certain to lead to John K. Paine (1839–1906), the Harvard professor who has been called "the Dean of American composers." One of the most fruitful lines descends from him to George W. Chadwick, and thence through Horatio W. Parker (1863–1919) to a host of moderns. Chadwick, who outlived his famous pupil some twenty years, characterized Parker as one who hated shams and pretense. The small number of his works for orchestra Chadwick felt resulted from Parker's need of words as a vehicle and poetry as an inspiration. This verbal inspiration would appear most favorable for solo songs, and there are twelve sets of them; but actually, for him, the solo voice seemed a weak medium compared to the chorus, whose mass, space, and contrapuntal organization spurred him to his best.

Parker, however, does not appear to have been hampered by the boundaries of *The Lark now leaves his wat'ry nest*, Op. 47, No. 6, the most admired of his songs. It is the last of the set entitled *Old English Songs* (1899). The poem by the seventeenth-century Sir William Davenant inspired Parker to something of an English musical style which trips gayly along. After the delicately scored introduction, the voice closes its five-measure phrase with a winged cadence, immediately echoed in the piano. The second vocal phrase leads to the relative minor, where a longer poising at the end of the imitative reply is necessary to get us ready for the return to the home key and a refrain, "Awake! Awake!" There is life in the sequence and in the countermelody of the bass, and the repetition (m.27) is varied in both voice and piano. The introduction (m.36) of the second stanza warns us that this is to be no mere routine repetition. Its second vocal phrase is telescoped; the interlude following leads not to the expected refrain, but to new material ("But still the lover wonders"). While the accompaniment attempts to draw away to new tonalities, the dominant of the home key persists and is finally rewarded by the refrain (m.63) with an extended close, in which at last the lark mounts "singing, until the clouds and sky about him are ringing." Strange to say, Parker, knowing full well that all singers are not larks, has scored an optional ending which is as common as a sparrow and twice as uninteresting. The ornamental cadences and the lift of the coda are most appropriate to the text, but there is much of the song that is earth-bound. Its melody is too square and angular, and the principal rhythmic motive,

$$\cup \mid \_ \cup \cup \cup \mid \_ \cup \cup$$

in its persistence and lack of imagination is far more like a woodpecker than a lark.

James H. Rogers

A LITTLE SPACE IS GIVEN to James H. Rogers (1857–1940) not only because of his own gifts to song, but also because he is typical of a group of composers in every generation, not one of whom becomes a cornerstone of the temple of music building in their day, yet each of whom has fitted his stone into the pattern and has given firm support to the common cause. Rogers never seemed to lack ideas. He broke into a tune easily, and, although his melodies seldom reached great depths, they are clear and graceful and have an air of health and wellbeing. Rogers was a natural composer, never seeking distinction through the sensational or recherché. He is never awkward and is always singable.

His accompaniments are graceful and contribute their fair share. They are never merely fussy when they get in motion, and everything falls into place and counts. His musical plans are firm, the keys well ordered and moving in the right direction. To liven the texture, there is often counterpoint, but never so much that it obscures the way. Much admired is his setting of Frederick Patterson's *At Parting*. While the voice moves in a simple, graceful line, the accompaniment swings to and fro; the right hand is active with a cunningly spaced sixteenth-note figure that adds a little piquancy by an occasional nonharmonic tone, such as the sixth in the opening pair of phrases. The B idea enters in m.9 and exactly balances A, offering, however, a pleasant change of key to the major third below and shifting the active accompaniment to the left hand. Smoothly turned is the way back to home key for the return of A (m.18), modified and extended in tranquil coda.

Stronger fibered, indeed, rising to a stunning climax and—what is a thousand times more difficult—receding from it with real dignity to close in quiet lyric mood, is *The Star*.[15] The contrast of the wide-sweeping arpeggios and sustained chords, the doubled support of the voice line, or little or no support, the difference of pulse, and drifting modulation in the mid-division—these are a few of the marks of a skilled craftsman and able builder.

Mrs. H. H. A. Beach

EVEN IN CHILDHOOD Mrs. Beach (1867–1944) could not stomach the diet of musical "gum-drops" which her playmates relished. The most effective punishment for her childhood indiscretions was not a spanking, but a rendition by her mother of Gottschalk's *Last Hope*.[16] When such a girl matured into a composer, naturally she had no taste for the trivial. Serious, dignified, an expert craftsman, though inclined to load the score fearing it

[15] Plato's lines are in *Greek Anthology*, Book VII, #699.
[16] J. T. Howard, *Our Contemporary Composers*, 16.

might seem thin, she worked in many media, but never with finer lyric results than in song. Most of the verse which she chose to set from Browning is quite free from involved artifice and concealed meaning. There is no friction set up between his lines and her music in *The Year's at the Spring* and *Ah, Love but a Day*. Commissioned by the Browning Society of Boston in 1904 to set the first to music, she had postponed the task because of her work on a violin and pianoforte sonata. Returning to Boston from its New York *première,* the composer tells us that she suddenly thought of the Browning Society, and, meditating on the poem, she allowed it to take possession of her. The song was sketched before she reached Boston, and, in her words, "It is the poem which gives the song its shape, its mood, its rhythm, its very being."[17] In the first section of the drama, *Pippa Passes,* from without is heard the voice of Pippa singing a gay, fresh, morning song, and Mrs. Beach's setting gives the feeling of a carefree, unpremeditated burst of song.

In the first poem of the *Dramatis Personae,* "James Lee's Wife speaks at the Window" of far different things, not of constancy and joy, but of change and fear. Mrs. Beach wisely omitted the final stanza, giving a loose unity to the through-composed music of the first two stanzas by repetitions of the rhythm of the first vocal phrase. In each stanza, she has immediately repeated the first pair of lines and returned to them for the close, which in both instances called from her a most sensitive reflection of mood. In the first stanza—after its pensive opening—the lines have led to the frightening realization that summer has stopped; and the repetition of the key lines (m.21–4) brings sudden anguish, almost directly suppressed, the phrase closing quietly, but filled with sadness. The second stanza opens with soft entreaty, aided by the tonic major and the slow-motion-tremolando accompaniment in triplets. Soon the doubts mount to fears, the triplets now *agitato,* pulsing in blocks of fours. The

[17] H. H. A. Beach, "The How of Creative Composition," *The Etude,* March, 1943, p. 151.

cry of the impassioned climax is suddenly broken. The voice resumes its note of entreaty, but closes wistfully questioning on the repeated dominant, "Wilt thou change too?"

Charles Wakefield Cadman

AGAIN, FROM A HOST of composers, we choose one not only for his unique contribution, but also as representative of those who shared his views. There have been many like Cadman (1881–1946), who more or less seriously worked for an American national school founded upon "American folk music." To some this meant music of the Indians, to others that of the Negro or cowboy. Nowadays people get a good deal less excited in discussing this subject of nationalism in music. The United States is a big country, and her peoples have sprung from such different heritages that a truly representative music can never be founded upon a single element of her greatness. We should recall William Billings' counsel that "each composer should be his own Carver." The important thing is that each makes the best music that he can in his own way, and thus we will hew our way to our musical destiny.

The composer takes inspiration where he finds it, and nothing roused Cadman's spirit or incited him to composition like a bit of Indian music. Although he collected some of his materials directly from the Omahas, his interest was never primarily ethnological. Indian themes were motives, which the composer translated into Cadmanese. He idealized these slender materials as the title page of his most successful group of songs illustrates: "Four American Indian Songs / Founded upon Tribal Melodies / Harmonized and Elaborated by Charles Wakefield Cadman, Op. 45." Best loved of all is *From the Land of the Sky-blue Water*. There is a haunting strangeness in the flageolet love call of the Omahas, with its twirl of whole tones at the end. The succeeding tribal melody, with its pentatonic outline and syncopated twist, is very singable. The harmonization is simple, the alto line of the right hand in the accompaniment offering now a countermelody, now doubling the voice, and the whole making good use of the rhythmic quirk of the love song. The ending of the first quatrain has risen to the dynamic climax of the song, reinforced by a new key, a major third higher. A short interlude brings us back to home key and the first phrase of the tribal melody, its *pp* suggested by the stealing "to her lodge at dawning." The accompaniment is lightened by being lifted an octave. There is real charm in Cadman's extension of the first phrase, the whole song seeming to be spun of the same lyric theme. A delicate reminiscence of the flageolet call closes this most popular of Indian idealizations.

Sidney Homer

THE EARLY TRAINING of Sidney Homer (1864–) was similar to that of Parker in that they both studied with Chadwick and then went to Munich for work with Rheinberger. Then, while Parker was gaining an international reputation through his choral works and finding time for many engagements outside his post at Yale, Homer was happy in writing songs under the inspiration of his wife, the superb contralto Louise Homer. That he was not anxious about rushing into print is evident from his delightful account in *My Wife and I,* where he tells how he bundled up a few songs and explained to the publisher that he had written songs for a number of years (seventeen in all) and wished Mr. G. S. to hear some of them.[18] At an impromptu musicale which then took place, a set of eight Tennyson songs was chosen first for publication.

Homer tells us how queer some of the great poetry appears to the song writer, who finds it now and again "angular, stiff, heavy, long-worded, stretched beyond the musical phrase, interrupted with parentheses. I should be ashamed to tell how many big things I started. I loved them but they didn't love

18 S. Homer, *My Wife and I,* 120.

music. They would not "make themselves," and unless a song makes itself the game is up. All the king's horses and all the king's men. . . . Much of my life has been wasted in vain attempts."[19] Homer is at his best when he sings of simple things in a simple musical style. He dares write a good jingling tune, as in *A Banjo Song*. The thirteen-measure setting of W. E. Henley's *Dearest* gives evidence of his concentration and warm emotional sweep. The definitive setting of R. L. Stevenson's *Requiem,* Op. 15, No. 2, required only eight measures—less if we subtract the final cadence's repetition of m.3–4. How tempting to most composers would have been changes in the second stanza, but Homer was content with the short phrases of his melody, undimmed by tears, and broad chordal masses with religious suggestion in their pauses on III (m.2) and II (m.6).

Sing Me a Song of a Lad That Is Gone

THE NATURAL MUSICAL REFLECTION of Robert Louis Stevenson's verse, whose first stanza becomes a refrain, would be a rondo, ABACADA. But note that while Homer gives the feeling of the couplets of a rondo, he is actually varying and transforming the basic materials, A (refrain) m.2–9, B (couplet) m.11–18; the form resulting is: ABA(19)b'(28) A(36) A'(45) A"(52). The verse might have jogged along in even eights, but Homer's music gives it a spirited gait with a quarter followed by two sixteenths, allegro. The melody has a fine, free, singable line that belongs to the faith and trust of a youth as he starts voyaging. The sea is a hard master, and as the poet asks where the glory of youth has gone, the melody has lost some of its open joy and the harmonies have become tensive. Even the repetition of the chord of the introductory measure seems strident, but it serves to reintroduce the refrain which recalls the youthful hopes. Then, as the man longs to be the lad that is gone, the meter is stretched to a 9/8, and the minor mode is strengthened by the

[19] *Ibid.,* 192.

determined pulsing of the repeated eighths of the accompaniment, supported by a closely bound descending bass. A sort of bravado marks the return of the refrain, *ff*. Soon, however, *più lento,* over a tonic pedal, the once jaunty melody seems broken. The accompaniment has lost its lilt, as it moves in even eighths, and the strength of the chords ebbs in their new rolled harmonies. The final transformation extends this mood as the refrain idea tries to fit the 9/8 measure, but at the last appears in its "youth's" tempo and meter. Is there a touch of bitter regret, at the thought of the man that might have been, suggested in the lowered seventh of the chord on "sea," and in the weak, single line of the right hand in the next to the last measure?

CHAPTER XXII

The Later American School

THE careers of several of the composers considered in the preceding chapter have extended well into this century, but
those dealt with here are more truly representative of the twentieth century trends of the Art Song in the United States. The
facets of the current scene are extremely diverse, and no attempt
will be made to throw the strongest light on the extremists, those
daring experimenters who for many are the true moderns. Unforced and honest reflections of romanticism and impressionism
still persist, and to some these modes of expression are inherently more compatible with song than are striking angularity and
dissonance, which seem more natural to contemporary expression in other media.

The experiments in subject and technique of expression ven-
tured in the first half of this century indicate that music has been
moving through the first phase of a new cycle. A definitive style
has not yet emerged. Some who were working toward it have
wearied in the reshaping of a tonal world or the establishment
of an atonal world, and there has been many a "masterly retreat to the heavily fortified Brahms Line," as Virgil Thomson
has pointed out. One composer who maintained his forward
position and who was one of the most courageous yet shyly sensitive spirits of his generation was Charles T. Griffes.

Charles T. Griffes

DESPITE THE tragic fact that his scrupulous scoring and early
death (he died in 1920 at the age of thirty-six) left us with so

few works, there is little difference of opinion regarding Griffes's high place in American music. A succession of forces from without—German, Russian, French, Oriental—by which his hypersensitive nature was attracted, contributed a bit of color here and there, but the glow of his music came from within. There is plenty of evidence of the struggle that was his in the shaping of new beauty. The elusive and ever changing goal he sought led to experiments. Griffes never allowed them to run rampant, but, on the other hand, he never curbed his imaginings in order to win an audience with a familiar music. Even though there is a note of the proud in his work, there is nothing smug or static about it; there is no posing and beating of the chest. He was a sincere and honest craftsman trying to reveal the rich fancies which he had imagined.

The first set of songs, captioned *Five German Poems for a Solo Voice with Piano Accompaniment,* published in 1909 without opus number, contains *Auf geheimem Waldespfade* ("By a Lonely Forest Pathway"), the most frequently performed of his twenty-four songs. One reason for its early acceptance was that it seemed to stem in an evolutionary line from Brahms and Strauss. It has maintained its favored place not so much because of its likeness to others as because of its unique beauty. N. Lenau's poem is a song of the longing of the loved one, who dreams of his dearest as he wanders down a secret path in the darkening, rustling woods. The trees speak to him of her, and in fancy he hears her voice singing in the distance, dying away.

An introductory measure sets up the basic sixteenth-note motion of this song and begins a tremulous dissonance that is seldom broken. Griffes is here intent upon mood, and this is not interrupted by any minute picturing of the text. The stanzas offer the natural punctuation of the flowing music with a measure of rest for the voice (m.10, 19), while the piano meditatively prepares the way for the succeeding verse. There is a new triplet figuration, introduced for the second stanza. Beginning quietly, its mounting climax in the relative minor (m.17–8) has been intensified by the chromatic descent of the bass. The $^6_4$ chord of the climax (m.8 in stanza 1; m.17 in stanza 2) has been "resolved," and the triplet motion stilled, when with radiance the music pushes outward to a new $^6_4$ in distant key, at the very beginning of the final stanza. The voice quietly arches to new heights and repeats and intensifies the high note from a skip, thence to sweep downward an octave and a fourth. The one

Till the mu-sic of thy sing-ing On the wa-ter dies a-way.

break in its diatonic descent, a small third from "ein*en*" to "*lieb*lichen," could not be otherwise, for m.26 reaffirms m.24, its repetition at the octave a chief reason for the great musical satisfaction one feels in this final phrase. It is interesting to compare Franz's setting of this last phrase, where the voice has quietly risen through a minor tonic chord to drop to the fifth, supported by a I$^6_4$, almost as if Franz were imagining the lover intently listening to catch the last dying echo of the loved one's voice.[1] Griffes, however, after a perfect mood-picture, has emphasized the lover's joy at the sound of her voice. He brings added unity to the song through the piano's epilogue, which resumes the opening measure and the rustling of the added sixth.

It often happens that a composer's most spontaneous songs occur early in his career. As he matures, he is inclined to question the impulse, and second thought leads to a third and often to inaction. He ponders and philosophizes. In the case of Griffes, "maturity" came early, and sustained joy was the rarest of experiences in his musical expression. Exceptional, then, is the gaiety of *We'll to the Woods to gather May,* Op. 3, No. 3. Even more surprising is the swashbuckling vigor with which he begins John Masefield's *An Old Song Resung,* Griffes's last song, dated July, 1918, and published posthumously. Marked "*Giocoso*

[1] R. Franz, Op. 2, No. 1, the first song in his only cycle, *Schilflieder.*

ma non troppo presto," the hearty rhythmic beat of the introductory chords, colored by open fifths and a yawning space between the right and left hands, swings into a sturdy tune, at first filled in and around the tonic chord. Interesting contrast of color is gained by the low pitch of the accompaniment (m.7–10) and by the above-center of the piano part through the second stanza. This is a repetition of the first stanza with modifications of the voice line, richer harmonic overtones which the high-pitched chords can easily absorb, and a new triplet figuration beginning in m.19.

While the "merry men were cheering" and "the tall ship rolled," the music has run ahead of the "summer wind" in somewhat objective ballad style. But there is only the hollow frame of this style in the final stanza, which is filled with a sharply sinister music driving to its dread climax. The stanza opens with the introductory chords carried on while the voice bravely begins the old refrain. But the desperate gaiety of the men "singing songs and drinking" while their ship was sinking demands a new music: tense, seemingly disordered in its chromatic veerings, and wildly exciting in its rhythmic vehemence. The crashing chords and leaping octaves of the graphic, powerful climax (m.34–6) are followed by a dramatic silence. A faint tolling in reflective mood (m.37) leads to the pictorial falling chords beginning on the word "sank." The strangely distant pedal (E-natural in the key of A-flat) is brought into focus by the enharmonic F-flat, which sinks to the dominant, soon quietly supported by the tonic. A wisp of the refrain returns. The moaning sixths begun in m.40 continue until all is wiped out with the final curt tonic chord, *sf.*

Lament of Ian the Proud

GRIFFES WAS NATURALLY attracted to the writings of Fiona Macleod, the pseudonym of William Sharp, under which he freely spun beauties in verse and "prose-rhythms" that were frequently colored with "the color of a lost day and of a beauty that is legend." Thus he wrote in the preface to *Foam of the Past* from which Griffes chose the *Lament of Ian the Proud,* first song in his Op. 11. *The Rose of the Night* and *Thy Dark Eyes to Mine,* from the same author, complete the opus.

Inspired by Gaelic legend, Fiona Macleod portrays the old and blind Ian the Proud, whose spirit is troubled. He is haunted and oppressed by grief. Is the crying he hears in the wind a foreboding of some new sorrow, or is it the old grief, the remembrance of one who lies buried on the moor? The verse is simple and direct with seldom more than one word a line other than monosyllables. This may have prompted Griffes to his syllabic melody, in which there are only two instances of a slur. He, too, like the poet, evidently felt the tendency of the verse to become an intoned chant in which repetition holds an important place. The leitmotif of this lament is stated at the very beginning over a primitive bourdon of root and fifth.

Of the number of melodic and rhythmic variations of the theme, let us note only the pathetic twisting of its strong profile at m.38, *tempo primo.* Over diminished harmony, the melody, *pp* and *flebile,* is unable to rise to its perfect fifth. This seems symbolic of the old Scot, stooped and bent, almost broken by the remembrance of a stone among the heather, on which is written: "She will return no more." And then, as it were, Ian the Proud squares his shoulders and faces the wind. Momentarily, there seems respite as the major is touched (m.44); but it can not be sustained, and while the voice intones its last phrase on the dominant, the simple chords in the quietest motion since the introduction sink to the tonic. The drama behind this has been reflected in the dynamics that have been mostly in the realm of piano, but have risen to strong climaxes. The triplet has woven a background, now restless, now peaceful. Pitch is an important factor, an air of the somber, even dour, furthered by the deep-voiced accompaniment. The dramatic device of the tremolando marks the mid-division of the poem, the piano interlude framing it on either side. Note the important role of the piano, which rises to solo status in twenty of the fifty-three measures. The song, although originally conceived for voice and orchestra, was published first for voice and piano. It has had no popular success, but each season since its *première* in 1919, *The Lament of Ian the Proud* has won a few devoted friends, who feel it to be one of the great songs.

Bainbridge Crist

CRIST (1883–) forsook the law after practicing it for six years, and since then his avocation has become his profession. For him, this was like emerging from the bailiwick of prose into the boundless domain of poetry. As might be expected of one who had been trained to perceive the exact, inescapable meaning of a verbal phrase, Crist as a composer has been consistently attentive to his text. He has written most discerningly of the rhythm and values of specific words and lines in *The Art of Setting Words to Music*. It appears that the solution of the problem is less an obedience of laws, strict as those of the Medes and Persians, than a choice resulting from a weighing of physical and spiritual values. Crist may be drawn particularly to the latter, but he is not one to believe in faith without works; inspiration and technique he holds to be "virtually inseparable."[2] He loves the highly imaginative, the exotic. These are combined and touched with whimsy in *Chinese Mother Goose Rhymes* (1917), based in part on actual Chinese themes.

[2] J. T. Howard, *Bainbridge Crist*, 8.

Crist is even more successful in capturing the tenuous fancies of mystical verse. Thus the poems of Walter De la Mare have attracted him again and again, but never has the meeting of the two been more propitious than in the song, *Into a Ship Dreaming*. Will the flaming sun ever be weary of wand'ring? Will ever a shepherd lead all the little stars like lambs to the fold? Will the wand'rer ever take us all into his ship, dreaming? Such imaginative dreams need a light touch. Yet, as Crist folds this fantasy into tones, he covers it with more than a filmy veil. Here is substance and direction. The accompaniment looks of fuller √ body than it is, because so much of the time the left hand keeps gently stroking a dominant pedal, alternating with a tenor countermelody. The voice and the right hand move in strangely independent melodic lines, considering the constant feeling, and seldom do the parts actually double. The pattering of eighth-notes is lulling. The harmonies are sweet with dissonance, so spaced that they produce a soft mist. Note, for example, the chord sustained in m.7 ("moon"), where five consecutive "letters" are sounding. Almost a quarter of the song moves in another notational world, sharps replacing flats. The climax, which needs only an *mf* in such an ethereal atmosphere, begins *pp;* the major chord is replaced by an augmented triad widely spaced ("far," m.27) and slowly filled in as the left hand rises; the harmonies then move through new channels, as if seeking where

the islands are in the clouds of the west. After the coda, they are still seeking as the left hand adds a sixth to the tonic chord.

Wintter Watts

WILLIAM TREAT UPTON once characterized Wintter Watts (1884–) as thoroughly American in his work, pointing out as typical his enthusiasm, his directness of expression, and the "elemental simplicity" of his harmonic backgrounds.[3] His accompaniments are the pianist's delight, although the singer may occasionally fear that the accompaniment is going to run away with the song. Unlike many songs with important piano parts, however, these songs never reduce the voice to a mere obbligato in a piano solo. The composer's reason for writing seems to have been, in the phrase of the poet who frequently set him singing, "beauty has filled my heart."

Sara Teasdale, author of the above line, created a pensive beauty as once she mused on twilight and a bird's calling. The opening line suggested to Watts the principal motive of his song *Wings of Night*. The repeated note (the dominant during the first seven measures) symbolizes the falling rain, but what gave rise to the composer's invention of the transparent, graceful, arching melody of the voice is one of the mysteries of creation

[3] W. T. Upton, *Art-Song in America* (Boston, 1930), 183–84.

Dream -i -ly o-ver the roofs - - The cold

which no one explains. The melody is doubled by the alto, and where the voice sustains the close of a line, the bass joins in thirds (m.4) or sixths (m.27). The most important change appearing in the opening of the second stanza is the lifting of the accompaniment an octave. There is a warm surge of new music for the last two lines, and the final repetitions of "calling" for a moment summon the deeper emotional undertones of the song, the voice's rise and fall of a half step being strangely effective. The coda does not respond to this, but continues its charming melody, trembling delicately before the final chord.

Rather meditatively, the lover thinks how "Blue are her eyes." As the melody sustains the dominant ("sea"), parallel fifths rock back and forth in the bass. Then he calls to mind her voice, the music beginning as before, but changing to 6/8, the accompaniment replying to the voice's new melody. And then as he remembers the touch of her lips, the music glows. The voice rises as the bass descends, a tenor adding intensity by its stubbornly repeated figure. This is followed by chords pulsing six to the measure until the climax, where the movement broadens to twos, and the fortissimo gradually dies away as the chords of the lover's first wondering (m.8–11) return.

High among cycles of American songs is *Vignettes of Italy,* nine songs to text by Sara Teasdale. *Stresa,* the last of the cycle, somewhat exceeds the bounds of a vignette, a dainty sketch. Within its six pages there are soaring climaxes, but its chief concern is a delicate beauty. *Ponte Vecchio, Florence* is filled with the sounds of the bells as they ring over the Arno, not once striking the second or seventh. The higher pitched bells begin an *ostinato* measure-long figure, pealing throughout. Offering some slight variation to its intriguing monotony are infrequent alterations of the third (first in m.8) and a momentary change of key (m.27–8). An additional jangling (m.19) and the clang of the big bourdon (m.21) accompany the poet's beseeching the bells to cease, for "time takes too much from me." But the bells continue to the end, returning to their simpler, calmer music as the poet considers eternity granted to rock and river. To the poet's meditations on the *Ruins of Paestum,* Watts has given a music that sounds distant, and lonely, and strange. The harmonies, although not at all "archaic," create a feeling of another time, as an expected resolution escapes in a different direction (m.7–8) or a cadence is blurred (m.10). *From a Roman Hill* has a most engaging running figure that moves in eighth-note motion with grace and freedom in the 7/4 measure. There is a sensuous color in the harmony, a free play of the decorative element, and a favored second key—as well as a coda—that remind one of Liszt. The rippling eighths are calmed as the poet would retain all beauty. Why should dawn pass "with unremembered things?" The voice then comes to a close with a gently sweeping phrase, inherently Italian.

John Alden Carpenter

ONE OF THE MOST distinguished personages of American song is John Alden Carpenter (1876–1951). With the passing years the orchestra had become his chief medium, but song was his first and for some time his only love. He was born to the purple, both economically and aesthetically, and his wealth and refinement have aided rather than hampered his musical independence. He was a "Sunday music maker," a man of business during the week, and in each field he prospered. His native refinement made him sensitive in the choice of texts and naturally influenced his setting of them. In his student days, the French impressionists were rapidly displacing the German romanticists in the affections of the young composers of this country. Carpenter was naturally attuned to their fragile imagery, but he was too sincere a craftsman merely to imitate their style. Some have charged him with being an eclectic, an objectivist, but his music is far too persuasive in its beauty to be other than in his own style.

His first group of songs appeared in 1912, "a memorable year in American song," and each of the eight has a distinct personality. Evidently Carpenter had no predetermined method and allowed each poem to shape its own song. *Don't Ceäre,* a poem in Dorsetshire dialect by William Barnes, is caught "to the life" by Carpenter, who begins with the frank squareness of a folk tune. There is the drone bass; the voice accents the first beat of the measure, and one can almost hear the peasant shoes joining in a hearty if not boisterous way. The cap line, "I don't ceäre if they do," is more subtly approached, the figure of the introduction accompanying it. The hold, which it leads to, is followed by a new single strand. The accompaniment of the second stanza, however, is enriched with a little counterpoint, and, as with folk musicians when they get warmed up, an embellishment is added (m.51) here and there. The accompaniment to the final stanza is more sustained, with the punctuation at the end of eights, "vull o' smiles." There is a gay abandon accompanying the last "do" and a strong but droll sense of finality in the ending open fifth.

The ability to imagine and create tone patterns of sharp contrast is one of the marks of the great composer. A mirthful scherzo may follow or precede a solemn andante. The spirited and almost facetious *Don't Ceäre* is by the same composer who discovered the mysterious enchantment of *The Sleep that flits on Baby's Eyes.* This is one of the six songs in *Gitanjali* ("Song Offerings"), the poems in prose by Rabindranath Tagore. The philosophy of this Indian mystic found a sympathetic follower in Carpenter, who could penetrate to its refuge of inward serenity or climb to its open sky flooded with a world-filling light. Illustrating the latter is the last of the cycle, *Light my Light,* whose heroic sweep and *fff* climax few have fully realized. Opposed to the refulgent brilliance of that world is one which is "dimly lit with glow-worms"; there great mysteries are made clear to the humble of heart. And in such spirit Carpenter set the text of *The Sleep that flits on Baby's Eyes.* Quietly he casts his spell of magic. There is warmth in his coloring, but no straining after the oriental. The introductory measures, both in

harmony and in alternation of meter, form a mystic prelude to
the tonic chord (m.4). The answer to the question of the first
section has a gentle repetition of tonic (m.12–3), then sixth
(m.14–5), then fifth (m.16–20). The alternation of the harmonies and of the right and left hand produce a feeling of a
world where nothing presses. Lovely in color is the harmony as
it drops on "glow-worms" and "buds." The octave jumps of the

tonic pedal (m.34–8), as voice and chord sustain, are like little
bells accompanying the mystic's revelation. The cadence repeats a three-measure falling pattern with slight but significant
changes, closing in the soft haze produced by the added sixth.

The first of the cycle, *When I bring to you colour'd toys,* is
concerned with the understanding that comes through gifts to
a child. His eagerness and joy bring fresh realization of the inner
significance of things. Carpenter has suggested the new-found
joy in the lilt of the first melodic kernel, its importance to the
color of the song shown in seventeen repetitions. The three paragraphs of text bring the three natural divisions of design. Something of childish pitch is found in the high accompaniment of
the first part, colored largely by parallel fourths and fifths. The
mid-division (m.33–50) centers in dancing figures, jumping
octaves followed by skipping arpeggios. New keys are touched
before the return (m.52). The final section gives unity through

its clear reference to the first division, but both voice and accompaniment are freely modified. The coda (m.69–79) turns back to the first motive, closing in gentle gaiety.

Charles E. Ives

A PULITZER PRIZE was awarded in May, 1947, to Charles E. Ives (1874–) for his *Symphony No. 3,* composed in 1911. He appeared little more interested in the honor than did Stephen Foster when *Jeanie with the Light Brown Hair,* composed in 1854, topped the "Hit Parade" in 1941. At least Foster had the satisfaction of hearing his songs as soon as they were scored, but Ives's musical adventures frightened performers, who generally decided not to waken the music from its troubled sleep. The composer, a successful businessman, found his fun in creation and could afford to ignore the public. This aloofness, coupled with his abhorrence of empty formulas and flabby "musical-muscles," led him to many experiments in which he anticipated modern devices such as polyharmony, polytonality, tone-clusters, and sustained use of dissonance. In the postlude to *114 Songs,* published and distributed at the expense of the composer in 1922, Ives freely admits that some of the songs "have little musical value," some "might be given to students as examples of what not to sing," and some "cannot be sung." He closes his homespun philosophizing with assertions and queries concerning the rights of a song. "If it feels like walking along the left hand side of the street, why not let it? ... Must it always be a ribbon to match the voice? Should it not be free at times from the dominion of the thorax, the diaphragm, the ear, and other points of interest? ... In short, must a song always be a song!" And the echoes rebounding from this volume shout "No!"

Some of the vocal lines certainly are free of the dominion of the thorax—not to mention the pharynx and larynx—resulting in what is awkward and ungrateful to the singer. One recalls a few exceptional artists who might be described as "singers without voices," but it seems to carry paradox beyond the realm of reason to issue "songs that cannot be sung." Let us ignore them, as well as the rather generous number which are of no musical value. Still to be reckoned with are a few songs which, in spite of (or because of) their unorthodox behavior, strengthen one's belief in the emotional and intellectual vitality of our American school. *Charlie Rutlage* is loaded with dynamite— such diverse and dangerous elements as the use of the speaking voice "following the piano," a quotation from a cowboy song, a passage in the accompaniment in which "the notes are indicated only approximately" (the composer's words), the fists being drawn into play—but the song survives. For this cowboy story sent to him by John Lomax, the composer set up a jogging accompaniment figure that refused to stay in the beaten tonal tracks. After the swinging motion, there is a strength in the four-square, on-the-beat chords ("the first that dies was Kid White"), closing with descending parallel triads. The narration of how Charlie Rutlage was sent to his grave is accompanied by a new, vivid, rhythmic figure, a rising *ostinato* in the tenor; "faster and faster" and "louder and louder" the music rushes to the horse's fall, when tremolando and fist clusters mount to *ffff*, but no grand pause. White-faced notes (the only ones in the song) appear ("Poor Charlie died"). The singing voice resumes and repeats the jogging music of the opening, flowing into a codetta, which closes without peroration in a new key. As for the logic of this, Ives once ridiculed the "sacred cow" of beginning and closing in the same key, saying it was as "silly as having to die in the same house you were born in."[4]

Of simple, warm sentiment is the conventional *My Native Land*. The setting of Wordsworth's *I travelled among unknown men* has a peasant-like tune, a unifying accompaniment figure, strength for "the mountains," and an imitative figure as voice and bass move in octaves in turning the wheel. But one comes

[4] P. Moor, "Horseback to Heaven: Charles Ives," *Harper's*, Vol. 197 (1948), 66.

to Ives not for those songs that are more nearly like other men's songs, nor yet for those that are unsuccessful experiments; rather, one comes for something of each of these, for there can be a golden mean (relatively), even for C. E. Ives. It is touched in *The Children's Hour,* a setting of a tiny fragment of Longfellow's poem. The two-voiced accompaniment sets up a neutral background in sixteenths that repeats its basic pattern during the first six measures, slightly modified in the four remaining measures of the first stanza. Its murmur is saved from dull monotony by the pivoting fifths of the bass, first echoed, then doubled (m.1) in the upper voice and in the high B and C-sharp in the left hand (m.2). The melody for voice moves in slight range, changing back and forth from 4/4 to 3/4 for the rhythm of the text. The next section needs two more meters; the sixteenth-note

Be - - tween the dark and the day - - light,

motion of the accompaniment is replaced with triplets; the chromatic chords seem rich after the two-part invention. The voice declaims the text simply, with suggestive mirroring on the "broad hall stair" and "laughing," while there is considerable glint on the "golden hair." With the latter, the motion of the first division returns, and soon a bit of its text and music, with a strangely suspensive close, creates a "feeling of sadness and longing."[5]

Quite a different approach to the world that revolves about children is *The Greatest Man,* an amusing text by Anne Collin

[5] H. W. Longfellow, "Children's Hour" (stanza three).

which Ives found in a newspaper. The teacher's assignment to "write about some great man" led the boy to "thinkin' 'bout his pa," who can ride and swim and hunt. The narrative in the vernacular leads to an "easy," graphic music, that moves unevenly through the child's recollections to a grand, boastful climax, "Dad's got 'em beat all holler." Then, after a pause, softly yet perkily, and a bit conscious of his boasting, the child ventures, "Seems to me."

Let us note in *Majority* the fattest clusters in song literature, where forearms full of tones cause the composer to advise a unison chorus, as "it is almost impossible for a single voice to hold the part in the score." As an example of his frequent avoidance of key signature (and key) and occasional omission of all bar lines, examine *Afterglow*. For musical satisfaction, experience *Disclosure* and *Night of Frost in May*. One may come from his study of Ives in absolute agreement with the composer's belief in "the right of man to the pleasure of trying to express in music whatever he wants to,"[6] but some may still doubt the wisdom of "trying to fly where humans cannot fly" and writing "songs that cannot be sung."[7]

Samuel Barber

MR. IVES HAS DOUBTED the wisdom of stimulants, such as prizes and contests, fearing the winners might be weakened rather than strengthened by this "kind of bait." The one who has been able to survive repeatedly these "enervating" experiences is Samuel Barber (1910–). The leisure that the awards have purchased for him has borne good fruits, creating a confidence in him on the part of both foundations and the public. These awards extend from 1935 to 1947 and include the American *Prix de Rome* and two grants each from the Pulitzer and Guggenheim foundations.

[6] C. E. Ives, *114 Songs* (Redding, Conn., 1922), 192.
[7] *Ibid.*, 262.

The urge for expression in song came early in Barber's student days and fortunately has never been crowded out by the challenge of larger forms and media or by the feeling of obligation to the foundations which expect big things. His lyricism feeds on other than sugar and water, and as early as Opus 2, No. 3 (*Bessie Bobtail*), one finds a bitter strength that calls to mind Moussorgsky. There is an overpowering drive and anguish in *I hear an army,* Op. 10, No. 3. More frequent is a gentle, intimate beauty, as in *The Daisies,* Op. 2, No. 1, whose melody flows with the graceful strength of an English folk tune. The diatonic line of the introduction is continued in the voice, the piano then setting up a scattered support, whose alternation of octaves in triple meter and duplication or omission of the vocal melody offer pleasant contrasts. Welcome, too, is the change of figure

In the scent-ed bud of the morn-ing O,

with sequence in m.69, while the reversed dominant pedal and counterpoint of a chain of thirds in m.17–20 enliven the lark's singing.

A year later (1928), Barber's setting of A. E. Housman's *With Rue my Heart is Laden* disclosed some late Brahmsian traits in the open filigree accompaniment, the division of the 3/4 measure into two dotted quarters, and the flexible changes of meter to match sensitively the rhythm of the text. The sentiment of the text, however, is less strictly translated, as if the years had softened sorrow and regret. The "way of mem'ries," which

James Joyce ponders in *Rain has fallen,* is more closely reflected in Op. 10, No. 1 (1936). An almost constant pattering of eighths is descriptive of the title. As the pattern of the introduction returns, the voice joins to sustain a chromatic, angular phrase that mounts three times to fall a perfect fifth in a stark cadence. The phrase that follows is freely drawn from the preceding, but its open cadence leads through a tense interlude to the return of the stanza. Here the piano is scored an octave lower; assertive chords take the place of the former running line and lead appassionato to an interlude heightened further by an inner voice leaping in sixteenth-note motion. The repetition of "speak to your heart" brings back the music of m.17–8, the suspensive unison dominant soon joined by an alto's intoning, which draws with it the old unyielding cadence, dropping to the bare tonic.

The songs of Op. 13, published in 1941, strengthen one's impression of the flexible technique of Barber, who invents a music as various as the poems he sets. He has a real gift of melody, which does not strain to be angular and crabbed. Its singability, in comparison with much of the music of his important contemporaries, makes one feel that he would agree with Gardner Read's evaluation of a good melody as being "worth a carload of exotic chords and perverse rhythms."[8] Barber has an imagination that seems to stay within bounds, a fancy that is relevant rather than wayward. In the matter of tonality, for example, he still finds plenty of freedom within established centers of key. When he obscures or disguises key, it is seldom arbitrary; there is usually poetic suggestion for it, as in *A Nun takes the Veil.* Its use of a free rather than a real church mode gives background. The signature of two flats ordinarily means B-flat major or G-minor; yet this song contains only one of each of those "tonic" chords, and neither is in a "key" position. By thus obscuring key, the mood of remoteness and other-worldliness is evoked.

Sure on this Shining Night begins and closes in canon, at

[8] Howard, *Our Contemporary Composers,* 215.

the tenth. Do you suppose a composer like Barber set out to make a song in canon? Probably not, and this is a wild guess why this song issued in that form. A composer, as he mulls over a poem, is open to a thousand refractions, and, consciously or not, the word "round" at the close of the second line of Agee's verse may have set the composer romancing in this way. But the important point is not that he wrote in canon, but that he made music that sings. Barber's flexible technique, which makes possible melody, harmony, tonality, and form that find their roots in the poet's verse, is not lacking in rhythmic sensitiveness. If he finds a just declamation within the frame of a single meter, he never feels that he has to jack up rhythmic interest by arbitrary changes of metric signature. When the poet's varying lengths of line and changing accents within them command different musical meters, the composer obeys. *The Secrets of the Old* by W. B. Yeats is, for Barber, an extreme example of metric oscillation, nine changes within the first twelve measures, with only four metric signatures: 5/8, 2/4, 3/8, 5/4. In all this change, there is a stubborn constancy of the value of the eighth-note, which adds to the gaiety of this trifle that bumps along on an "oom-pah" accompaniment. One can scarcely predict what his next songs will be like, although it seems certain that he cannot deny for long his natural gift for lyric expression.

THIS WOULD BE THE PROPER PLACE for a chapter listing the author's sins of omission. Never have they appeared more flagrant in his eyes than in the discussion of the current American scene. He resists, however, the temptation of a catalogue of names. A highly selective list, without discussion, is only a little better than a cumbersome inclusive one. Indeed, the most satisfactory list is one that each musician must make for himself after some exploring, after touching strange ports and examining many cargoes containing "ivories . . . diamonds . . . and cheap tintrays."[9] The "ivories" include those carefully fashioned songs

---

[9] J. Masefield, "Cargoes."

which are rather too coolly perfect, occasionally abstract, the products of busy minds. The "cheap tin-trays" are made to sell in a highly competitive market. Their garish colors and flashy designs soon fade and become dull. The "diamonds," however, retain their brilliance and are valued through the years. There has never been a period when there has not been traffic in all three types of songs. The lapse of years makes it relatively easy to choose the good songs of the past, but we can only hope that we know the "diamonds," when we happen on them, in the full cargoes of contemporary song.

Bibliography

THIS BIBLIOGRAPHY includes only the most fruitful sources consulted. It frequently omits works which have yielded a quotation or a fact, duly recognized and listed in the footnotes. Instead of an alphabetical listing of all sources, there has been noted first a section of general references, followed by a bibliography for each chapter. Occasionally pages are given for a reference, especially when an index is lacking or when relevant materials are within a small part of the book. Seldom listed are the essays prefacing collections of the composer's music. Abbreviations employed include: *MQ* (*Musical Quarterly, New York*) and *M&L* (*Music and Letters,* London).

General References

Finck, H. T. *Songs and Song Writers.* New York, 1900.

Kagen, S. *Music for the Voice.* New York, 1949.

Taylor, D. C. and Moderwell, H. *The Art Song.* Vol. V of *The Art of Music.* New York, 1915.

Upton, G. P. *The Song, Its Birth, Evolution, and Functions.* Chicago, 1915.

Walker, C. *The Art Song and Its Composers.* Vol. III in *Fundamentals of Musical Art.* New York, 1926.

Wodehouse, A. H. "Song," *Grove's Dictionary of Music and Musicians.* New York, 1935. 3rd ed.

Woodside, J. *The Evolution of the Art Song.* Boston, 1942. 7 vols.

I. Problems of the Art Song

Bie, O. "Melody," *MQ,* Vol. II (1916), 402–17.

Castelnuovo-Tedesco, M. "Music and Poetry: Problems of a Song-Writer," *MQ,* Vol. XXX (1934), 102–11.

Clinton-Baddeley, V. C. *Words for Music.* London, 1941.

Colles, H. C. *Voice and Verse.* London, 1928.

Davies, W. *The Pursuit of Music.* Chap. 26. New York, 1936.

Dickinson, E. *The Education of a Music Lover. Pages* 142–70. New York, 1911.

Drew, W. S. *Singing, the Art and the Craft.* London, 1937.

Gibbon, J. M. *Melody and the Lyric.* London, 1930.

Greene, P. *Interpretation in Song.* New York, 1926.

———. "The Future of English Song: The Singer and the Public," *M&L,* Vol. 1 (January, 1920).

———. "The Future of English Song: The Singer and the Composer," *M&L,* Vol. 1 (April, 1920).

Gurney, E. "The Sound Element in Verse," *The Power of Sound.* Pages 423–50. London, 1880.

———. "Song," *The Power of Sound.* Pages 451–75. London, 1880.

Henderson, W. J. *Art of the Singer.* New York, 1906.

Honegger, A. "What is True Vocal Music?" Rice Institute Pamphlets (XVI). Houston, Texas, 1929.

Kramer, A. W. "The Things We Set to Music," *MQ,* Vol. VII (1921), 309ff.

Lehmann, L. *More than Singing.* New York, 1945.

Schauffler, R. H. *Florestan, the Life and Works of Robert Schumann.* New York, 1945.

Stanford, C. V. *Musical Composition. Pages* 127–44. New York, 1922.

Williams, C. F. A. *The Rhythm of Song.* London, 1925.

II. Italian Song

Dent, E. J. *Alessandro Scarlatti, His Life and Works.* London, 1905.

Fellowes, E. H. *William Byrd.* London, 1923.

Floridia, P. *Early Italian Airs and Songs.* Boston, n.d. 2 vols. (Foreword, biographical sketches, and notes.)

Gatti, Guido. "Respighi," *International Cyclopedia of Music and Musicians.* Pages 1534–38. New York, 1939.

———. "Pizzetti," *International Cyclopedia of Music and Musicians.* Pages 1415–18. New York, 1939.

———. *Ildebrando Pizzetti.* London, 1951.

Henderson, W. J. *Early History of Singing.* New York, 1921.

Jeppesen, Knud (ed.). *La Flora.* Copenhagen, 1948. 3 vols. (Preface, notes on composers and compositions, text translations, and translations. Excellent in every respect.)

Kramer, A. W. "Malipiero," *International Cyclopedia of Music and Musicians.* Pages 1079–83. New York, 1939.

Luciani, G. A. "Respighi," *La Revue Musicale,* January, 1927, pp. 51–54.

Parisotti, A. *Anthology of Italian Song.* New York, 1894. 2 vols. (Preface and biographical sketches.)

Prunières, H. "G. F. Malipiero," *La Revue Musicale,* January, 1927, pp. 5–25.

Weber, R. von. "Castelnuovo-Tedesco," *Book of Modern Composers.* Ed. by D. Ewen. Pages 394–99. New York, 1942.

III. Early German Song

Bekker, P. *Beethoven.* Pages 251–60. London, 1927.

Bie, O. *Das deutsche Lied.* Berlin, 1926.

Burke, J. N. *The Life and Works of Beethoven.* Pages 335–44. New York, 1943.

Curzon, H. de *Les lieder et airs détachés de Beethoven.* Paris, 1905.

Einstein, A. *Mozart—His Character—His Work.* New York, 1945.

Elson, L. C. *The History of German Song.* Boston, 1888.

Friedländer, M. *Das deutsche Lied im 18 Jahrhundert.* Stuttgart, 1903. 3 vols.

———. *An die ferne Geliebte.* Pages 45–72. Leipzig, n.d.

Geiringer, K. *Haydn, A Creative Life in Music.* New York, 1946.

Moser, H. J. *Das deutsche Lied seit Mozart.* Berlin, 1937. 2 vols.

Mozart-Goethe. *Das Veilchen.* New York, 1948. (Facsimile with foreword by P. Nettl.)

Reissmann, A. *Joseph Haydn.* Pages 237–56. Berlin, 1879.

Rolland, R. *Goethe and Beethoven.* New York, 1931.

IV. Schubert

Bie, O. *Das deutsche Lied.* Berlin, 1926.

Capell, R. *Schubert's Songs.* New York, n.d.

Colles, H. C. *The Growth of Music*. Vol. III, pages 43ff. London, 1928.

Deutsch, O. E. *The Schubert Reader*. Trans. by E. Blom. New York, 1947.

Flower, N. *Franz Schubert, the Man and His Circle*. New York, 1935.

Istel, E. "Goethe and Music," *MQ*, Vol. XIV (1928). 221ff.

————. "Schubert's Lyric Style," *MQ*, Vol. XIV (1928), 575–95.

LeMassena-Merx. "The Songs of Schubert." New York, 1928.

Robertson, A. "The Songs of Schubert" in *The Music of Schubert*, ed. by G. Abraham. New York, 1947.

Schubert, Franz. *Fünf erste Lieder*. Foreword by O. E. Deutsch. N.p., 1922. (Facsimiles of manuscript and first editions.)

V. Loewe

Bach, A. B. *The Art Ballad*. Edinburgh, 1890.

Northcote, S. *The Ballad in Music*. London, 1942.

VI. Schumann

Fuller-Maitland, J. A. *Schumann*. London, 1884.

Reissmann, A. *The Life and Works of Robert Schumann*. London, 1886.

Schauffler, R. H. *Florestan, the Life and Works of Robert Schumann*. New York, 1945.

Schnapp, F. "Robert Schumann and Heinrich Heine," *MQ*, Vol. XI (1925), 615ff.

Untermeyer, L. *Heinrich Heine, Paradox and Poet*. New York, 1937.

VII. Franz

Aldrich, R. "Robert Franz on Schubert and Others," *MQ*, Vol. XIV (1928), 410ff.

Davies, W. *The Pursuit of Music*. New York, 1936.

Kleeman, H. "Robert Franz," *MQ*, Vol. I (1915), 497ff

Saran, A. *Robert Franz und das deutsche Volks-und Kirchenlied*. Leipzig, n.d.

VIII. Liszt and Mendelssohn

Cooper, M. "Liszt as Song Writer," *M&L*, Vol. XIX (1938), 171ff.

Ford, W. *The Heritage of Music*. Vol. II, pages 248–49. London, 1934.

Hughes, E. "Liszt as a Lieder Composer," *MQ*, Vol. III (1917), 390–409.

Istel, E. "Peter Cornelius," *MQ*, Vol. XX (1934), 334–43.

IX. Brahms

Adler, G. *Handbuch der Musikgeschichte*. Pages 949ff. Berlin, 1930.

——. "Johannes Brahms," *MQ*, Vol. XIX (1933), 113–42.

Colles, H. C. *Brahms*. London, 1908.

Evans, Sr., E. *A Handbook to the Vocal Works of Brahms*. London, 1912.

Friedländer, M. *Brahms's Lieder*. Trans. by Leese. London, 1928.

Fuller-Maitland, J. A. *Brahms*. London, 1911.

Hadow, W. H. *Studies in Modern Music: Second Series*. London, 1913. 2nd ed.

May, F. *The Life of Johannes Brahms*. London, 1905. 2 vols.

Specht, R. *Johannes Brahms*. Trans. by E. Blom. London, 1930.

X. Hugo Wolf

Aiken. "Spanish and Italian Songs," *M&L*, Vol. XXV (1944), 194ff.

Ford, W. An essay, *Heritage of Music*. Vol. II, pages 224–63. London, 1934.

Fox-Strangways. "Comparison of Schubert and Wolf," *M&L*, Vol. XXIII (1942), 126ff.

Newman, E. N. *Hugo Wolf*. London, 1907.

Rolland, R. An essay, *Musicians of Today*. Trans. by M. Blaiklock. Pages 168–98. New York, 1915.

XI. Strauss

Bie, O. *Das deutsche Lied*. Berlin, 1926.

Finck, H. T. *Richard Strauss*. New York, 1917.

Newman, E. N. *Richard Strauss*. London, 1908.

Specht, R. *Richard Strauss und sein Werk*. Leipzig, 1921. 2 vols.

XII. Contrast of German and French Song

Amiel's Journal. Pages 73, 186. New York, 1928.

Ellis, H. *Fountain of Life*. Pages 34, 53–54, 74, 209. Boston, 1930.

Faure, E. *The Spirit of the Forms*. Page 220. New York, 1937.

Fouillé, A. *Psychologie du peuple français*. Paris, 1898.

Jean-Aubry, G. *French Music of Today.* Trans. by E. Evans. London, 1919.

Lockspeiser, F. "French Song in the Nineteenth Century," *MQ,* Vol. XXVI (1940), 192–99.

Parry, C. H. H. *Style in Musical Art.* Chap. 9. London, 1911.

Rolland, R. *Jean Christophe.* New York, 1910–13. 3 vols. *Revolt,* 372–75, 394; *Market Place,* 49–60; *The House,* 355–60, 366–67, 411; *The New Dawn,* 365–97.

———. *Musicians of Today.* Pages 246–324. New York, 1915.

Staël, Mme de. *French Literature of the Nineteenth Century.* Ed. by Bradley and Mitchell. Pages 47–50. New York, 1936. *De la Litterature et des arts,* Chap. 1; *De L'Allemagne,* Vol. II, Chap. 1.

Thomson, V. *The Musical Scene* (The French Style). Pages 298–301. New York, 1945.

———. *The Art of Judging Music* (French Rhythm). Pages 293–95. New York, 1948.

Tiersot, J. *Un demi-siècle de Musique Française* (1870–1917). Paris, 1918.

XIII. French Song

Barzun, J. *Berlioz and the Romantic Century.* Vol. II, pages 282–93. Boston, 1950. 2 vols.

Bertelin, A. *Traité de composition musicale.* Vol. III. Paris, 1931.

Combarieu, J. *Histoire de la Musique.* Vol. III.

Lavignac, A. *Encyclopédie de la Musique.* 1re Partie, pages 1562–1697. Paris, 1914.

Lockspeiser, E. "The French Song in the Nineteenth Century," *MQ,* Vol. XXVI (1940), 192–99.

Lyle, W. *Camille Saint-Saëns.* New York, 1923.

Pater, W. An essay on Joachim du Bellay, *The Renaissance.* Pages 200–27. Portland, 1924.

Rolland, R. *Musicians of Today.* Pages 1–64. New York, 1915.

Wooton, T. S. *Hector Berlioz.* Pages 124–30. London, 1935.

XIV. Gabriel Fauré

Bruneau, A. *La vie et les Oeuvres de Gabriel Fauré.* Paris, 1925.

Chalupt, R. "Fauré, et les poètes," *La Revue Musicale,* October, 1922.

Copland, A. "Gabriel Fauré," *MQ,* Vol. XXVI (1942), 576ff.

Fauré, G. *Opinions musicales.* Paris, 1930.

Hill, E. B. *Modern French Music.* Boston, 1924.

Jankelevitch, V. *Fauré et ses mélodies.* Paris, 1938.

Jean-Aubry, G. *French Music of Today.* London, 1919. *Fauré,* 62–68; *Verlaine,* 191–203.

Koechlin, C. *Gabriel Fauré.* Paris, 1927.

Orray, L. "Songs of Gabriel Fauré," *Music Review,* Vol. VI (1945), 72–84.

Ravel, M. "Les mélodies de Gabriel Fauré," *La Revue Musicale,* October, 1922.

Rostand, C. *L'oeuvre de Gabriel Fauré.* Paris, 1945.

Servières, G. *Gabriel Fauré.* Paris, 1930.

Suckling, N. "Gabriel Fauré, Classic of Modern Times," *Music Review,* Vol. VI (1945), 65–71.

Vuillemin, L. *Gabriel Fauré et son oeuvre.* Paris, 1914.

XV. Franck

Cooper, M. *French Music.* New York, 1951.

Emmanuel, M. *César Franck.* Paris, 1930.

D'Indy, V. *César Franck.* Trans. by R. Newmarch. London, 1930.

Jean-Aubry, G. *French Music of Today.* Pages 132–36. London, 1919.

Koechlin, C. *Encyclopédie de la Musique.* Ed. by A. Lavignac. 2me Partie, Vol. I, pages 63ff. Paris, 1914.

Revue Musicale, La. The special issue (Chausson) of December, 1925.

Tiersot, J. *Un demi-siècle de Musique Française* (1870–1917). Paris, 1918.

XVI. Debussy

Bernard, R. *Les tendances de la Musique Française Moderne.* Paris, 1930.

Boucher, M. *Claude Debussy.* Paris, 1930.

Daly, W. H. *Debussy.* Edinburgh, 1908.

Dumesnil, M. *Claude Debussy, Master of Dreams.* New York, 1940.

Grey, C. *A Survey of Contemporary Music.* Pages 95–103. London, 1924.

Jean-Aubry, G. "Claude Debussy," *MQ,* Vol. IV (1918), 542–44.

———. *French Music of Today.* London, 1919. *Debussy,* 69–96; *Baudelaire,* 171–190.

Liess, A. "Harmonie," *La Revue Musicale,* January, 1931.

Lockspeiser, E. *Debussy.* Chap. 11. London, 1936.

Northcote, S. *The Songs of Henri Duparc.* New York, 1950.

Prod'homme, J. G. "Claude Achille Debussy," *MQ,* Vol. IV (1918), 55–71.

Revue Musicale, La. The special issue (Debussy) of December, 1920.

———. "La Jeunesse de Claude Debussy" (May, 1926).

Rosenfeld, P. *Musical Portraits.* Pages 119–31. New York, 1920.

Sabaneev, L. "Claude Debussy," *M&L,* Vol. X (1929).

Thompson, O. *Debussy, Man and Artist.* Pages 276–306. New York, 1937.

Vallas, L. *Claude Debussy, His Life and Works.* London, 1933.

———. *The Theories of Claude Debussy.* London, 1929.

XVII. Russian Song

Abraham, G. E. H. *Borodin, the Composer and His Music.* Pages 159–74. London, n.d.

Bowen, C. D. *Free Artist—Story of Anton and Nicholas Rubinstein.* New York, 1939.

Brewerton, E. "Rachmaninov's Songs," *M&L,* Vol. XV (1934), 32–36.

Calvocoressi, M. D. *Musorgsky.* Trans. by E. Hull. Pages 91–133. London, 1919.

Calvocoressi and Abraham. *Masters of Russian Music.* New York, 1936.

Lyle, W. *Rachmaninoff, a Biography.* London, 1938.

Leyda and Bertensson (eds.). *Musorgsky Reader.* New York, 1947.

Oliphant, E. H. C. "A Survey of Russian Song," *MQ,* Vol. XII (1926) 196–230.

Rachmaninoff, S. *Recollections as told to Oskar von Rieseman.* London, 1934.

Rimski-Korsakov, N. A. *My Musical Life.* Trans. by J. A. Joffe. New York, 1933.

Seroff, V. I. *The Mighty Five.* New York, 1948.

Schindler, K. See the foreword, *A Century of Russian Song.* New York, 1911. See the foreword, *Masters of Russian Song.* New York, 1911. 2 vols.

Weinstock, H. *Tchaikovsky.* New York, 1943.

XVIII. Grieg and Dvořák

Abraham, G. (ed.). *Grieg: A Symposium.* Norman, 1950.

Desmond, A. "Grieg's Songs," *M&L,* Vol. XXII (1941), 333-57.

Finck, H. T. *Grieg and His Music.* New York, 1909.

Fischl, V. (ed.). *Antonin Dvořák, His Achievement.* London, 1942. (Contains a chapter on songs by Astra Desmond.)

Hadow, W. H. *Studies in Modern Music: Second Series.* Pages 173–228. London, 1913.

Horton, J. "Ibsen, Grieg, and Peer Gynt," *M&L,* Vol. XXVI (1945), 66 ff.

Mason, D. G. *From Grieg to Brahms.* New York, 1902.

Monrad-Johansen. *Edvard Grieg.* Princeton, 1932.

Newmarch, R. *The Music of Czechoslovakia.* Pages 125–75. New York, 1942.

Robertson, A. "Dvořák's Songs," *M&L,* Vol. XXIX (1943), 82–89.

Sourek, O. *Dvořák—Leben und Werk.* Vienna, 1935.

———. "Dvořák," *Grove's Dictionary.* New York, 1935. 3rd ed.

Stefan, P. *Anton Dvořák.* New York, 1941.

XIX. Elizabethans and their Successors

Bridges, J. F. *Twelve Good Musicians—from Bull to Purcell.* London, 1920.

Chappell, W. *Popular Music of the Olden Times.* London, n.d. 2 vols.

Colles, H. C. *Essays and Lectures.* (Essay on John Dowland.) Pages 5–8. New York, 1945.

———. *Voice and Verse.* London, 1928.

Cummings, W. H. "Our English Songs," *English Music, 1604–1904.* New York, 1906.

Davey, H. *History of English Music.* London, 1895.

Evans, W. M. *Henry Lawes, Musician and Friend of Poets.* New York, 1941.

Fellowes, E. H. *William Byrd.* London, 1923.

Hadow, W. H. *English Music.* New York, 1931.

Heseltine, P. *The English Ayre.* London, 1926.

Holland, A. K. *Henry Purcell—The English Musical Tradition.* London, 1932.

Kidson, F. "A Study of Old English Song and Popular Melody, prior to the Nineteenth Century," *MQ,* Vol. I (1915), 569–82.

Langley, H. *Doctor Arne.* Cambridge, 1938.

Naylor, E. W. *Shakespeare and Music.* London, 1896.

Sear, H. G. "Charles Dibdin," *M&L,* Vol. XXVI (1945), 61–65.

Walker, E. *History of Music in England.* London, 1907.

Westrup, J. A. *Purcell.* London, 1937.

XX. Later English Song

Colles, H. C. *Essays and Lectures.* New York, 1945.

Dent, E. J. "On the Composition of English Song," *M&L,* Vol. VI (1925), 224–35.

Holbrooke, J. *Contemporary British Composers.* London, 1925.

Kimmel, W. "Vaughan Williams's Choice of Words," *M&L,* Vol. XXIII (1938), 132–42.

Scholes, P. A. *The Mirror of Music, 1844–1944.* London, 1947.

Simpson, H. *A Century of Ballads, 1810–1910: Their Composers and Singers.* London, 1910.

Sullivan, H., and Flower, N. *Sir Arthur Sullivan, His Life, Diaries, and Letters.* New York, 1927.

XXI. Song in the United States
General References

Cowell, H. (ed.). *American Composers on American Music.* Berkeley, 1933.

Farwell, A. and Darby, W. D. *Music in America.* Vol. IV in *The Art of Music.* New York, 1915.

Howard, J. T. *Our American Music, 300 Years of It.* New York, 1931

———. *Our Contemporary Composers.* New York, 1941.

Hughes, R. *American Composers.* Boston, 1900.

Overmyer, G. *Famous American Composers.* New York, 1944.

Rosenfeld, P. *An Hour with American Music*. Philadelphia, 1929.

Thorpe, H. C. "Interpretative Studies in American Song," *MQ*, Vol. XV (1929), 94.

Upton, W. T. *Art-song in America*. Boston, 1930.

———. "Recent Representative American Song Writers," *MQ*, Vol. XI (1925), 387.

———. "Aspects of Modern Art Song." *MQ*, XXIV (1938), 11–30.

Composers in Historical Sequence

Hastings, G. E. *Life and Works of Francis Hopkinson*. Chicago, 1926.

Milligan, H. V. *A Washington Garland*. Boston, 1918.

Sonneck, O. G. *Early Concert Life in America*. Leipzig, 1907.

———. *Francis Hopkinson and James Lyon. Two Studies in Early American Music*. Washington, D. C., 1905.

Gombosi, O. "Stephen Foster and Gregory Walker," *MQ*, Vol. XXX (1944), 133–46.

Howard, J. T. *America's Troubadour*. New York, 1934.

Jackson, G. P. "Stephen Foster's Debt to American Folk-song," *MQ*, Vol. XXII (1936), 154–69.

Milligan, H. V. *Stephen Collins Foster—A Biography*. New York, 1920.

Morneweck, E. F. *Chronicles of Stephen Foster's Family*. Pittsburgh, 1944.

Finck, H. T. "Edward MacDowell, Musician and Composer," *Outlook*, Vol. 84 (1906), 983–89.

Gilman, L. *Edward MacDowell—A Study*. New York, 1908.

———. "MacDowell, an American Genius." *Review of Reviews*, XXXVII (1908), 301.

Engel, C. "George W. Chadwick," *MQ*, Vol. X (1924), 438–57.

Rogers, F. "Some Memories of Ethelbert Nevin," *MQ*, Vol. III (1917), 360.

Thompson, V. *The Life of Ethelbert Nevin*. Boston, 1913.

Chadwick, G. W. *Horatio Parker*. New Haven, 1921.

Semler, I. P. *Horatio Parker*. New York, 1942.

Smith, D. S. "A Study of Horatio Parker," *MQ*, Vol. XVI (1930), 153.

Beach, H. H. A. "The How of Creative Composition," *The Etude*, Vol. 61 (1943), 151.

Tuthill, B. C. "Mrs. H. H. A. Beach," *MQ*, Vol. XXVI (1940), 297–310.

Cadman, C. W. "Idealization of Indian Music," *MQ*, Vol. I (1915), 387–96.
———. "On Writing a Successful Concert Song," *The Etude*, Vol. 50 (1932), 167–68.
Homer, S. *My Wife and I*. New York, 1909.
· Thorpe, H. C. "Songs of Sidney Homer," *MQ*, Vol. XVII (1931), 47.

XXII. The Later American School
Composers in Historical Sequence

· Maisel, E. M. *Charles T. Griffes*. New York, 1943.
Robinson, E. "Life and Death of a Composer," *American Mercury*, Vol. 30 (1933), 344–48.
Upton, W. T. "The Songs of Charles T. Griffes," *MQ*, Vol. IX (1923), 314–28.
Howard, J. T. *Bainbridge Crist*. New York, 1929.
· Borowski, F. "John Alden Carpenter," *MQ*, Vol. XVI (1930), 449.
· ———. "A New Spirit in American Musical Composition," *Current Opinion*, Vol. 54 (1913), 32–33.
Downes, O. "John Alden Carpenter—American Craftsman," *MQ*, Vol. XVI (1930), 443–48.
· Bellaman, H. "Charles Ives, the Man and his Music," *MQ*, Vol. XIX 1933), 45–58.
Copland, A. "The Ives Case," *Our New Music*. Pages 147–61. New York, 1941.
Cowell, H. "Charles E. Ives," *American Composers on American Music*. Pages 128–48. Berkeley, 1933.
"Charles Ives," *Current Biography*, June, 1947.
Moor, P. "Horseback to Heaven: Charles Ives," *Harper's*, Vol. 197 (1948), 63–73.
Slonimsky, N. "Composers of New England," *Modern Music*, February, March, 1930.
———. "Bringing Ives Alive." Saturday Review of Literature, Vol. XXXI (Aug. 28, 1948), 45.
·Broder, N. "Music of Samuel Barber," *MQ*, Vol. XXIV (1948), 325–35.
"Samuel Barber," *Current Biography*, September, 1944.
· Horan, R. "Samuel Barber," *Modern Music*, Vol. XX (March, April, 1943), 161–69.

Index

Figures in italics indicate musical illustration and/or analysis.